The Underground Railroad
in Western Illinois

The Underground Railroad in Western Illinois

Owen W. Muelder

McFarland & Company, Inc., Publishers
Jefferson, North Carolina, and London

LIBRARY OF CONGRESS CATALOGUING-IN-PUBLICATION DATA

Muelder, Owen W., 1941–
The Underground Railroad in
western Illinois / Owen W. Muelder.

p.   cm.
Includes bibliographical references and index.

ISBN-13: 978-0-7864-3141-0
illustrated case binding : 50# alkaline paper ∞

1. Underground Railroad — Illinois.
2. Antislavery movements — Illinois — History —19th century.
3. Abolitionists — Illinois — History —19th century.
4. African American abolitionists — Illinois — History —19th century.
5. Fugitive slaves — Illinois — History —19th century.
6. Illinois — History —1778–1865.
I. Title.
E450.M84   2008   973.7'115 — dc22   2007039582

British Library cataloguing data are available

On the cover: Phelps barn; reproduced from George Thompson,
Prison Life and Reflections (Dayton, Ohio: United Brethren Printing, 1860).
Illustration courtesy of Michael Godsil, Godsil Photography.

Manufactured in the United States of America

*McFarland & Company, Inc., Publishers
Box 611, Jefferson, North Carolina 28640
www.mcfarlandpub.com*

To Susan, Kirrie, and Caitlin

Acknowledgments

This book has benefited tremendously from the suggestions, advice and support of numerous people, but I would like to call special attention to the following individuals. First of all, I would like to thank Dr. Robert Seibert, R. W. Murphy Professor of Political Science at Knox College, who first suggested I take on this project. In addition, I must recognize Dr. Rodney O. Davis, co-director of the Lincoln Studies Center at Knox College, for his many suggestions. I would also like to express appreciation to Dr. Douglas Wilson, co-director of the Lincoln Studies Center at Knox College, for his support along with that of Dr. Lawrence Breitborde, dean of the faculty at Knox, and Roger Taylor, president of the college.

There are many faculty members, administrators, staff members, and students at Knox College who have helped me throughout the writing of this book. They include David Amor, director of Corporate and Foundation Relations; Jeffrey Douglas, director of Seymour Library; Carley Robison, curator of manuscripts and archives; Julie Mills, assistant archivist; Kay Vander Meulen, special collection librarian; Matt Norman, special collection librarian; Sharon Clayton, associate librarian; Anne Giffey, assistant librarian; Laurie Sauer, information technologies librarian; Irene Ponce, reader service librarian; Peter Bailley, manager of media relations and photography; Karen Irwin, Alumni Office secretary; Vicky Romano, computer center technology specialist, Christin Kjelland, student research assistant; Allyson Cooper, student research assistant; Mary Kiolbasa, student archives assistant; and Lucas Street, special collections student assistant.

There is an additional group of people outside the Knox College community who also lent me invaluable help and advice. They include Dr. James McCurry, Rex Charrington, Sue Lindsay, and Frances Stafford. I am particularly grateful to Brenda Patterson who designed and created many of the book's illustrations. I also recognize my sister, Dr. Marcia Eaton, retired professor of philosophy at the University of Minnesota, for her critical analysis and Peter Robinson, retired editor at American College Testing, for his many important contributions. I am obliged to University of Minnesota theoretical statistician, Dr. Morris L. Eaton, for warning me about the pitfalls of statistical projections. Finally, let me thank my wife Susan who helped me with nearly every aspect of my research and writing.

Table of Contents

Preface

The reader of this book must understand from the outset that the primary difficulty facing anyone who examines the history of the Underground Railroad (UGRR) is one of reliable verification. Those individuals most directly affected, fugitive slaves, were not, for the most part, able to leave accounts because usually they could not read or write, and literate free blacks and whites who were Underground participants tended not to make written records of their illegal activities. The Fugitive Slave Law of 1793, and a stronger version of this law passed as part of the Compromise of 1850, subjected anyone who aided runaway slaves to the possibility of fines and imprisonment. There were some firsthand accounts created by Underground operators at the time of their involvement, but most stories were written by these activists or retold to interviewers after 1865. The children, relatives, friends and acquaintances of some Underground operators who witnessed these clandestine events or were told of these events later wrote them down in letters and reminiscences or as contributions to county histories or newspaper articles. Many of these stories were highly embellished, fraught with nostalgia, and grossly exaggerated tales of daring family "heroes." Therefore, with so many examples of sketchy sentimental narratives and overreaching praise, generations of historians have, to a great extent, been leery of extensively examining this subject. County histories, for example, are considered by many academic historians as unreliable resources and often with good reason — *but not always.* The same skepticism is usually maintained toward anniversary speeches delivered by former UGRR "agents" years after actual events occurred or newspaper interviews given by relatives of "operators" decades later, but sometimes these accounts are most likely true and in some cases are in fact accurate.

The challenge then is to differentiate between self-serving mythical rhetoric and honest and legitimate accountability. Much of the time, the real story lies somewhere between the two. To throw the baby out with the bathwater may also distort the truth.

Preface

The necessarily secretive nature of the UGRR activity during the time of its operation, and its illegality, not surprisingly created ambiguity about the subject when it was discussed and written about after the Civil War.

I have attempted to evaluate the writings of others regarding the Underground Railroad in western Illinois with considered skepticism. In doing so I have tried to examine documents with both a critical eye and an open mind in hopes that they will reveal much, but certainly not all, of what really happened. The materials I have used include monographs, newspaper articles, accounts from county histories, pamphlets, personal journals, proceedings from professional meetings, letters, historical encyclopedias, historical society articles, obituaries, speeches, sermons, and books. The reader should always keep in mind that rarely do these accounts provide absolute proof but they do give, at the very least, a glimpse or faded impression of an important time in American history about events that are hard to trace because they were usually conducted in shadows. As much as possible I have quoted these materials directly, as the language used in them gives a sense of the time and place as well as the sensibilities of the writers in ways that are lost through paraphrasing.

This book is a documentary edition. The original writing is moving and often, in many cases, truly eloquent. My aim is to do justice to both the subject and to those who chronicled the events.

"Two things fill the mind with ever new and increasing admiration and awe, the oftener and the more steadily we reflect on them: the starry heavens above and the moral law within."
— Immanuel Kant, *The Critique of Practical Reason*, 1788

"He is blowing out the moral lights around us who contends that whoever wants slaves has a right to hold them."
— Abraham Lincoln, Fifth Lincoln/Douglas Debate, October 7, 1858, Old Main, Knox College, Galesburg, Illinois

I

The Military Tract

On any cloudless evening in western Illinois, in any season, just after twilight as darkness sets in, anyone scanning the sky can easily see the Big Dipper and the Little Dipper's North Star come into view. In this part of Illinois, from the end of the War of 1812 to the end of the Civil War, these celestial designs were a road map toward freedom in Canada. African American slaves had learned methods from their parents and other relatives for knowing the five basics for directions. They were: (1) the sun rises in the east and sets in the west; (2) you're walking north when the sun rises over your right shoulder and sets on your left, or if your shadow is on your left side in the morning and your right in the afternoon; (3) when you're facing north, south is behind you, east is to your right and west is to your left; (4) moss almost always grows on the north side of trees; and (5) at night the North Star, Polaris, can be your heavenly marker toward safety.[1] Black sailors passed along this important information about navigating by the stars to friends and family. In Charleston, South Carolina, ordinances were passed requiring black sailors to be jailed while they were in port in order to prevent the spread of these facts.[2] Runaway slaves also applied, as best they could, what they had been taught throughout their lives about methods for not being tracked or caught. These included (1) staying close enough to a river bank to use the river to get a sense of direction; (2) wading in streams to confuse dogs trying to follow their scent, even though some trained canines could pick up a trail even in water; (3) rubbing the bottoms of their feet with onion, turpentine, or pepper to cover their scent[3]; (4) occasionally going south rather than north, which might fool their pursuers; and (5) remaining very still all day.[4]

Along the way these "travelers" received much needed help from northern abolitionists, antislavery sympathizers and free blacks who sheltered them, fed them and transported them along a secret escape network on the ground, by water and sometimes by rail. A major advantage for these northern fellow travelers of the fugitives

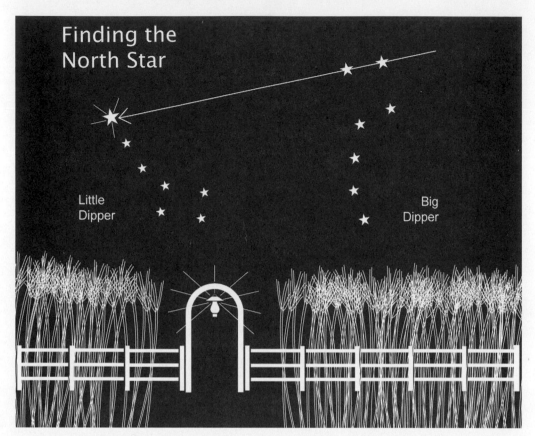

Finding the North Star

Little Dipper

Big Dipper

was their knowledge of the areas where each lived, of timber groves, rivers and streams, caves, and old Indian trails that they knew like the backs of their hands. They were people willing to *break the law* in order to serve the cause of liberty. Though contemptuous of the three-fifths compromise in the United States Constitution that counted slaves thus for the purpose of representation in Congress and gave disproportionate political and economic influence to southern states, these people were first and foremost opposed to slavery because they believed it was evil. Most succinctly put, these were individuals who refused to abide by a system of law that allowed one person to own another person and therefore they attached themselves to the Underground Railroad movement. Scores of "stations" or hideouts were dotted upon the prairie landscape of western Illinois. One of these was a signal station barn belonging to William J. Phelps, who lived south of Elmwood, Illinois. The barn had a cross-shaped opening carved into its top eastern gable. The cross, difficult to see by day unless one happened to be looking for it, was easily visible at night when a lantern was placed closely behind it. Runaway slaves had been alerted by their abolitionist friends that when the gable cross beamed light after dark, it was safe for them to pass in order to reach the next place of concealment.[5]

One of the most difficult things facing slaves who were about to flee was knowing that after they escaped they would probably never see family members or close friends ever again. Some runaways waited for months, weighing options for success before they sought freedom while others left abruptly if an opportunity arose that gave them confidence they wouldn't be caught. The ideal time to leave was during holidays or over a weekend when time elapsed before a slave's departure would be discovered. The slave's journey usually started on foot and sometimes covered long distances by walking. Fugitives on the run in slave states often found refuge with families and friends on a slave owner's property before making it into a free state. If a connection was made with an Underground Railroad "agent," after crossing over into free territory,[6] slaves might travel over land in a "conductor's" rig making the trip faster, less exhausting and also allowing the "cargo" to travel out of sight. Runaways sometimes hid in an empty cider barrel,[7] a wagon with a false bottom or under stacks of hay. Occasionally runaways took a horse from their master's barn, rode horseback on a fresh mount provided by a UGRR "operator,[8]" or simply "appropriated" a mule or mare from a settler's shed. But countless fugitives required *no* help at all from underground operators during their long journey to freedom.[9] Emma Chapin whose father, William T. Allen, was one of the most seriously involved antislavery advocates in Illinois before the Civil War wrote in 1896:

> Some groped their way alone, with only the north star to guide them.... Sometimes two or three were in company, and the terror & loneliness were lessened by being shared, as they hid in the forest by day, or burrowed in some farmer's [hay]stack on the treeless prairie, & patiently picked their way by night, thro storm, cold & heat.[10]

Most slaves were dependent on information about the antislavery movement and escape being transmitted to them by other slaves[11] through word of mouth passed along the secretive "slave grapevine." Ira Berlin writes the following in *Generations of Captivity*:

> Rumors of the demise of slavery elsewhere in the world and the upswell of abolitionist strength in the North entered the slave quarter in fragments of conversations, newspaper accounts, and — perhaps most significantly — their owners' increasingly exaggerated and vitriolic public denunciation of antislavery fanatics and "Black Republicans." ... By the 1850s, few slaves did not know of the struggle between slave and free states or appreciate how that conflict might affect their future.[12]

Thirty-four years after the Civil War ended, Galesburg abolitionist Hirim Mars recalled, in a speech presented at the Galesburg Public Library, that Missouri slaves were sometimes made aware of the Illinois UGRR through information given to them by daring antislavery crusaders. Mars said that "some [abolitionists] people from Quincy under the guise of peddlers, had gone into Missouri and had scattered among the slaves their plans on how to get to Quincy and where to go when they got there."[13]

John Hope Franklin and Loren Schweninger write in *Runaway Slaves* that "among the most significant characteristics of runaways was their intelligence."[14] They were often described as "smooth with words and quick with speech."[15] Quickness, in general, was often required in order to escape the pursuit of "Negro dogs." Slave catchers had specifically trained breeds of dogs that were kept away from slaves intentionally except during training exercises and actual tracking. These vicious dogs were capable of tearing a fugitive to pieces if not restrained. "The most salient characteristic" for runaways according to Franklin and Schweninger "was courage."[16]

The region the runaways moved through in western Illinois fell within the boundaries of three significant rivers. The northern boundary, the Rock River, enters the state at about the midpoint along the Illinois/Wisconsin border and flows south before turning sharply west and eventually emptying into the Mississippi. The Mississippi, known to some slaves as the "River Jordan," was the western border. The third river, the Illinois, was the eastern and southern boundary.[17] It moves gradually west from its headwaters in northeastern Illinois, then flows south passing Peoria before angling in a southwesterly direction until it, like the Rock, meets the Mississippi. This roughly shaped triangle was given the name "Military Tract" by Congress when it was set aside to be offered in sections as bounties to War of 1812 veterans. Most veterans decided not to pioneer in Illinois, so they sold their "grants" to land speculators. Lands not set aside for veterans were available to other frontiersmen.

The Military Tract, a domain slightly larger than Massachusetts, possessed three major ingredients favorable to running a successful Underground Railroad: (1) runaways bolting from a "slave state" bordering a "free state" and coming in large enough numbers; (2) to require a sufficient cluster of UGRR "agents," "conductors" and "operators" to support their movement to Canada; and (3) waterways to enhance quick passage through the north. But a fourth important factor in Illinois and Iowa[18] was the existence of tall grass prairie.[19] The long grass, not found in most parts of the United States, was a crucial "extra" that helped slaves on their northern journey.

Prairie grasses and an astonishing variety of wild flowers covered the area inside the rivers, stretching for miles and miles. To be sure, there were timber groves[20] and trees and wild brush growing by rivers and creeks, but vast stretches of the land were covered by this grass. The vista was breathtakingly beautiful and the prairie was filled with an abundance of wildlife.[21] Some varieties of the prairie grass grew as high as seven feet and higher. It must have seemed as incredible to most of the runaway slaves as it did to the awestruck settlers who saw it for the first time. The grass followed and shadowed the slope of the countryside, rose and fell as it stretched unfenced and boundless. The grass reminded some Europeans, who had crossed the Atlantic Ocean, of the swells of the sea as they watched the wind toss it to and fro blowing it across the landscape. On a clear night in the summer, there was only the Milky Way, the stirring tall grass, and the immense sound of crickets as the slaves moved through the "free state." Glennette Turner in her comprehensive work on the Illinois Underground Railroad writes:

> While most prairies did not shield UGRR passengers as much as forests, they had their advantages. They were easier to walk across than wooded or rugged terrain. And they were easier to survey. A passenger who was hiding in the woods at the edge of a prairie could see anyone who approached. However, in the northern portion of the state, grasses sometimes grew to stand taller than a rider on horseback.[22]

Illinois Military Tract

BRENDA PATTERSON, BG PATTERSON GRAPHICS.

Moving across the prairie was not always an easy thing to do which made Underground operators familiar with the landscape even more crucial to those on the run. A Scottish traveler, James Caird, new to the Illinois prairie, left this record of getting lost in the grass after heading north from Springfield before the Civil War:

> The horses struck without hesitation into the long coarse grass, through which they pushed on with very little inconvenience, although it was in many places higher than their heads.... We had fixed our eye on a grove of timber on the horizon as our guide, and drove on for about an hour in a straight line, as we believed, toward it. But stopping now and then to look at the soil and the vegetation, we found that the grove had disappeared. Without knowing it we must have got into a hollow, so we pressed on. But after hours' steady driving we could see nothing but the long grass and the endless prairie, which seemed to rise slightly all round us. I advised the

9

Counties
cut out of the
Illinois Military Tract

BRENDA PATTERSON, BG PATTERSON GRAPHICS.

driver to fix his eye upon a cloud right ahead of us, the day being calm, and to drive straight for it. Proceeding thus, in about half an hour we again caught sight of the grove, still very distant, and the smart young American driver "owned up" that he had lost his way.[23]

Though the term "Underground Railroad"[24] has long served as a powerful metaphor to help one picture the antislavery highway, it is equally important to think of it, in this part of Illinois, as a cluster, a web or network; indeed, more like the maze of a large maple tree's root system. The most important cities located in this web did follow a more or less straight line from Quincy to Galesburg to Princeton. This course was sometimes called the Quincy Line. But in reality, throughout the entire area, a web of numerous possible hideouts existed for fugitive slaves on the run. "The Underground Railroad in Illinois was not a single passageway along which escaped slaves were forwarded. There were a number of routes that ran northward at irregular intervals."[25] A runaway might be taken on a course that darted and zigzagged, sometimes weaved back and forth and occasionally backtracked like a U-turn. The stations along the course should be envisioned as a cluster of optional stops instead of a progressive succession of fixed points, albeit generally arranged in a north by northeast direction.[26] If, for example, slaves were hiding at the home of Fountain Watkins, who was an ally and neighbor of William J. Phelps, and a lantern was not showing at the Phelps' barn a few miles away, then a route frequently taken from there north to Galesburg would not be followed. Instead, Watkins would most likely take the runaways northeast to Freeman Miles's place and then to the Huey homestead in Brimfield.

It was not unusual for "conductors" on the UGRR to be watched by proslavery men or individuals indifferent to slavery who simply wanted to catch a fugitive slave in order to collect reward money. Radical abolitionists knew this and they would often use imaginative ruses to outsmart their adversaries. The members of a deeply involved UGRR family might be disguised and overdressed, whisked from the back door to the barn and loaded quickly into a wagon or a buggy (a sleigh or bobsled in the winter) and hurriedly driven in one direction at high speed. They would be chased down by those spying on them only to enjoy the last laugh when their pursuers found no slaves. Meanwhile, after the initial chase had ensued, the runaways would be taken in a different direction to another stop within the local web or cluster. The quality most needed when working undercover was the ability to make calm, thought out, measured decisions — instead of rash judgments or overreactions. Recklessness could mean trouble for an Underground operator but it might doom a captured runaway. If fugitives were caught, the punishments included branding, whipping, crippling, and even death. There were various kinds of painful instruments of torture used for beatings that included clubs, hickory sticks, buggy whips, paddle boards with bore holes, braided rope cords, the flat side of handsaws, leather straps, and bullwhips.

In any case, from Adams County on the Mississippi River runaways moved northward through a broad band of counties: Hancock, Henderson, McDonough, western Schuyler, Fulton, Peoria, Warren, Mercer, Knox, Stark, Henry, Rock Island, Marshall, Putnam, and finally Bureau. In all of these counties, antislavery men and women functioning as "agents" were waiting, planning and gaining valuable experience in ways to safely transport their human cargo. These trips were planned in secret, rarely discussed with the children, never revealed to strangers and were filled with danger, excitement, stealth, daring, intrigue, and subterfuge.

The three counties at the southern end of the triangle, Calhoun, Brown, and Pike, did not have as many "stations" but this is not surprising since these counties were close to St. Louis.[27] The largest city in the slave state of Missouri was a dangerous place for runaway slaves. Runaways were vulnerable to capture in river towns due to the presence of police and bounty hunters but nonetheless countless escapees passed safely through these communities. Larger cities lured many who fled slavery, but once reached, cities were often unsafe and fugitives were frequently nabbed and jailed. Runaways from a rural setting were often easily discovered due to their dress, dialect and ignorance of how to function in an urban setting. Escapees did pass through Calhoun[28] and Brown counties and "stations" did exist in Griggsville and New Philadelphia in Pike County. New Philadelphia was a small community of "free blacks" that thrived for decades and its residents ran a significant UGRR operation. This was a community established by Frank McWorter, a free black, who moved to Pike County, Illinois, after he purchased his own freedom in Kentucky. The town gradually disappeared after the Civil War. This remarkable man returned to Kentucky throughout his life to buy other family members their freedom as well and take them back to New Philadelphia. Runaway slaves who passed through this community were either ushered north to Quincy or taken east to the Illinois River or to Jacksonville. But given the strong proslavery element in this area, it made much more sense for slaves escaping on the water to wait and disembark farther north whether moving up the Mississippi or Illinois rivers. A map of the UGRR published by the National Park Service in 1998 shows four thick arrows revealing the primary ways slaves moved through the north. The farthest west of these arrows passes through and along the area of the Rock, Illinois, and Mississippi rivers. James and Lois Horton's map of the Underground Railroad in *Hard Road to Freedom* also shows the same escape pattern through western Illinois and up the Mississippi River and it also reveals that some fugitives traveled all the way north to St. Paul, Minnesota.[29]

One route existed in the counties just north of the Rock River, again moving in a north-easterly direction, following the natural course of that waterway. This track proceeded from the cities of Rock Island, Moline, Port Byron, and Albany on the Mississippi over to the Rock and from there proceeded to Hillsdale and Erie past Sterling and Dixon and finally turned north to Oregon, Grand Detour and Byron. This liberty line crossed over into Wisconsin to "stations" at Beloit, Milton and Janesville before heading toward Lake Michigan. A second major artery originated at Alton,[30] across the river from St. Louis, and moved fugitives up and along the Illinois River with spur lines off that basic route into Jacksonville and Springfield. This course continued due north toward Havana on the Illinois River before swinging east of Peoria (but sometimes took escapees west through Fulton County) and then again north, through Tazewell, Woodford, eastern Marshall and eastern Putnam counties. Stationmasters were wait-

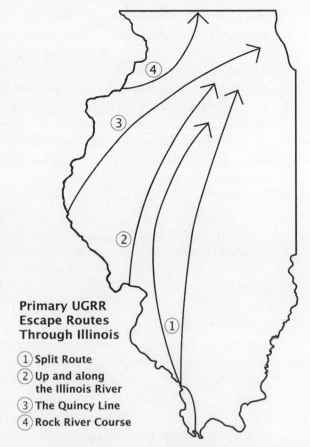

Primary UGRR Escape Routes Through Illinois

① Split Route
② Up and along the Illinois River
③ The Quincy Line
④ Rock River Course

BRENDA PATTERSON, BG PATTERSON GRAPHICS.

ing when fugitives arrived at Princeton, LaSalle, Peru, and Ottawa[31] and they were then moved along the last leg of the Illinois trip to Chicago.[32] A third UGRR route started in Cairo and moved toward Chester,[33] Sparta and other points in southwestern Illinois and ushered fugitives in two directions. One line headed toward Alton joining the Illinois River escape route. The other course used by runaways coming north from Cairo, followed a jagged track out of Randolph County to Centralia and then moved through the middle part of the state to Vandalia, Pana, Decatur, Bloomington, and Joliet, before it turned toward Chicago. The fourth highway to freedom was the previously mentioned Quincy Line that carried escapees through the heart of western Illinois. It is not surprising that Jesse Macy wrote 55 years after the Civil War that this part of Illinois was "honey-combed with refuges for patrons on the Underground Railroad."[34]

There were also a good number of northern men and women who helped fugitive slaves even though they were in no way associated with antislavery groups or Underground Railroad agents. These were people who unexpectedly found themselves in circumstances that forced them to choose between giving help to or turning away from fugitives they came upon who were in dire straights. The sympathetic impulse they felt toward these runaways often resulted in them aiding the fugitives' escape. This support, spontaneously given and frequently determined on the spur of the moment, helped many trying to evade capture.

The circumstances or conditions that led to slaves deciding to risk running away varied, but certain common factors frequently existed. Franklin and Schweninger in *Runaway Slaves* write:

> The events surrounding the death of a master ... not only created anxiety and concern among bondsmen and women but sometimes provided opportunities for escape. Some feared being sold to distant lands or being turned over to a slave trader, others were apprehensive about losing their privileged positions, and not a few simply saw it as a good time to run. In any event, that blacks would choose a grieving period to break their ties with the master class suggests a combination of hostility and opportunism.[35]

There were other reasons common to most slaves that hastened them to flee their bondage, including sexual abuse of a slave woman by her master or overseer, physical cruelty due to a slave's "insolence," all the way to punishment for an attempted escape. Particularly traumatic was dealing with a family breakup due to the selling of a family member to other slave owners.[36]

One Missouri slave's account of this heinous cruelty paints a picture similar to thousands that were seen throughout the nation's slave states until 1865:

> Why down at Bonnville, woman and a baby was put up to be sold, and de buyer he want de woman, but he don't want de baby, so they separated 'em, and was gettin' ready to put 'em on de boat for Noo Orleans, and ship 'em down de river, and de woman she ran back to kiss de baby goodbye, and de tradar picked up a whip and cracked it and shouts, "A bellerin cow will soon forget its calf!" She was sold down de river and navar saw de baby again. Now dat was sad.[37]

Another significant fact uncovered by Franklin and Schweninger had to do with the heavy drinking and alcoholism common among southern slave owners[38]:

> They knew when masters drank to excess, experienced health problems, encountered family and marital difficulties, or faced financial woes. They witnessed or learned about the arguments, hostilities, jealousies, and hatreds among family members, the violence of husbands against wives, and the excessive attention of some masters to their female slaves. When these problems, conflicts, and involvements impaired the ability of the masters to manage their slaves, when they became careless or lackadaisical or preoccupied, slaves then exploited the situation. In not a few instances, they responded by lying out[39] or running away.[40]

It was also true that some former slaves who had escaped to freedom later returned to help their family and friends get away. These former bondsmen knew exactly where the UGRR "stations" were or where escapees might follow routes and required no help at all. In western Illinois the runaway, "Charlie," appears as a noteworthy example of a slave, who once free, decided to return through the Underground chain again and again in an effort to retrieve his family and others. His story will be told in later chapters.

In the Prairie State and throughout the nation the most important secret operators were northern blacks and former slaves who gave their support to the operation of the Underground Railroad. These black conductors and agents had often escaped earlier or had been born free in the north. They helped organize escape routes and networks and were frequently led by the leadership surrounding black ministries. One can easily imagine what horrors would befall a black conductor if he or she were caught giving aid to fugitives trying to escape. There are numerous stories throughout the north of former slaves who, once free, reached back to help others find freedom such as Frederick Douglass, Henry Highland Garnet, and Harriet Tubman along with many, many others. Blacks were the first to organize northern resistance and prod their white brethren to join them. In the east, as early as 1829, black author David Walker wrote *The Appeal to the Colored Citizens of the World*— a document considered to be the most extreme anti-slavery publication of its time. Walker's *Appeal* not only demanded the immediate abolition of slavery but also called upon blacks to rebel against it everywhere. His *Appeal* was circulated widely in the north and was disseminated by sailors throughout the south. Northern blacks and ex-slaves communicated facts to those still in bondage about geography, mileage or relative distance, dangerous places along the way, possible safe havens and other valuable escape information. But at the western edge of the nation in sparsely populated western Illinois, there were few blacks, so most Underground Railroad activity was overwhelmingly carried out by whites.[41]

Sometimes slave catchers or detectives hired by enraged slave masters[42] to pursue their escaped human property were so hot on the trail of runaways that fugitives needed real ingenuity to figure out how to avoid being spotted. They used whatever means they found at their disposal for any device that might buy valuable minutes that could retard pursuers. Fleeing wayfarers might hide in the rafter beams of a covered bridge, a remote cave, a tree hollow inside a forest grove, or tall prairie grass or cornfields. Exposed to the elements, with only the sky as their umbrella, they could only hope to find someone to help them the following day. If escaped slaves were connected or reconnected to a "station conductor," a more comfortable shelter might be found. "I remember the low uncertain rap they gave at our back door, their hearts in their mouth in fear least they had mistaken the place"[43] wrote Emma Chapin in

January 1896 recalling her family's UGRR involvement in western Illinois. Fanciful lore, passed down over decades, about secretly constructed Underground Railroad hideouts are most often found to be untrue but occasionally, reliable accounts surfaced of hiding places that were built with real imagination. One example of such a secret place was accidentally discovered by John V. Henry when he was a child growing up in DeKalb County, in northern Illinois. It illustrates the extent to which truly dedicated agents would go, in order to fool slave catchers:

> One day ... we were playing on top of a straw stack when suddenly the straw gave way and we found ourselves in a rather circular room about eighteen feet in diameter, with upright posts about seven feet, with old rails and brush behind to keep the straw like a wall, and overhead poles running upward to the center pole for a roof. The center pole or support was a dead tree, the whole top having been cut off, leaving only a few lower stub lines for the roof poles to rest on.
>
> Though we searched for a long time, we could find no way of exit, and finally managed to climb the dead tree and make our escape from this "Underground Station."
>
> We told of our escapade at the house, but the family did not enlighten us as to the uses made of the straw-stack room. After my return from the army, when secrecy was no longer required, I learned that had we searched the room closely on the ground, *exactly* in the north center (toward the "North Star") we would have found an exit, then packed with straw and that the straw was thinly lain on top where we fell through, for the purpose of ventilation.[44]

Small paneled spaces in a private home, trap doors leading to a basement hideout or tunnel, the hayloft of a barn, or an old log cabin abandoned by a rural family after they moved into their more substantial farmhouse could provide cover, warmth and a place to be kept out of sight. In addition to avoiding professional trackers and law officers, runaways had to dodge "vigilante committees" created at antiabolitionist gatherings in Missouri for the purpose of pursuing fugitives in Illinois.[45]

Dense fog was the most beneficial weather condition for fugitives while hiding but it was disorienting for freedom seekers on the run. However, UGRR "carriers" familiar with the region they were traveling through welcomed fog. Conversely, a slave tracker looking for runaway slaves would have hated to see foggy weather move into an area where they were searching. In eastern Iowa and western Illinois dense fog, defined by meteorologists as visibility less than one-fourth of a mile, exists on an average of only 17.5 days per year. However, thick fog occurs at an average of nearly 2.5 days per month during December, January, and February.[46]

Slavery existed throughout the north before the colonies struggled for independence, but it was mostly eliminated legally north of the Mason-Dixon Line by the early 19th century. By the end of the Revolutionary War there were many antislavery societies being formed in the north. There was even limited sentiment growing against slavery in the south[47] at that time, but the cotton gin, patented by Eli

Whitney in 1793, which made it possible to eliminate the seed from cotton quickly and thoroughly, cemented slavery's existence thereafter. Whitney's new machine had sawtooth disks on rollers to de-seed long and short staple cotton. A crank would be rotated, the cotton was then snared by the teeth, and the seeds, too big to pass through a combing screen, were brushed away. A slave could now "clean up" 50 pounds of short staple cotton a day, compared to one or two pounds a day before gins were used. The textile mills in the north and in England needed cotton and southern planters could now meet that demand by clearing more land and planting more acres. In addition to cotton, sugar cultivation and production, particularly in Louisiana, also contributed to the call for more slaves. Tobacco and rice were other products central to the slave-based southern agricultural system. Consequently, the demand for slaves grew by leaps and bounds and this financial condition had a profound impact on the nation as a whole.[48] It appeared that the United States had adopted the position that, without slavery, America would see its national economy crippled if not destroyed. Most Euro-Americans in the United States adopted and reinforced deep-rooted prejudices about African Americans passed down over generations. The result was a majority view that saw whites as racially superior to blacks (as well as Indians, Mexicans or any other "colored race") and that this was the "natural" state of things. The poison of slavery and racial prejudice therefore seeped deeper and deeper into the fabric of the American character, north and south, fundamentally scarring it thereafter.

It should never be lost on a student of the Underground Railroad and the antislavery movement that women were central contributors and practitioners in this crusade. On no matter what level one studies the subject, women's examples are there to be found. Famous Underground Railroad conductors, like Harriet Tubman, were literally on the frontlines and no orator or writer achieved more influence in spreading the antislavery message than Harriet Beecher Stowe, author of *Uncle Tom's Cabin*. Stowe's book struck the nerve of the nation. According to Princeton University historian James McPherson, it sold "300,000 copies in the United States within one year which would be like 3,000,000 today."[49] In 1862 when President Lincoln met Stowe, he reportedly said to her, "So you're the little woman who wrote the book that made this great war."

Funding for the antislavery cause was often provided by sales conducted at the bizarres and fairs that were organized by women. There were numerous women school teachers who were devoted to the antislavery struggle and were therefore in a position to have a substantial influence on the attitudes of their pupils toward slavery. Direct and invaluable service to the UGRR was regularly dispensed by women in the form of nursing, feeding, and clothing fugitives. To quote Macy again:

Women were not a whit behind men in their devotion to the cause of freedom — the women of the west were already better organized than the men and were doing work which men could not do. The "Library Associations" of Indiana which were in fact effective anti-slavery societies, were to a large extent composed of women. To the library were added numerous other disguises, such as "reading circles," "sewing societies," and "women's clubs." In many communities the appearance of men in any of these enterprises would create suspicion or raise a mob. But the women worked on quietly, effectively, and unnoticed. The matron of family would be provided with the best riding horse which the neighborhood could furnish. Mounted upon her steed, she would sally forth in the morning, meet her carefully selected friends in a town twenty miles away, gain information as to what had been accomplished, give information to the work in other parts of the district, distribute new literature, confer as to the best means of extending their labors, and return in the afternoon.[50]

Several women were present at the organization of the American Anti-Slavery Society[51] in Philadelphia in 1833. Lucretia Mott, a well-known Quaker minister, took part in the society's proceedings. The female influence in west central Illinois can be traced to the writings of Mary Brown Davis as well as the efforts of Lucy Pettingil, Mary Allen West, Irene Allen and Mary A. Blanchard, the wife of the second president of Knox College, Jonathan Blanchard.

Galesburg and Knox College[52] were recognized from the very beginning as one of the most important stops, if not the primary downstate stop, on the Illinois Underground Railroad.[53] In a speech given in Galesburg to a packed audience 35 years after UGRR operations ceased, Booker T. Washington thanked the town for its past support saying, "I assure you the colored people of the south appreciate the opportunities the people of Galesburg gave us in the dark days when we could not help ourselves."[54] Many in the Galesburg[55] community were proud of this reputation, and the town's founder George Washington Gale was once indicted and brought before the county court for helping runaway slaves. In Elijah P. Lovejoy's *Alton Observer Extra*, printed on September 26, 1837, he lists ten Knox College trustees among those calling for the first State Anti-Slavery Convention that was held in Alton a month later.[56] The college's first president, H. H. Kellogg, attended the World Anti-Slavery Convention in London in 1843. Despised by the majority of the area's citizens as extremists, they were, however, well-known to regional and sectional "conductors" in a wide circle surrounding the college town. George Avery,[57] the Reverend Edward Beecher[58] (Harriet Beecher Stowe's brother), A. S. Bergen, President Blanchard,[59] Mary Blanchard, George Davis, R. C. Dunn, R. C. Edgerton, William Mead and Mary Ferris Mead, Charles Gilbert, Samuel and Catharine Hitchcock,[60] William Holyoke, Charlie Love, Abram and Charlotte Neely, Lucius Parker, Hiram Revels, Susan Van Allen Richardson, John Waters, Julia Wells, John West, Mary Allen West, Nehemiah and Catherine West, and Sherman Williams were forthright and unabashed about embracing the UGRR.[61] Others, though less flamboyant and blunt about their true loyalties to the movement, were nonetheless openly recorded members of antislavery societies and attended local and state meetings of these societies. The abolitionist movement and the Underground Railroad were not one in the same. Some abolitionists disapproved of aiding fugitive slaves and wanted nothing to do with the illegal activity of the UGRR. Consequently, the group of abolitionists who were directly involved in helping to organize the escape network were a smaller group within the larger abolitionist community. But in Galesburg there was a remarkable concentration of people who, to one degree or another, associated themselves with fighting the curse of African slavery. This was so much the case that the town functioned as a kind of sanctuary for runaways. There is not a single record of an escaped slave being captured and returned to bondage after arriving within the city limits. The men and women mentioned above as agents, both black and white, male and female, were supporting a mutually organized network in Galesburg that was part of the nation's first truly integrated social movement. Unfortunately, in Galesburg and generally throughout the nation blacks were not given leadership roles in antislavery societies.[62]

This town of mostly transplanted easterners[63] was overwhelmingly dominated by Presbyterians and Congregationalists, as were many abolitionist communities in other parts of Illinois and the nation as a whole. In fact, without these church leaders and loyal parishioners, the movement and its organization would have been minimal:

> One of the leading features of the antislavery movement in Illinois is the prominence of clergymen among its leaders and promoters. Foremost among them were Owen Lovejoy, John Cross, W.T. Allen, Chauncey Cook, and James H. Dickey. Moreover, in the

SPECIAL COLLECTIONS AND ARCHIVES, KNOX COLLEGE.

George Washington Gale is the founder of Galesburg, Illinois, and Knox College. He was indicted in 1843 for aiding the escape of fugitive slaves.

whole antislavery ranks it would have been difficult to find a single adherent who was not at the same time a strong religious believer. In fact, the organization had its birth in the conviction which seized upon a number of conscientious, sincere, and zealous souls, that slavery was forbidden by the Bible, and therefore a sin.[64]

By way of their religious association with the American Home Missionary Society, abolitionists were bound together with other kindred colonies throughout Illinois. The Quakers,[65] small in number in Illinois, were also longtime supporters of ending slavery in the United States and many of them, but not all, along with some Baptists, Catholics, Lutherans and Methodists, were also known to help support the success of the illegal activities of the UGRR.

During the 1820s and 30s many churches chose a tepid course regarding their response to the antislavery crusade, out of fear that real commitment would drive away proslavery membership. Abolitionists did not hesitate to characterize any religious sects' empty gestures to the cause as a compromise with conscience and a denial of the fact that slavery was a sin. By the late 1830s and early 40s many denominations had split over the slavery question.

Like the civil rights and anti–Vietnam war dissenters and demonstrators a century later, these were 19th-century practitioners of a very similar civil disobedience. The Fugitive Slave Law, passed by Congress in 1793 and signed by George Washington, and a stronger version passed by the federal government as part of the Compromise of 1850 made it illegal for any American, anywhere, to help or harbor runaway slaves. Imprisonment, stiff fines and the threat of physical violence were the stakes if one decided to attach himself or herself to working on "freedom's highway." Men and women gallant enough to address a gathering called to present abolitionist views were often furiously attacked. They were sometimes showered with rotten eggs and stones and were occasionally whipped and driven from the premises.

Attacks on abolitionists did have the beneficial effect of publicizing the fact that moderate white Americans as well as vocal antislavery advocates were both, in the ultimate scheme of things, vulnerable to proslavery forces that might eventually destroy free speech and the principles of due process. Many calculating abolitionists knew that drawing attention to these attacks and emphasizing them as threats to free speech and civil liberties would eventually further the cause. The lesson abolitionists taught went beyond the "slavery issue" only, for in due course they helped convince others to stand up against the advocates of slavery or later risk much greater consequences. Antislavery crusaders were not only standing up for the dignity and status of all human beings but, at the same time, were defending fundamental values of a truly democratic society; the rights to unfettered inquiry and open discussion. When people allied themselves to the proslavery position, they were joining forces with those who opposed a citizen's right to speak freely. The liberty to argue, disagree, hear an idea that might change your mind or follow your own conscience was at stake.

In the late 1830s an incident occurred in rural Knox County that illustrated the extreme antiabolitionist sentiment of many while it simultaneously revealed the wish of others who wanted an open hearing. An account found in E. P. Chambers's *Reminiscences of Early Days* (he was the son of Matthew Chambers, a highly regarded community leader) describes a band of rabble shouting down and egging the well-known Illinois abolitionist lecturer, Chauncey Cook. Though no date is found on Chambers's manuscript, the same incident was reported by Benjamin Lundy in *Genius of Universal Emancipation*, June 28, 1839. E. P. Chambers's firsthand observations detail much more than a description of roughnecks bent on breaking up an antislavery gathering. His story also shows the reluctance of many individuals in attendance to give up their right to hear a controversial speaker, whether they agreed with him or not. There were clearly some pioneers on hand at the lecture who were not enthusiastic watching the principle of free speech trifled with so casually:

> While living in Knoxville I was witness of an event unique in the history of Knox county. It was the mobbing of Rev. Chauncy Cook, a dignified Congregational minister, father of the Honorable Burton C. Cook, a prominent lawyer and for several years representative of the Ottawa district in Congress. While no blood was shed, nor any bodily injury inflicted, and it turned out almost a fiasco, it was sufficient to show the bad passions and prejudices aroused during the early period of the antislavery agitation.
>
> Mr. Cook had come to Knoxville to deliver an anti-slavery lecture ... I was surprised to see the kind of crowd going there and immediately inferred the preacher who was speaking then must be very popular to draw such a crowd which seldom, and some of them perhaps never attended church, and asked my older brother, clerking in the store, what it meant. He smiled and said I had better go over and see. I accepted this advice and hastened over.
>
> Conspicuous in the crowd as I now recall it, was its leader, a very lame man and "Old Bland," as he was called with his usual four or five feet hickory staff. Bland was one of the characters of his time, smart, but usually got drunk every Saturday he came to town and gathered a crowd around him listening to his sometimes witty, but more often nonsensical speeches. These were no doubt representative of the whole crowd which came from the grocery stores as the saloons were styled in those days. Mr. Cook, while able and dignified, was pleasant and winning, even to children, as I can testify.
>
> I was therefore disappointed greatly upon entering the building to find the crowd I was going there, seated at the rear end of the room interrupting the speaker with loud remarks, singing darkie songs, stamping, and old Bland's hickory staff doing full duty, thumping on the floor. Finding they could not prevent his speaking the leader arose and said: "Those opposed to the preacher will leave the house." Immediately the crowd arose, when Mr. Cook very pleasantly invited them to remain. Mr. Holcomb at the same time warned the mob that he would hold them responsible for any damage done, believing they had some ulterior bad purpose in withdrawing. To this

the leader replied to Mr. Holcomb: "You are not the man we thought you were." To which old Mrs. Jackson, a high spirited Southern woman, notwithstanding, she had two sons who were rich slaveholders, but she a good Presbyterian Christian, instantly shouted back to the leader: "he is just such a man as we took him to be." The woman showed as much courage as the men, not one leaving I think during the whole disturbance. After the mob left the meeting proceeded pleasantly for a time, but after a while by the uneasiness of the audience and the rush of some to the windows to hold them down and others to the door to keep it closed, I knew, for I could not see out, that the mob had returned. The windows were mostly kept down, but after a struggle the door was forced open, when in came a rapid succession, a volley of rotten and fresh eggs, aimed at the speaker, who though considerably past middle age and inclined slightly to corpulency, was an expert dodger and none of the eggs hit him and he maintained his place in the pulpit.

But the young pastor of the church, the Rev. John J. Miter,[66] was driven out of it. The egg throwing continued for some time and one of the mob rushed up to a small boy and ordered him to hold the basket from which he picked the eggs to hurl at the ministers.[67]

One notable aspect of the Underground Railroad movement was that it was not beholden to any of the traditional power bases in the country. Abolitionists and UGRR operators alike usually turned a cold shoulder to both major political parties. They did not necessarily need financiers, wealthy manufacturers or businessmen to fund them. Woven into all of this, in many cases, was the element of family loyalty. In the majority of counties within the three rivers, fathers, mothers, sons and daughters working with aunts and uncles, nieces and nephews and even grandparents with grandchildren were all actually involved with the operation of the Underground Railroad. Slave catchers and law enforcement officers found it impossible to suborn one member of a family to betray the others.

Many of the abolitionist settlers who moved into the Military Tract from the east were friends and neighbors well before they arrived in Illinois. This was true of most of the families in the early Galesburg settlement and of a good number of people in western Peoria County, northeastern Fulton County, and much of Stark County. Their longstanding connections were deep and strong.

The Galesburg group extended itself out and into the area Underground network and, indeed, had two Knox College[68] trustees operating as "agents." Samuel G. Wright, a trustee from 1849 to 1872, lived in Stark County not far from Galesburg and kept a fascinating diary that included notes about "carrying fugitive slaves." The other college trustee, who served in that capacity from 1852 to 1883, was the same William J. Phelps whose barn lantern, south of Elmwood, signaled safe passage to those traveling the fugitive highway. However, the Yankee prairie town of Galesburg was clearly the regional base station for the organized resistance. One Galesburg newspaper said Gale's town was called by some in Quincy "the little nigger stealing town ... a nest of nigger thieves" and the *Chicago Times* wrote before the Civil War that the town was a "center of abolitionism in the state."[69]

Throughout its early history, when its population was concentrated in its southern counties, Illinois was technically a "free state," but in reality, the southern part of Illinois was a slave state.[70] That part of Illinois was settled by southerners who brought slaves and indentured servants to the territory via the Carolinas, Virginia, Kentucky, Tennessee and Missouri. When Illinois joined the Union in 1818, slavery was forbidden, but indentured servitude was permitted. In 1819 several laws were passed which, in effect, stripped blacks of their full legal rights and these laws, called "black codes," grew even harsher in the years ahead.[71] Scores of residents in northern Illinois, many of whom were "Yankees," rejected slavery's existence in any form. Here, many aspiring northern wage earners and small farmers did not want to compete with slave labor in their own backyard. They were joined by another group of former New Englanders[72] whose religious convictions and moral idealism caused them to stand with the wage earners and farmers against the "peculiar institution." Two very different American cultures collided in the counties of west central Illinois before the Civil War. E. P. Chambers recalled a story that bluntly showed the differences:

> To show how low Yankees were rated here at this time, a remark of old Bland's will indicate. Some movers stopped in front of the Knoxville [Illinois] court house, while being constructed, evidently desiring information, Bland stepped forward and offered his services. An amusing conversation ensued, and when the immigrant asked what kind of people had settled here, Bland replied: "White folks, niggers and Yankees."[73]

Illinois, it must be remembered, extends 385 miles from top to bottom. The tension between the down-staters and up-staters created profound differences in Illinois until the beginning of the Civil War. The Prairie State became a microcosm of the nation as a whole regarding the slavery issue:

> Illinois was the fractured Union in a mirror: divided in its allegiance, north and south, by its own sectional slant. Most of the upper half of the state had been settled by New Englanders; the lower, by pioneers from Georgia, Kentucky, and Tennessee.[74]

Central and west central Illinois were flash points where these two forces clashed.

Underground railroad historian Larry Gara[75] goes to great lengths to properly point out that numerous fugitives were required to go it alone in order to successfully achieve freedom.[76] In fact, most runaways who found their way to freedom did so through their own effort, wit, and guile. To the scores of those trying to find their way by themselves, without underground support, the North Star was enormously important:

I did not know north from south, east from west. I looked in vain for the north star; a heavy cloud hid it from my view. I walked up and down the road until near midnight, when the clouds disappeared, and I welcomed the sight of my friend — truly the slaves friend — the north star![77]

There were surely runaway slaves who did not have enough information about where or how to find "operators." Others might have had directions to a "station," but were simply unable to connect with an "agent." Many runaways were understandably suspicious of whites[78] in general and others had been intentionally misled about the work of abolitionists. The extent of distrust many fugitives felt toward anyone who was white, even if aid and comfort was offered, was captured in an account left by O. A. Garretson, a relative of an active southeastern Iowa UGRR operator. There were undoubtedly numerous runaways who decided to be as independent as possible over the course of their desperate passage:

At one time a stalwart and athletic negro was found in hiding on the farm of Joel Garretson. He was armed with a heavy club and a dangerous looking knife, and permitted no one to approach within reaching distance of him. He would accept food offered him if placed where he could reach it without coming in contact with the donor, but he always kept a safe distance between himself and would-be friends. In vain did Garretson and Hoag try to convince him that they would give him aid if he would trust in them: he departed as he came, unseen by friend or foe, determined to fight his own way to his intended refuge.[79]

The confidence felt when fugitives were given help by a free black UGRR "shepherd" was a particular source of security to runaways:

Many of the escaping fugitives were armed, and sooner than be taken, would have used their weapons.... A mulatto named Free, living at Springfield, had a fine team of horses, and plied regularly between Springfield and Chicago, helping many a slave to freedom. He was once pursued and shot, near Washington, Ill., but upon displaying an old rusty musket his three assailants fled in mortal terror, and he delivered his load safely. The shot lamed him for life.[80]

But making a connection with a UGRR "keeper," black or white, made a huge difference to escapees. Operators would feed the runaways who were usually desperate for food when they were connected to "agents." "Conductors" also distributed supplies of extra clothing to men, women and children who often appeared at a "station" with nothing more than the clothing they wore when they escaped.[81]

Frequently a fugitive's interaction with helpers along the way was only intermittent or accidental. In John W. Blassingame's massive work, *Slave Testimony*, one of the most gripping stories is based on an interview with John Anderson in the *Toronto Weekly Globe*, February 22, 1861. Anderson was a Missouri slave[82] whose six-week journey to Canada included passage through western Illinois. He accomplished most of this trip on his own but was aided as well by both blacks and whites along the way. The following selections are taken from the interview:

I. The Military Tract

John Anderson was born in the year 1831, in Howard County, state of Missouri. His mother was the slave of one Burton, a carpenter, who lived on a small farm near Fayette. His father, who was almost white, served as a steward on board a steamer, which sailed on the Missouri, but made his escape to South America while Anderson was young....

... Anderson acquired great proficiency in running, jumping, and other athletic amusements, usually practiced by slaves in the evening, which afterwards proved of great service to him....

... In September, 1853, when he had been about two months with McDonald [his owner] he made his escape....

... He usually traveled by night, and got what rest he could during the day. He suffered much from want of food, sometimes not tasting any for several days, and often he had to content himself with corn, hazel nuts, pawpaws (papayas) and raw potatoes. A dollar and a half was all the money he had when he started on his perilous journey, and of this he never spent any except when compelled to do so by extreme hunger.

One day, while resting himself by the wayside, a man on horseback rode up and attempted to capture him, but Anderson fled to a neighboring field and found protection among the stalks of corn....

... Near a Mississippi [River] village he met with a colored man, and gave him ten cents to buy some crackers for him. This man, in whom Anderson placed little confidence, after some delay brought him the crackers, which he greedily devoured. He crossed the Mississippi by night, using for that purpose a boat which he found near the river, and keeping clear of the ferry for fear of detection. It was now Saturday night, and about two weeks since he had left McDonald, and he had reached the free State of Illinois; but from the attempts made to capture him in this State, he was convinced that he was almost in as much danger there as he had been in Missouri.

On Sunday night he went into the house of a white man, an Englishman, who gave him a good supper and a bed.... His entertainer lent him a razor, by which he was enabled to indulge in the luxury of a shave. Having got breakfast, and after the good-hearted Englishman had prevailed on him to take some bread and apples in his pocket, John again set out with renewed strength and spirits....

... After two days, he struck a branch of the Illinois river, which he crossed, and after proceeding some distance, he came to a railway track, with the use of which he was acquainted. He next came to Bloomington, where he obtained some provisions. He availed himself of the railway track for a short distance north of Bloomington. Confused and bewildered, he met a man who promised him a ride if he would help him with his cow. Anderson consented to do so, and rode with the man to a certain village, when he was requested to leave. After leaving the village, Anderson again encountered him and accompanied him, notwithstanding his attempts to shun him. At this man's house he got his supper and a bed, and started early next morning before breakfast.... Overtaking some teams that were on the road to Rock Island,[83] he got on one of them and reached that city by daylight. Here he hired himself a barber, though he was quite uninstructed in the art of shaving. Remaining in that city for two days, he went to Chicago, the Abolition Society paying his fare.[84]

The haphazard nature of escapes and the unpredictable encounters runaways experienced were recounted by Indiana's most notorious UGRR operator, Levi Coffin, in his book *Reminiscences*. One such account, entitled "Narratives of a Nameless Woman," describes a fugitive's lengthy journey, which started in Mississippi and eventually took her through Illinois on her way to safety in Canada. This story also suggests that food and other kinds of aid were given along the way by both blacks and whites:

> There lived in Mississippi, a black woman who was poor, ignorant, and a slave, but rich in the knowledge of the truth as it is in Jesus, and strong in unwavering faith. Working in the field under the driver's lash, or alone in her little hut, she never ceased praying to God, asking him to help her to escape, and assist and protect her on the long journey to the North. She had heard there was a place called Canada, far to the northward, where all were free, and learned that, in order to reach it, she must go a long way up the Mississippi River, then cross over and steer her course by the north star....
>
> ... This slave woman managed to evade the dogs by wading in pools and streams of water, where she knew they would lose the scent and be thrown off her trail....
>
> ... She had a long journey after that, lasting for several months, and encountered many dangers, but was preserved safe through them all. She traveled at night and hid in the thickets during the day, living most on fruit and green corn, but venturing now and then to call at negro huts and beg for a little of the scanty food which they afforded. When she came to rivers and streams of water too deep for wading, she made rafts of logs or poles, tied together with grape-vines or hickory withes, and poled or paddled herself across as best she could. Reaching Illinois, she met with kind people who aided her on to Detroit, Michigan. Here also she found friends and was ferried across to Canada.[85]

The web of "agents" and "stations" in Illinois was at the western margin of the national antislavery and Underground Railroad network. The antislavery movement, of which the western Illinois wing was a part, had been tremendously influenced by writers and orators in the east, like William Lloyd Garrison, publisher of *The Liberator*.[86] Garrison's one-time associate, Benjamin Lundy, moved to Putnam County in Illinois in 1838 and began publishing again his abolitionist newspaper, *Genius of Universal Emancipation*. The nearly larger-than-life former fugitive slave and abolitionist leader Frederick Douglass, lectured inside the three rivers before the Civil War. The significance of his lectures in Illinois was described by James and Lois Horton in *Hard Road to Freedom*: "for many whites attending these lectures, it was the first time they had heard a black speaker."[87] The work of the American Colonization Society to do away with slavery by purchasing slaves and sending them to Sierra Leone and Liberia in Africa, were familiar to the people of the Prairie State. The national antislavery forces (particularly those composed of people who supported political solutions) eventually gave birth to the Liberty Party. Founded in 1840, only a few years after the great abolitionist martyr Elijah P. Lovejoy was murdered in Alton by a proslavery mob, the Liberty Party was put together by totally committed abolitionists. Its first nominee for the

United States' presidency was James Birney in 1840. The Liberty Party stood for "free soil, free speech, free labor, and free men." By the end of the 1840s, a greatly expanded version of the Liberty Party called itself the Free Soil Party. Many of the Party's leading figures in Illinois came from the state's western counties. John Cross, for a time a Knox County resident, who was also a well-known radical "outside agitator" and one of Weld's "Seventy," was a member of the Liberty Party in the state. Theodore Weld, one of the nation's leading abolitionists, had at one time been a student of George Washington Gale's in New York State. Historian S. E. Morison described Weld as "a great bear of a man himself ... capable of cowing a mob or whipping an assailant which he often had to do."[88] Weld, with others, helped organize his "Seventy" to spread the crusade's word throughout the north.[89] "The harvest is great," he told them — "behold, I send you forth as lambs among the wolves." In Illinois, Cross took Weld's message in earnest and before long was given a title that pleased him: "Superintendent" of the Underground Railroad. If the overwhelming majority of people associated with the UGRR wanted to keep their efforts a secret, it was Cross's goal intentionally to do otherwise. He succeeded.

The Illinois Anti-Slavery Society was composed of numerous individuals who were eventually involved with the establishment of the Liberty Party in the state. Though some free soilers argued for political solutions that would restrict slavery to the south, others who addressed the slavery issue much more broadly were of a more radical stripe. In time, as has often happened in American history, both dominant political parties, the Whigs and Democrats, had to make compromising overtures to the third party. The antislavery crusade, therefore, had both national and local structures and this situation was a benefit to the Underground Railroad.

Against this backdrop, it is important to remember that after 1812 the huge Mississippi Valley Territory experienced a great population influx as Americans moved westward. Many experimental communities arose in the "new west." Robert Owen's New Harmony community in Indiana and the communal Amana Colonies in Iowa are particularly well-known examples of these experimental societies.

In western Illinois, along with the reforming abolitionists, two rather remarkable religious sects attempted to establish themselves at this time. The best known, and ultimately most successful, were the Mormons, who based themselves and built their temple at Nauvoo in Hancock County. Their belief in polygamy was just one of many practices that infuriated their neighbors. The murder of their prophet, Joseph Smith, in 1844 began the dissolution of the Mormons in Nauvoo. Two years later they fled Illinois under the leadership of Brigham Young, most moving west to Utah. At roughly the same time, the Scandinavian Janssonites, led by Eric Jansson, were settling south of Cambridge in Henry County. This group, which called its community Bishop Hill, had fled Sweden as religious dissenters in order to follow the teaching of their charismatic leader, who established his "utopia on the prairie" based on communal principles. This community was brought down when Jansson was murdered in 1850. His followers waited three days hoping for his resurrection, which failed to manifest itself, and the colony gradually disbanded thereafter. In some ways abolitionists and antislavery loyalists, though considered by most in the state to be people who "went too far" on the slavery issue, did not seem nearly as extreme as the Mormons or Janssonites.

Waterways were central to the success of the Underground Railroad movement. To appreciate this, one need only look at a map of UGRR routes in western New York and in west-central and western Pennsylvania. Underground railroad historians have uncovered and verified a truly remarkable number of escape routes and clusters existing from there all the way to the Mississippi River. But a large gap in the Underground Railroad existed between the western Indiana border and central Illinois. The map in Professor Wilbur Siebert's[90] highly regarded 1898 book, *The Underground Railroad from Slavery to Freedom*, highlights this untraveled ground.[91] This map does not list a single station in east-central or southeastern Illinois. Some "depots" have been discovered since the publication of Siebert's book, but not many. One reason for this dearth of stations may well be the fact that no major rivers flow through this part of Illinois. None of the rivers in this region match, in size, the Rock, Mississippi, or Illinois. As was previously mentioned, one western Illinois escape route hugged the Rock River and another "way to freedom" moved close to the eastern side of the Illinois River. In addition, four smaller western Illinois rivers fell inside or close to the boundaries of the big three: the Green,[92] Edwards, LaMoine, and Spoon. Most people at this time, including slaves, knew that all but a few rivers flowed south. By moving against the current runaways could be reasonably confident that they were heading north. All seven of these rivers were fed by countless creeks, streams, runs, and forks, and their high banks, deep ravines and low-level flood plains with trees and scrub brush served as cover. Flatboats were normally used to descend the rivers, but keelboats and barges could travel in either direction. By 1815, many steamboats plied the Mississippi and in the early 1820s the first steamboats appeared on the Illinois River. By the 1850s, almost all riverboats on the Illinois and Mississippi had slaves working as deckhands, cabin boys, cooks, and stevedores. In addition, many slaves were onboard these boats serving as valets, maids and nurses to their owners. If escaping slaves coming off these waterways did make it to this part of Illinois, they needed to know these basic points: (1) stay east of the Mississippi; (2) stay west of the Illinois; and (3) stay close to the Rock. By so doing, they could follow the course of any of these three rivers to ultimate freedom in "Victoria's domain."[93] (Some fugitives did not travel all the way to Canada, but decided to take up residence in various free states instead.) There were rivers in every county but one (Warren) inside the Military Tract. An absconder who disembarked at Oquawka in Henderson County, or in Keithsburg or New Boston in Mercer County need only find and follow the Edwards River, Henderson Creek, or Pope Creek to get to clustered stations in Sunbeam, "Carnahan's Place," or New Windsor. Just east, escape routes formed a mendota[94] at Andover and Cambridge in Henry County.[95] The Spoon River, which meanders through Stark, Knox, and Fulton counties, provided a remarkable number of "scattered waywagons"[96] near to its course. It is worth noting that waterways could also be a safe means of travel in the middle of the winter when they were frozen solid. A slave could rapidly move on top of the hard surface and in extremely cold weather it was unlikely a fugitive would be seen by friend or foe if a runaway stayed close to the shoreline.

The eastern and southeastern counties in Illinois were pioneered by Hoosiers with strong southern loyalties. There were relatively few "Yankee" settlers. These counties were filled with "Copperheads"[97] during the Civil War and most people there were more inclined to capture than to help runaway slaves. Verna Cooley wrote this in an article entitled "Illinois and the Underground Railroad to Canada" that appeared in the *Journal of the Illinois State Historical Society* in 1917:

> Few lines were known in the South except those developed by some Covenanter Communities between Chester and Centralia. The Southeast was the enemy's country for the fugitive. Bitter animosity was felt by the people of this region toward any person aiding the slave and also toward any section which distinguished itself in that respect. This feeling is expressed by the Shawneetown *Gazette* as a result of the satisfaction expressed by Chicago over the discharge of a slave from the claims of a slave agent. The paper says, "We of the South do not regard Chicago as belonging to Illinois. It is as perfect a sink hole of abolitionism as Boston or Cincinnati."[98]

Therefore, the combination of Hoosier settlers and no major rivers (plus a lack of tall prairie grass in southeastern Illinois) seems to help explain the empty area in Siebert's map. A slave crossing into the state from Kentucky or southwestern Indiana was much better off following the Wabash and White Rivers north to where they would find a heavy concentration of Underground Railroad safe havens. As mentioned earlier, river towns could mean trouble and were often avoided. There, law officers, slave catchers, and bounty hunters were likely to be lurking, and many slaves on the run knew of this danger, and left the waterways to dodge the larger river towns.

The challenge of finding a way to cross the Mississippi, Illinois, or Rock River was alarming, if not frightening. Even the difficulty of making it over smaller rivers if they were swollen by floods could be very discouraging. Fugitives were fortunate if they found a boat or skiff to cross any river. William Wells Brown wrote the following account of crossing the Mississippi River with his mother in a skiff he found:

> The time at length arrived, and we left the city just as the clock struck nine. We proceeded to the upper part of the city, where I had been two or three times during the day, and selected a skiff to carry us across the river. The boat was not mine, nor

did I know to whom it did belong; neither did I care. The boat was fastened with a small pole, which, with the aid of a rail, I soon loosened from its moorings. After hunting round and finding a board to use as an orr, I turned to the city, and bidding it a long farewell, pushed off my boat. The current running very swift, we had not reached the middle of the stream before we were directly opposite the city.

We were soon upon the Illinois shore, and, leaping from the boat, turned it adrift, and the last I saw of it it was going down the river at good speed.[99]

Runaways often put together crude rafts or floats built from logs or large tree branches tied together; sometimes they swam. Escapees would sometimes attempt to gain passage on a ferry, but this was very dangerous. In Missouri it was illegal to do business with a slave without approval from the slave's owner. A ferryboat operator or any other boatman found guilty of carrying a slave across the water without the owner's permission could be made to pay for the value of the slave plus damages to the master. Nonetheless, the opportunity to bribe boat captains did arise and some fugitives found ways to hide on boats and ferries in order to make it across the Mississippi to Illinois.

It is likely that a river played a crucial part in what is one of the most compelling and widely told stories about the UGRR in Illinois. Its main characters were a black woman, Susan Van Allen Richardson, and her former slave master, Andrew Borders. Borders was from Randolph County in southern Illinois, where legal authorities were sympathetic to slavery. In fact, slavery had existed continuously in that county from the time the French first occupied

PHOTOGRAPH BY THE AUTHOR.

View of the Mississippi River from its eastern shore in the free state of Illinois looking west from Henderson County.

the region.[100] Borders had a reputation for harsh treatment of his slaves and upon hearing of a disagreement between Susan and his wife one afternoon, he decided he would flog the slave the next day. However, when Susan overheard the Borders discussing this incident and their decision to beat her, she decided to flee north that night. Susan fled with her two young children, her older half-grown son, and another slave woman named Hannah. She went to the home of William Hayes, a known antislavery man who lived close to Borders's homestead. We know of William Hayes thanks to the research and writing of Carol Pirtle. Her book, *Betwixt Two Suns*,[101] is the best account we have of the Susan "Aunt Sukey" Van Allen Richardson tale. Hayes lived for a time near Peoria and had relatives in Knox and Stark counties. His uncle, Sylvanus Ferris, helped found the city of Galesburg and Knox College. Hayes's story is an intriguing one in its own right. A member of the Reformed Presbyterian Church, he was sued for helping Susan and her party escape to Knox County. That litigation eventually reached the Illinois Supreme Court, where Hayes lost. When he died in the mid–1850s, Hayes left his wife and children financially strapped because of his legal expenses and lost income.

On September 1, 1842, these five runaways fled north using Hayes as their guide. Pirtle believes it was likely that the group traveled part of the way by boat up the Illinois River. On September 6th, having slept the night before near Farmington, they were moved by "brakeman" Eli Wilson across Knox County to the property of the Reverend John Cross, the aforementioned radical UGRR activist. However, after a long chase, they were caught on Cross's homestead hiding in a cornfield. The runaways were incarcerated in the Knox County Jail and when Borders learned of their whereabouts, he came to Knoxville to claim all except Hannah. Local abolitionists argued that he could not prove that they were his slaves and Borders was forced to return to Randolph County to get papers to verify his claim. The fugitives were eventually released by the sheriff, but were ordered not to leave the area. Susan, or "Aunt Sukey" as she was called, found employment doing laundry and her oldest son found a job doing chores on a nearby farm. A day after Susan had started living in her own place, Borders and his son returned. The sheriff, Peter Frans, helped round up Susan's children, and Borders assumed that once he had the children, Susan would come to him. But abolitionist friends talked her out of giving herself up, disguised her, and spirited her off in a sleigh to Galesburg. After months of legal wrangling that involved prominent local citizens, such as George Washington Gale and Nehemiah West, weighing in on Susan's behalf, Borders returned to southern Illinois with her children. Susan eventually took up residence in Galesburg, joined the old first church, helped found the first black church in town, and became a local UGRR operator; she never saw her three children again.[102] She married H. Vanolar/Van Allen in 1846, married Thomas Richardson in 1857 and lived in Galesburg until the turn of the century. In the early 1900s she moved to Chicago to live with her

LIBERTY LINE.
NEW ARRANGEMENT---NIGHT AND DAY.

The improved and splendid Locomotives, Clarkson and Lundy, with their trains fitted up in the best style of accommodation for passengers, will run their regular trips during the present season, between the borders of the Patriarchal Dominion and Libertyville, Upper Canada. Gentlemen and Ladies, who may wish to improve their health or circumstances, by a northern tour; are respectfully invited to give us their patronage.
SEATS FREE, *irrespective of color*.
Necessary Clothing furnished gratuitously to such as have "*fallen among thieves.*"

"Hide the outcasts---let the oppressed go free."---*Bible*.
☞For seats apply at any of the trap doors, or to the conductor of the train.
J. CROSS, *Proprietor*.
N. B. For the special benefit of Pro-Slavery Police Officers, an extra heavy wagon for Texas, will be furnished, whenever it may be necessary, in which they will be forwarded as dead freight, to the "Valley of Rascals," always at the risk of the owners.
☞Extra Overcoats provided for such of them as are afflicted with protracted *chilly-phobia*.

FAC-SIMILE OF UNDERGROUND RAILWAY ADVERTISEMENT
(*From "The Western Citizen," July 13, 1844*)

SPECIAL COLLECTIONS AND ARCHIVES, KNOX COLLEGE.

This widely reproduced advertisement of the Underground Railroad first appeared in Chicago's *Western Citizen* in July 1844. John Cross submitted the illustration to the antislavery newspaper while living in Knox County, where he openly defied the Fugitive Slave Law.

daughter, Mary Van Allen Fleming. Susan Richardson died in 1904 and was buried in Galesburg's Hope Cemetery.[103]

The lasting effects in this part of western Illinois of the whole Borders/ Susan/Hayes affair encouraged more open and tolerant attitudes toward runaways than had previously existed among the general public. Boastful, even mocking quotes, from the Reverend Cross appeared in Chicago's antislavery newspaper, the *Western Citizen* in July 1844. Cross drew what is now a famous Underground Railroad illustration for the same issue of the Chicago newspaper, advertising his role as a Knox County UGRR conductor. This observation is supported by the Revered Samuel G. Wright's correspondence to Milton Badger in December 1842. "A better move for the cause of the oppressed probably could not have been started. Many of whom before were full of prejudice are now enlightened and their confidence gained."[104]

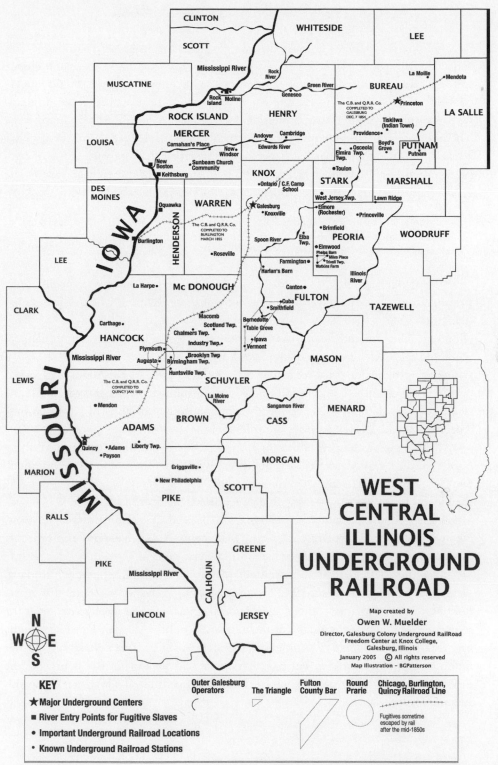

WEST CENTRAL ILLINOIS UNDERGROUND RAILROAD

Map created by

Owen W. Muelder

Director, Galesburg Colony Underground RailRoad
Freedom Center at Knox College,
Galesburg, Illinois

January 2005 © All rights reserved
Map Illustration – BGPatterson

KEY

★ Major Underground Centers
■ River Entry Points for Fugitive Slaves
• Important Underground Railroad Locations
• Known Underground Railroad Stations

Outer Galesburg Operators

The Triangle

Fulton County Bar

Round Prarie

Chicago, Burlington, Quincy Railroad Line

Fugitives sometime escaped by rail after the mid-1850s

BRENDA PATTERSON, BG PATTERSON GRAPHICS.

Despite the changed attitude that Wright describes in his letter to Badger, an active UGRR operation was very much needed for many years after the Susan Richardson affair was over. As late as the autumn of 1859 there were reports of kidnappers prowling the area trying to capture blacks in order to return them to servitude.[105] Until the end of the Civil War, professional slave catchers continued to kidnap blacks whether they were runaway slaves or freedmen.[106] All blacks had to constantly keep a wary eye out, but the haunting memory of slavery enhanced their sense of self-preservation. On September 10, 1875, Dr. J. T. Stewart, in a speech he gave to the eighth annual reunion of "Old Settlers Union of Peoria," recalled:

> Among my earliest recollections is ... old Black Fanny and her broadsword. Fanny was a runaway slave from Kentucky, who carried a large sword to protect herself against anyone who might attempt to capture and take her back into slavery.[107]

The danger of being stolen in the north and taken into captivity in the south was something black parents taught every one of their children. The possible loss of liberty to "mansteallers" was a regular lesson preached from the pulpits of black churches. The fact that many northern whites acted in concert with kidnappers required that blacks never let their guard down.[108]

The region inside the three major rivers of the western Illinois triangle remained deeply involved with the operation of the Underground Railroad and the abolitionist cause until Abraham Lincoln's death. Until 1865, any blacks in Illinois, or anywhere else in the United States, were vulnerable.

The following chapters of this book will take the reader along a rough, north by northeast route that runaway slaves might very well have followed in western Illinois. Some journeys were described by Underground Railroad participants during the time the Liberty Lines were functioning or were recalled by them after the Civil War ended. Other accounts were left by their children or the next generation of their relatives. Though not directly involved with the UGRR themselves, these reporters had either witnessed the events themselves or had heard descriptions of them directly from former operators. There are also descriptions that are taken from reputable historians; county, city or regional histories; a few contemporary newspaper articles that reveal new UGRR information; and one story published in the *Elmwood Gazette* under the sobriquet H. B. These accounts, for the most part, tell the story of Freedom's Highway from the standpoint of people who participated in it. The descriptions do not follow a chronological order, but represent events that took place in Illinois from the early 19th century when Illinois joined the Union, until 1865, when the Thirteenth Amendment was ratified.

II

Adams County — Free Soil but Not Free

Quincy, in Adams County north of St. Louis, was famous or infamous depending on which side one was on, as the "jumping off point" on the western Illinois Underground Railroad. The community was on free soil, but fugitive slaves were far from being free in the river town. Named after John Quincy Adams,[1] it was located across the Mississippi River from the slave state of Missouri. By 1860, the largest concentration of Missouri slaves lived in the north central part of the state, directly west of Quincy. This belt of widespread slavery followed the course of the Missouri River from its mouth all the way across the state to its western border.[2] In many Missouri counties, 10 to 30 percent of the population were slaves; in a few, slaves comprised 30 to 50 percent of the total population.[3] Quincy was home to several abolitionists, some of whom became active "operators" of the UGRR, eager to liberate slaves from across the river.

In the 1840s, as antislavery societies were being formed in communities across western Illinois, Missouri counties along the Mississippi River such as Marion, Lewis, and Ralls were organizing antiabolition meetings. Here were heard strong denunciations of the work of abolitionists as well as calls to organize direct action against them.[4] These antiabolition groups conducted slave patrols that roamed the countryside at will checking the papers of slaves and even investigating white strangers traveling through the region. These patrolling parties destroyed boats and rafts found unattended by rivers and streams. The vigilante bands helped to track down runaways said to be passing through the vicinity.[5] In Clark County, at the extreme northeast tip of the state, the Des Moines River forms the border between Iowa and Missouri, weaving a distance of approximately 25 miles before emptying into the Mississippi. North of this stretch of water, only a short distance away, UGRR "sta-

35

tions" thrived in the Iowa communities of Denmark, New Garden, and Salem. The resistance operators in this area sent runaways across the Mississippi River into Illinois.

In 1837, just outside Quincy, Dr. David Nelson, who stood 6'2" with broad shoulders and a sturdy build, founded the Mission Institute. Like Knox College, it was established as a manual labor school, its main purpose being to train young men for the ministry and missionary work. Like Knox, it clearly associated itself with antislavery theology, emphasizing the basic idea that to hold people in bondage was a sin. Hugh Ferris, the son of Sylvanus Ferris, one of Galesburg's most prominent early settlers, was once enrolled at the institute.[6] The ties between Quincy and Galesburg were established almost immediately. In 1838, Nelson, who had been a surgeon for the United States Army during the War of 1812, was joined at the Mission Institute by Moses Hunter, an abolitionist zealot from New York. Hunter's appearance must have seemed very strange to the residents of the frontier river town, as he moved about wearing robes that emulated Biblical garb. In 1836, Nelson, a committed antislavery advocate, was forced by a threatening mob to flee Palmyra, Missouri. His harrowing escape required him to hide in brush and move only at night before he made it safely across the river to Quincy. It was believed that, from time to time, Mission Institute students crossed the river "and tapped stones together on the Missouri side; from the woods runaway slaves emerged to be guided across the river and sent 16 miles inland to a barn [Mission Institute], which, ... served as a 'waiting room' of the Underground Railroad."[7] However, after thriving for about five years, the Mission Institute was burned in March 1843 by Missourians, whose tracks through the snow revealed they had left the scene of the crime by departing toward the river. No arrests were ever made for this obvious case of arson. Dr. Nelson died the next year and the institute faded away a few years later, but he was long remembered in Adams County for his powerful antislavery addresses.[8]

Abolitionists like Nelson had come to learn of one very effective way to sway some people to their way of thinking. They would sponsor, advertise, and deliver powerful public lectures on what antislavery crusaders had witnessed firsthand while traveling or living in the South. Audiences were often stunned and shaken to hear in detail what it was like to endure slavery on a daily basis. The descriptions included not only scenes of brutal floggings and whippings but also instances of cruel and casually handed out punishments to slaves for the slightest mistakes. Five years before his death, Nelson returned East and delivered an address in South Hampton, Massachusetts, where, included in his remarks was the following story reflecting abrupt, horrifying, and painful punishment meted out to a slave:

> I have not attempted to harrow your feelings with stories of cruelty. I will, however, mention one or two among the many incidents that came under my observation as

family physician. I was one day dressing a blister, and the mistress of the house sent a little black girl into the kitchen to bring me some warm water. She probably mistook her message; for she returned with a bowl full of boiling water; which her mistress no sooner perceived, than she thrust her hand into it, and held it there till it was half cooked.[9]

Dr. Richard Eels, a physician who moved to Quincy in 1833, was another well-known Underground Railroad operator in the town at that time. Eels, who was once

PHOTOGRAPH BY THE AUTHOR.

Anti-slavery activist Dr. Richard Eels resided in this house in Quincy. He was one of the most committed Underground Railroad operators in Adams County.

convicted and fined for aiding a Missouri slave, lived in a handsome brick house on Jersey Street, only a few blocks from the river. His crime had been providing dry clothes for a runaway and giving him a ride in his wagon to the Mission Institute. The slave was eventually captured. The abolitionist physician thought he might not be implicated but the sheriff came to his house, found wet clothing left behind by the runaway, and Eels was indicted. He fled Quincy for Chicago (with the help of Underground Railroad operators to the north, like the Reverend Samuel G. Wright[10] of Stark County) when he feared the governor of Illinois was going to hand him over to Missouri authorities for aiding runaways. Later, once Eels was convinced he would not be extradited, he returned to Adams County for his trial and eventual punishment.[11] He was fined $400 by Judge Stephen Douglas. It was during this period, following intensified contact between Quincy and Galesburg operators, that the UGRR began to move "passengers" to Chicago.

One of the most audacious tales of women acting alone while conducting a UGRR operation was reported in a public address given by an early resident of western Illinois. In the early 1900s, Hirim Mars recalled a plan hatched by three females in Quincy during the 1850s:

> One night a runaway slave had been captured by the Quincy police and was being detained at the police station.
>
> Quincy was one of the first stations on the railway, and a base of supplies for the Galesburg station....
>
> There were women in Quincy who were specially strong abolitionists and they were always active.
>
> It was the women who came to the rescue of the slave who had been captured.
>
> On the evening of his capture, three women of that city, Mrs. Dr. Foote, wife of the Rev. Dr. Foote, for many years a trustee of Knox college and at one time a pastor of the first church in this city; Mrs. Willard Turner, and the wife of Dr. Eels, called at the police station and requested that they be admitted to bring the slave his supper.
>
> The jailer was a kind-hearted old man, knew the women well, and he granted their request. He allowed them to enter the cell and then he withdrew to the end of the corridor. After a while the women announced they were ready to go, and the jailer escorted three women from the jail and locked the cell.
>
> The next morning when he went to the cell to feed his prisoner he was greeted by a bright and cheery "Good morning!" by one of the women who met him at the cell door. In reply to his questioning she told him that he had locked her in the cell the night before, and that she was ready to get out. He could not or would not detain her, and by that time the negro was well on his way.[12]

Quincy's controversial reputation was sealed in 1841 when three abolitionists, George Thompson, Alanson Work and James E. Burr, were caught in Missouri aiding the escape of runaways. Thompson and Burr were students at the Mission Institute and Work taught and lived at the school with his wife and four children. They were arrested, tried, found guilty, and sentenced to 12 years each in the Missouri state

REPRODUCED FROM THOMPSON, GEORGE. DAYTON, OHIO, UNITED BRETHREN.

George Thompson, Alanson Work, and James E. Burr, from Quincy's Mission Institute, were incarcerated in the Palmyra, Missouri, jail for attempting to help slaves escape to Illinois. When their trial ended, they were found guilty and were sent to the Missouri state penitentiary.

penitentiary. The news of this incident spread like a prairie fire throughout the region. Work spent a little over three years in jail before he was paroled; Burr was released after four and a half years; and Thompson was incarcerated for nearly five years. Even in the midst of their nightmare experience in prison they took some solace from the fact that the story of their ordeal was circulated so widely that it was reported to have been passed along the Missouri slave grapevine.

The account of their brutal imprisonment, after they had been set up for capture by slaves used as decoys, was recorded in a book published by George Thompson before the Civil War. Before moving to Illinois, Thompson had lived in Ohio, where he was greatly influenced by the antislavery speeches of Theodore Weld.[13] What follows are excerpts from Thompson's book about what befell these three abolitionists:

> The Mission Institute being situated near the Mississippi River, and just across the River from a Slave State (Missouri), we could, as it were, hear the crack of the over-seer's whip — the shrieks and groans of those who were suffering its cruel inflictions. Their earnest cries for help — their sighs for deliverance — their importunate

entreaties, as they rehearsed to us their tales of woe, reached our ears, and our hearts melted with pity, while the resolution was formed to respond to their call; and if need be, risk our own liberty and lives to effect their rescue....

... About the first of July, 1841, James (Burr), with another brother, made a tour of mercy in to Missouri, which resulted in an agreement with two slaves, to meet them at a certain point of the river, on a certain evening, to assist them across the river, on their way to freedom. On the day appointed, we went, arriving at the place about the middle of the afternoon. Alanson and James went into the country to view and reconnoiter, while I remained in the skiff to fish, and await their return....

... After dark, a number of slaves came to Alanson and James, in the prairie, and pretended they were going with them. They had proceeded but a short distance, when on a sudden, the slaveholders arose out of the grass, with their rifles, and took them prisoners — placing the muzzle of their guns to their breasts, and threatening, "I will shoot him any how," — but the mercy of the Lord prevailed. They were bound and taken to a house, where they were kept, while the blood-hounds came in hot pursuit of me. I was in the skiff. At first three or four slaves came, and approaching the bank very cautiously, one asked, "Are you a *friend?*" I replied, "I am." I had talked with them but a short time, when suddenly I heard another kind of a salutation, "Come out of that, or I'll blow you through!" I looked up, and two guns were pointed at me from the bank. I was obedient to my new commanders — dropped my fishing pole, and marched up to them....

... I was bound, and marched barefoot, over hubs, roots, and stones. Host after host came with all speed to meet us, and "the earth rang again" with their fiendish yells. It seemed almost as if the infernal regions had been uncapped, and had vomited forth their legions to hail our approach, as if some long dreaded monster had been captured....

... We awoke refreshed and strengthened to endure the reproaches and sufferings which were before us, with patience, fortitude, and I trust submission. That morning a man came in to see us, who asked many questions, and made threats of shooting us on the spot....

... We were then tied together, and led by the slaves (to mortify us) five miles, to Palmyra. The city was moved at our approach, many saying, "Who are these?" "Well, you've made a fine haul," &c. In the court house, we had a mock trial before a magistrate and were "thrust into prison," to await the sitting of the court, two and a half months from that time....

... Last night there was a rabble around the jail nearly all night, carousing, and thirsting for our blood. Night gatherings around the jail are frequent....

... This morning a company came, gazed, talked, mocked, sneered. "This," said one, "is a *Gospel ship*"....

... To-day I have heard more of the feelings of the people here, than I have since I came. It is amazing what passions can dwell in the human heart.

"Brethren Brown and Turner came here about noon, and we talked with them through the grates. A crowd immediately gathered round, with savage wildness and hellish madness depicted in their countenances. They looked upon Brethren B. and T. with a fiendish, blood-thirsty eye, as they talked to us through the grates....

... At first they branded us with the name of Mormons, that which, *Abolitionists* excepted, there was not a more odious name in Missouri. This was soon known to be falsely applied. Then they called us Dr. Nelson's satellites — a name we were proud of—

and he had been driven from their midst and hunted like a wolf, fleeing, in dead of night, for his life. In the papers they published us as dyed-in-the-wool abolitionists....

... Not knowing what will be the issue of my trial, I desire to record a summary of my feelings, that it may be known what they are, should I suddenly be killed or thrust into States prison.

I do not regret the step I took more than seven weeks ago; nor have I at any time been sorry for it, although thousands condemn and call me a thief, rascal, liar, and all that is vile and abominable — though many who love the Lord, and feel for the slave, and are my friends, disapprove of my course, yet I cannot see wherein I acted contrary to my master's direction or the spirit of the Gospel. My conscience approbates my course.

That helping the poor is *right*, I have no doubt; and although the slave holders may plead it is taking their *property*, I feel, and am bold to affirm, that there is no such thing as their having property in man. It is all a sham. The slaves, by the law of God, own themselves, and if we can relieve them in any proper way, we are bound, by the laws of our king — by the bonds of humanity — by the feelings of mercy — by the spirit of the blessed gospel — to do it....

... To-day, the slaves we would have helped, were here, among many others, who came to see us. They looked very much ashamed, and seemed to regret what they did, since they have ascertained that we were friends, and wished to do them good. But we have not the least hard feeling toward them — would just as soon help them to freedom as any others, though they may have voluntarily betrayed us, as some say. We have rather felt inclined to think that it was whipped out of them, by their masters — yet there are some things which strongly favor the former. It is said that the one who was foremost in the affair, belonged to a genuine *kidnapper* — if so, he may have feared we were like his master, and consequently betrayed us. And it is a well known fact, that slaves in general are taught that abolitionists are their worst *enemies*. It is not therefore to be wondered at, that they should be suspicious of them, till this idea is corrected — and this has been, and will be one good result of our imprisonment. The slaves will learn the true character of abolitionists, and fly to them for help from every quarter.

Another thing, that favors the idea that they betrayed us. The slaves informed us, that they got together one night — tied the one who was leader in the matter, to a tree, and gave him *fifty* lashes! So incensed were they at him, for treating in such a manner, those who loved them....

SLAVE WHIPPED

... Last night a slave passing the Jail, was ordered by Esq. Wilson to stop. "Where are you going?" "My master sent me after the Doctor." "It is a d — — d lie!" said Wilson — "Pull off your shirt." "I can't do that," said the slave, and took hold of Wilson. The guards came to his help, and held the slave while Wilson gave him twenty lashes! "Now go home," said he. "I shan't, I shall go after the Doctor," replied the slave, and ran, Wilson pursuing him....

SALE OF HUMAN BEINGS! — JOURNAL

... I know not in what words to express my feelings — my mind is filled with mingled emotions of amazement, indignation, pity, and horror. At noon, eight or ten horses were sold, at sheriff's sale, and then a woman and her child, for four hundred and sixty-five dollars — lastly, a man for five hundred and "Seventy"-one dollars! Of such things I have often *heard*, but never before *saw* them. O! the scene!

A crowd gathered round, and these immortal beings — bound to eternity, bought with the sweat, groans, blood, and death of Jesus Christ — destined to heaven or hell — bearing the impress of their Maker's hand — possessing feelings, emotions, and affections like ourselves, and the consciousness that they were *born* with the "inalienable rights of life, liberty, and the pursuit of happiness" — *these* were set up, cried, and knocked off under the hammer, to the highest bidder, for gold and silver...!

SENTENCE

... Monday morning, we again went before the court. After the different instructions were given to the judge, and he had charged the jury, that we were *guilty*, &c., they retired a short time, and returned with a verdict of "*Guilty, and twelve years in the penitentiary.*" Clapping of hands, and shouts of "good, good," filled the house. Though they had so strongly declared they would hang us, if we were sentenced for less than twenty years, they appeared to be satisfied, when this sentence was pronounced. "There," said one, "we've got clear of mobbing them!"...

... After we had been in the Penitentiary, nearly four years, a man who at the time of our trial (I believe he was present) lived in the adjoining county, said to us, "To your trial, twenty men came from Hannibal prepared to *hang* you in case of an acquittal.

THE JOURNEY TO THE PENITENTIARY

... The morning of the first of October, 1841, was cold and very stormy. We arose as usual — but about nine o'clock we were called to start for Jefferson. A crowd again assembled to take their farewell gaze at us. The rain was pouring down almost in torrents, but the stage came, and we, after bidding the jailer adieu, were seated, on the middle seat — the driver before, and the sheriff behind us....

THE MISSOURI RIVER

... In the afternoon of the third day, we came to the Missouri River, opposite the city of Jefferson, and the penitentiary. A messenger who went over for the ferry boat, reported that the abolitionists had come, and a multitude crowded the bank to behold the sight....

... A large concourse awaited our arrival, on the opposite bank, that they might meet and welcome to their city, those of whom they had heard so much. The mass of the male population, old and young, rich and poor, bond and free, were there — each one striving eagerly to get one view of an *abolitionist*! And from their running, and gazing, it was evident they expected to see something wonderful.

So elated were the people at our arrival among them, that many followed in our train, while others ran before, and on either side, like so many obedient servants, rejoicing to show their master honor, or homage to their king. I think the arrival of the President would not have caused greater "joy in that city...."

The Rules

... 1. "You must not speak to any prisoner, out of your cell, nor to each other in your cell."

... 2. "You must not look up at any visitor — if it is your own brother; if you do, I'll flog you."

... 3. "You must always take off your cap, when speaking to an officer, or when an officer speaks to you."

... 4. "You must call no convict, 'Mr.'"

When I was before them, I used the expression, "Mr. Burr." "No, no; there are no *Misters* here." "Well, brother Burr, then." "No, there are no *brothers* here." "Well, what shall I call him?" "Why, *Burr*, in just the roughest way you can speak it." Frequently afterwards, we were checked for applying Mr. to a convict.

With the repetition of these rules, we were threatened with severe punishment upon the violation of them; and charged, "carry yourselves straight...."

Our Cell

... We were all allowed to be in one cell. This was a great mercy. Had we been separated and scattered among the wicked, I know not what would have become of us....

... Our cell is twelve feet by eight — arched — brick, and plastered — a window, on hinges, in the corner at the top, defended by two large iron bars — an iron door, about four feet by twenty-two inches, with a thick wooden door on the outside. When we went into it, there were two beds — one double, and one single one. The covering of the double bed, consisted of two small, very poor, and thin Indian blankets, under which Alanson and myself *tried* to sleep; but the cold would frequently so molest us, that we could sleep but little the whole night. They were both too thin, short, and narrow — but these, or nothing....

Flogging

... When Brother Edward Turner was talking with us at our jail window, about coming to the penitentiary, he remarked that we would probably find Missourians *semi-barbarians*. We have found the saying fully verified. As our cell was next to the guard-room, we could hear the charges, the threats, the curses, the rage of the officers, and the blows they inflicted. We could hear the cries and groans of the poor sufferers....

The Runaways

... About the first of November, as I was walking home from the chopping, about three miles distant, with twelve or twenty others, in double file, with a guard before, and two behind, with their muskets, two of the hands, as we were passing a thicket, dropped their axes, and suddenly broke into the woods, bounding through the thicket with almost incredible swiftness. Each had on a chain, but the thoughts of liberty made them light and nimble. Both were in danger of being shot, but the love of liberty nerved them to risk even their lives. The sensations produced in my mind cannot be described by words. One was wounded and taken; the other escaped. That evening the wounded man was punished very severely, and another heavy chain put on him....

That "Salt" Again

... Not far from this time, a slave was put in here for punishment. This slave was a Christian, could read, and loved his Bible. He has a family. He soon found us out, and was eager for conversation — said he saw us when we came — knew what we came for, &c. He wanted a "*writing*" — we told him we could not, in our circumstances, give one — but we placed the "salt" before him. We told him of Canada — we told him of where he would find friends — and assisted to plan for getting his family away....

"Abolition All the Time"

... As James was at work, outside, with two others, on the Fourth of July, a slave watching his opportunity, when James was alone, asked, "Are you one of the three abolitionists who came here last fall?" "I am." "Are you *abolition* ALL THE TIME?" — meaning if he still continued to be an abolitionist, though in prison and suffering on account of it. James answered, "I *am* abolition all the time." Then came up another prisoner, and asked the slave, "Why are you not keeping *Fourth of July*?" The slave, very beautifully and expressively answered, "Ah, when I am FREE, I will keep Fourth of July — I'll keep it then, Sundays, and *all* days."...

Cutting Hair, and Shaving Heads

... It was the usual custom of the officers to cut the hair close, on one half of the head — and in cases of misconduct, to shave the head.

For a year and a half or two years, our hair was cut in this fashion. Then it was suffered to grow naturally. Most of the prisoners thought it a great trial to have their heads thus disfigured — and indeed it did present a singular appearance — but I never thought it of sufficient consequence to ask for — if they "gave me my hair," well and good — if not, it was all the same. They were welcome, as I frequently told them, to a half, or the whole, if they wished it. The *character* was not affected thereby. It is done to keep prisoners from escaping, but it is all folly — for if a man is resolved to run away, he will go just as quick without, as with hair....

Shaving on the Sabbath

... It was the custom to have all the shaving done on the Sabbath, because they could not spend time on a week day — so much gained, they thought! We felt that the practice was very wicked — endeavored to leave no means untried to be shaved on a week day — talked with wardens and overseers — besought and plead, but in vain. We talked and prayed together about it in our cell. On the third of April, Alanson refused to leave the cell and go down to be shaved. A great stir followed. A guard came and said, "Work, why don't you come down to be shaved?" "I feel that it would be wrong." The overseer came, threatened and coaxed — now flashing with rage, then speaking kindly. Capt. B. was quickly present, fiery and raging — his eyes flashing fury — he threatened, commanded, and stormed — "Do you not know the rules?" "I feel that I ought to obey God," "Well, put him in the dark cell, and see if that will be obeying God!" Alanson was then taken from us and put alone in a dark cell. The next morning one side of his head was shaved with a razor, and a heavy chain fastened to his leg. That evening he was summoned before the grand council, questioned and insulted, but not injured. The next morning early Alanson was brought back to us, and all hands kept in their cells that day. A general inquisition was held, and all were examined and questioned, which occupied most of the day. We spent our time in reading and prayer, not knowing what was before us.

When I was called to the guard-room, among many other things I was asked, "Has there not been an agreement between you that Work should refuse to be shaved?" "No sir." "Did he not try to persuade you to join with him?" "No sir. We talked and prayed about it, and each did as he thought best...."

THE SLAVE AND HIS CRIME

... A slave was brought here in chains, handcuffed and barefoot. What was his crime? Why he had been torn away from his wife, whom he dearly loved, and went one hundred miles to see her! And for this was he brought here, with a special charge to our tyrant, "Work him hard, feed him lightly, and flog him for every offence," all which was eagerly fulfilled....

... He was also flogged very severely for nothing, except that he was a poor slave. After three months he was probably sent South, for an infamous dealer in human flesh was around here buying up all he could, to take to the low countries....

A CASE OF CRUELTY

... Two prisoners dug through the cell wall, unlocked another cell, and let out two others, intending to scale the outside wall. They were discovered, and terribly punished immediately. Some who celled near by, said, they "never heard such hot times in the guard-room before." Others said they heard "much whipping and loud cries," and while they were whipping one, they heard Bradbury say, "Now get up." "I can't Mr. B." He then whipped him again, "Now get up, or I'll kill you." "Judge Brown, do stop Mr. B. I can't get up." "Then *drag* him to his cell." And as he was crawling to a cell near by, he was heard, "Do stop, Mr. Davis. I am going as fast as I can." He probably was kicking him along. In the morning, Capt. G. came to me and said, "Go there into the hall, pick up S., and carry him to his cell, he has the *backache*." Backache! O, what hard-heartedness...!

THE SLAVE'S REQUEST

... Soon after James left, a slave, with whom I had long been acquainted, came to me, and was very urgent that I should write him a free paper. "I am about to leave this place, and want a favor." I told him that I could not do such a thing. He entreated. Said I, "Try without." "I shall be caught." I told him where he would find friends. And when I made his case known to a wicked fellow prisoner, he said, "Do you have nothing to do with it. I'll attend to him." He wrote for the slave a "pass," and gave him all needful instruction. Whether he succeeded I cannot tell....

THE AGED FATHER'S VISIT TO HIS SON IN PRISON

... My old father came to see me, and labor for my release. When I was first brought into his presence, the *father* overcame him, and he wept, unable to speak. I said, "Weep not, father, 'it is the Lord, let Him do what seemeth Him good.'" His mind became composed, and we conversed together.[14]

The state of Missouri continued to imprison those found guilty of giving aid and comfort to fugitives trying to escape slavery[15]; by the end of 1852, seven such people were locked in the state penitentiary for enticing blacks to follow passages to freedom. The largest number of slave owners in Missouri reported lost slaves in the northeastern part of the state, not far from Quincy.[16]

The following is taken from John Tillson's *History of the City of Quincy, Illinois*, published in 1866 and revised and corrected by William H. Collins in 1886 at the direction of the Quincy Historical Society:

> On Maine west of Fourth, on both sides, were houses as far as Mount Pisgah on Second street, among them Anderson's store, on the corner of Third, Peabody's wool-carding factory, midway between Third and Fourth. South of the square, on Fourth street, on the west side, was the church — "God's barn," as a long, low frame building (which was the earliest, and at the time, the only structure devoted to religious purposes) was called.
>
> Associated with the remembrance of that ugly, clapboarded shed (for it was but little better than a shed) are many eventful associations that should be put on record....
>
> ... It was fostered in its earlier days by the faithful fervor of the lamented Turner, and made influential by the learning of Nelson and the originality of Foote. It had another and a higher mission. It was freedom's fortress when here "freedom's battle first began," when the "Nelson riots" arose, when humanity's duty to shield an innocent and eminent fugitive from pro-slavery barbarism was disputed, when that highest of American privileges, the right of free thought and free expression of thought was denied and assailed with threatened violence by men from abroad and men at home, among them, officials who should have been the guardians as they were the nominal representatives of good government and law. Then and there rallied from out the excited and divided community, true and fearless men (fearless because of their being right) and there organized in defense of free speech and quelled the threatened lawlessness. This was a turning period in Quincy's history. The old church was the place of rendezvous. It was prepared for defense, and beneath the platform of the rough pulpit, were hidden the arms of every sort, including hickory clubs, ready for instant use if needed. Religion and freedom will alike keep green the grateful memory of "God's barn."[17]

The Nelson Riots mentioned in this account were two antiabolitionist confrontations that occurred in Quincy in 1837. The first gathering directed threats toward a meeting organized by Dr. David Nelson and the Reverend Asa Turner, but members of Turner's church, along with others, came to both men's defense. This so-called riot amounted to little more than a gaggle of slavery sympathizers who passed "some resolutions *versus* Abolition — a word that has scared a great many wise men since that day; drank a little too much, fought a little too much among themselves, and went home."[18] The second mob action though, was much more serious.

In this case a band of rioters marched on a group attending an antislavery lecture inside a meeting hall. The threatening gang tossed missiles obtained from the site of a nearby uncompleted hotel. The crowd inside refused to be intimidated and as Asa Turner recalled, "friends of law and order [went] out and put down the mob. They went out [lecture suspended, and the brickbats returned] and applied brickbats as fast and as hard to the mob as they had done to the meeting-house. They ran for dear life, and whether some of them have stopped yet is a matter of opinion."[19]

The correspondence below was sent to Professor Wilbur Siebert, author of the previously mentioned classic book *The Underground Railroad from Slavery to Freedom*. It is one of numerous pieces of information about the Illinois Underground Railroad accumulated by Siebert. Though many of the letters sent to Siebert are difficult or impossible to verify, the following letter refers to "stations," schools and individuals that are confirmed by numerous other sources. Among those referred to in the letter is John Vandorn, one of Quincy's most active Underground Railroad agents. In 1838, Vandorn arrived in Quincy where he became the owner of a sawmill on Front Street. He was said to have helped large numbers of fugitives escape and when he died in 1875 many former slaves attended his funeral, some tossing flowers on his casket. This letter strongly suggests that the writer was well acquainted with the UGRR in Adams County:

SOME FACTS ABOUT THE UNDERGROUND RAILROAD IN ILLINOIS
By the Reverend H.D. Platt.

... Route, from Quincy & vicinity to the N. E. toward Chicago — (I) Was intimately acquainted with the line for 45 miles, through (or near) Mendon to Plymouth or Augusta, Hancock Co. In a general way, I know that beyond these last two points, it passed thro or near Macomb, Farmington & Galesburg.

Quincy, on the Mississippi, was a *noted* station — with "Keepers," & Conductors, Dr. Eels, Rasselas Sartle, J.K. & Wm. Vandorn & others less noted. Two miles E. of the public Square of Quincy, was Mission Institute, (a School for the Education of Missionaries,) whose students & villagers near were nearly all ready to help in any way. I was a student there, constantly from Dec. '41, to May '47.... Prominent Conductors were Alanson Work, Burr, Geo. Thompson, Lewis Andrews, John Reynard, Geo. & Andrew Hunter, Ed. Griffin, Wm. Mellen & myself. A couple of miles further East were Deacon Ballard, Mr. Safford, & Deacon Brown,[20] all farmers.

About 1840, Burr, Work, & Thompson were caught, on the Mo. side in a skiff, (the negroes, supposing them to be kidnappers, had betrayed them), were put in jail, held till (t)he Mo. Legislature could pass an ex post facto law to fit their case, & (they) were sentenced each to 12 years in the Penitentiary. They were pardoned, one at a time, after they had all together made up what was equal to 12 years for one man.

Mendon, 15 miles N. E. of Quincy, was a very prominent station — not so much the village itself as the farms in the vicinity. As "Keepers," or Conductors, or both, were Eastus Benton, Levi Stillman, Nathan Clark, Darwin Bartholomew, Wm. Battell, Dea. L. A. Weed, Deacon Jireh Platt & Sons: & some others.[21]

On November 7, 1926, the *Chicago Daily Tribune* published a detailed article about the Underground Railroad written by Oney Fred Sweet. Sweet specifically identified six UGRR places of concealment in the middle west; three in Ohio in Ripley, Jefferson, and Amesville; one in Green Bay, Wisconsin; and two in Illinois. Galesburg's Old Colony Church is cited, as is the "hazel thicket" in the pasture lot of Deacon Jireh Platt in Mendon.

Also found in Siebert's notes is a fascinating letter written to him on March 28, 1896, by J. E. Platt. It describes the Liberty Line, which ultimately headed north[22] to Mendon and the last northernmost set of hideouts in Adams County. In Mendon, lived Levi and Henry Stillman, prominent "operators" who took responsibility for transporting several fugitives to the next set of hideouts in Hancock County. The Stillmans were known to have given fugitives on the run fresh horses to get away quickly if pursuers were close behind:

> ...Mr. W. H. Siebert,
> Cambridge, Mass.
>
> Dear Sir,
>
> In answer to your request for information in reference to the "Underground Railroad" I will make the following statements.
> The route of the road from Quincy Ills, to Chicago, lay through Mendon, Plymouth, Macomb, and Gaylesburg, on to Chicago. My Fathers house was at Mendon the first station from Quincy. The second lay 30 miles N.E. of us — Plymouth, and the station Keepers were Marcus Cook and Mr. Adkins, I am not acquainted with names farther on....
> Runaways crossing the river near Quincy somehow found friends, who would escort them to some of the Conductors, of which there were several, A Mr. Van Dorn being a prominent one, and Mission Institute two miles east of Quincy was full of them. Some of those Conductors would lead them in almost every conceivable way, usually in the night to my Fathers who by some member of the family, or a neighbor, would escort them to Plymouth the following night. Sometimes a carriage would drive into my Fathers barn in the day time with a colored man dressed up in fine clothes, and a Stove pipe hat, for a driver, with the conductor on the back seat. Sometimes a person with a lady's cloak, hood and veil on would alight from the back seat of a carriage, with the conductor driving. Fathers barn or the haymow used to be the place for refreshment and retiring. In the summer time, the hazel thicket in the pasture was used for the same purpose.
> One night in Aug. of 1843 when I was a ten year old boy, a man came to my fathers escorting four strong hearty negroes, who had walked all the way from Quincy. Father gave them something to eat, then took them to the hazel thicket.
> Their pursuers were so close behind them on horse-back that the Quincy conductor met them a quarter of a mile from our house on his return trip.
> The hunters stopped at the Mendon Hotel a mile further on, and early in the

morning were again on the road looking for tracks. It was very dusty. One of the colored men had a shoe a little too short, and had cut off the toe of it, and as he walked in the road, his longest toe made a mark in the dust. His master knew that mark right well, and tracked it to our gate, and no farther. He was positively certain that his four colored men worth $1000. apiece were upon our premises, and he was determined to catch them. He asked permission to search the house, which was granted after which the party mounted their horses and rode down through the pasture within a stones throw of where his darkies were concealed.

That night they were spirited away somewhere and somehow, the particulars of which I never learned.

That master hired some fifty men to help him, and they hunted night and day for two weeks, watched all the roads, and could not understand why they could not find them, hence the name Underground R.R. They watched our place with great vigilance, blacked up a white man, and sent him there as a runaway slave, caught our chickens, to draw father out at night. Whet their knives on our front fence, and called out to us to be up and saying our prayers for we had but three minutes to live. They caught me one day about a mile from home and a dozen of them surrounded me and threatened to shoot me, and hang me and cut my throat from ear to ear if I did not tell them where the negroes were.

It was well that I did not know where they were at that time, for I thought surely they intended to kill me, but they got nothing out of me. After two weeks incessant search the master returned to Missouri and offered $1000 for my fathers head, dead or alive, and five hundred dollars for my older brothers head. A singular fact connected with this case is that about nine years ago in Comanche Co. Kan. I organized a Sunday School in the private house of that very man's son, who had been born since the war, and had made a new home in Kansas. I did not tell him that his father once offered $1000, for my fathers head. I could spend a whole day in writing up remarkable incidents, but time will not permit. One man came to our house with a bullet hole through his arm, which his master had shot so closely was he pursued. A runaway was being taken to the house of Erastus Benton, another Mendon Conductor, and they were so closely pursued that the horse was shot which drew the vehicle in which the slave was riding, but they escaped through a cornfield and were not captured.

When about 14 years of age, my father started me off on horseback at nine o'clock one evening, with a colored man on another horse by my side. We made the thirty mile trip all right and I led the horse home the next day. When I was about 17 years old, eleven slaves came along at one time some of them women. We put them into two tightly covered wagons, and I drove one of the teams. It was not practicable to stop at the Plymouth station, so we had to drive to the next sixty miles from home, took the day time for the last thirty miles. Keeping the darkies well covered with hay in the wagon body. Did not reach home until the fourth day, and you can well imagine that our folks were pretty well frightened about us. I suppose that nearly one hundred slaves passed the Mendon station of the Underground R.R. and I never heard of but one being captured. That was near McComb, McDonough Co. Ills.[23]

Close proximity to Illinois was part of what motivated a short-lived and ill-fated slave revolt in Lewis County, Missouri, in November 1849. In the northern regions of that county, a slave woman named Lin organized a group of bondmen belonging to four white families. According to the plan, 25 slaves were to kill all but one of the members of these four families, and then attempt an escape into the Prairie State. Lin mixed gunpowder with coffee to inspire bravery, and then added a special potion that she believed would make the band of conspirators invulnerable. The group's activities, immediately prior to overt action, aroused suspicion and the plot was discovered. A larger group of whites came upon and confronted the slaves gathered behind a barricade at the McCutchan's farm. The revolt fell apart after one slave was shot and killed and those remaining gave up. Subsequently, the conspirators who were perceived as the most dangerous were sold south. This incident solidified white Missourians' fears of slave uprisings and thus strengthened their antiabolitionist zeal against those who might help induce slaves to seek freedom.[24]

III

Hancock County— Remote Hideouts

If the initial stages of an escape were successful in Adams County, the next phase of the runaways' journey usually took them to a remote tall-grass range resting on top of what was called Round Prairie. Two small villages, Augusta and Plymouth in Hancock County were communities around which existed this important stage of the UGRR operation. Strong Austin, who moved to Augusta in 1843, was that community's most notorious UGRR "agent" and he was not secretive about his activities. Underground Railroad operations in this area were also conducted in western Schuyler County, close to the tiny hamlets of Birmingham and Huntsville.

One of the fullest regional accounts of the Underground Railroad in Illinois is in *A History of Round Prairie and Plymouth 1831–1875* by E. H. Young. His book, published in 1876, details the lives of the people who settled the isolated corner of southeast Hancock County. Young wrote with moral conviction and fervor while crafting a particularly effective literary style. He recorded the efforts to establish the first churches and business enterprises in the area, recalled Fourth of July barbecues, and the dispatching of the region's young men to fight for the Union in the Civil War. Young was less than enthusiastic when discussing Mormons,[1] who lived in Nauvoo, northwest of Round Prairie on the Mississippi River. The Round Prairie area was populated initially by many Presbyterians and Congregationalists who, according to Young, "converged and intermingled" for a number of years. The region's ties to Galesburg were strong because Augusta's Congregationalist minister, the Reverend Milton Kimball, was a member of the Knox College Board of Trustees. It is particularly significant to note that Young identified George Thompson of Quincy's Mission Institute as being familiar with many residents of Round Prairie. The final part of his book details the region's illegal UGRR operation, which gave aid to fugitives traveling north, on the "Gospel Train." The following are selections from his book:

> *Crooked Creek* ,[2] with it margin of timber, forms the eastern and most of the northern boundary of Round Prairie....
>
> ... A considerable tributary of Crooked Creek, known as *Bronson's* Creek, completes the northern boundary of Round Prairie; a small tributary of this, with its margin of timber, bounds it upon the west....
>
> ... The creek upon our south, with its flowery banks, woody slopes, quarries of rock, precipitous bluffs, and probable deposits of coal, has much about it both of beauty and a utility....
>
> ... Between the creeks of which we have spoken, lies Round Prairie, its general form corresponding quite nearly to its name — (leaving off the narrow neck jutting out toward Birmingham.)
>
> The average diameter of the prairie will not vary much from three miles.
>
> Of the wild, native beauty of this locality, we may gather some idea by remembering that its gently undulating surface was swept clean by the annual prairie fires, only to be reclothed with a rich carpet of grass profusely ornamented with the greatest variety and abundance of prairie flowers. The picture presented by this scene is spoken of by early settlers as one of surpassing beauty. The frame-work of this picture — the margin of timber surrounding it — was not a tangled mat of undergrowth amid the trees, inaccessible, almost, to man or beast, as we now find it in many places — but a clear, open growth of timber, through which one might travel unobstructed in any direction. This freedom from undergrowth was due to the same agency that renovated the surface of the prairie — the prairie fires....
>
> ... In 1819 the United States surveyors struck their temporary camps, leaving their "stakes and mounds" in the prairie, and their "witness trees" in the timber, as the only evidences that were to be perpetuated of the civilized occupation of Round Prairie until its permanent settlement in 1831–2.
>
> We get an introduction to our notorious fellow citizens of the Mormon persuasion about the time Round Prairie was settled.... The emigration of the Mormon community from Ohio to Missouri passed through the lower part of Round Prairie, leaving a well-marked and beaten road, traveled by hundreds of teams, and that continued to be used for years afterwards. This highway — the first made on Round Prairie — was known as the *Mormon Trail.* It crossed the Illinois river near the mouth of Spoon river, Crooked Creek just above Birmingham, and Flour Creek south of Mr. Fielding's present residence, thence along the north side of the Augusta prairie, crossing the Mississippi river at Quincy....
>
> ... Rev. Elijah P. Lovejoy, a Presbyterian minister, was killed by a mob in Alton, Illinois, October,[3] 1837. The difficulties leading to this result grew out of his attempt to establish an anti-slavery newspaper at that place.
>
> Round Prairie, the subject of our history, for many years was an important station of a prominent line of the so-called *Underground Railroad....*
>
> ... The death of Lovejoy was one of the links in the chain of educational agencies that God used to train men in the principles of universal freedom. "The blood of the martyrs is the seed of the church." That Lovejoy was a martyr to his earnest convictions no one doubts. His blood produced a bountiful harvest in the agitation of the slavery question through all this region. That agitation and discussion

brought with it light, knowledge, sympathy for the oppressed, and active effort in their behalf.

Another historical event may be stated here, having a direct personal influence upon a number of the citizens of Round Prairie, giving a keener edge to their sympathies for the oppressed, and to their feelings against the oppressor. We refer to the capture, and confinement in the Missouri penitentiary, of Alanson Work, James E. Burr and George Thompson, on the charge of "stealing slaves." The first named had been, for a time, a well-known resident of Round Prairie, and at the time of which we write, residing at the Mission Institute, near Quincy, for the purpose of educating his children. The other two persons were young men preparing for the ministry, the latter, George Thompson, then engaged, and afterwards married to a daughter of Lamarcus A. Cook, of this place. These men were captured on Missouri soil, arranging with slaves for their escape to freedom — confessedly an act of imprudence. There is a further fact to be stated, however: viz., at that time, and for nearly three years later, there was no law in Missouri designating that act as crime, and consequently no *penalty* provided therefore; yet these men were tried, and sentenced to the penitentiary for twelve years. They were pardoned after serving the following terms respectively: viz., Work, three years and a half; Burr, four years and a half; and Thompson, five years....

... The capture of these men occurred in July, 1841. Our record of local incidents commences at about the same time and extends up to the time of Lincoln's Emancipation Proclamation, January 1st, 1863.

The cases cited above are merely illustrative of the thousands of incidents that added fuel to the flame of anti-slavery excitement throughout the entire north. An important form this general movement took on in particular localities, was that of an organized system for aiding refugees from bondage on their way to a land of freedom. This system was designated the Underground Railroad. The secrecy of its workings justified the name. It is too late now to judge the men who carried on this business, by the then prevailing standard of human judgment. We have clearer light, and in that light must recognize God's plans, and the instruments He used in carrying them on.

Much complaint was made by pro-slavery men, against their abolitionist neighbors, for bad citizenship, as manifested in their disregard of the requirements of the slave laws. While it must be admitted that the charge contains a technical truth, as viewed in a legal light, we think the taunt well met in the answer sometimes made to it: viz., "That if, in the free State of Illinois, men and women, guilty of no crimes save wearing a black skin that God gave them, and a love of liberty, were permitted to enjoy the right of passing at will, by day or night, upon our public highways, there would have been no just cause of complaint. But while such persons did not dare to show themselves in public without the risk — aye, certainty — of being hunted down like wild beasts, it was only the dictates of a common humanity to aid them in their journey by ways concealed from public observation."

Again, this work was deeply imbedded in religious convictions, and warm, earnest human sympathies for the oppressed.

The work, and the workers, thus imbued, were invincible. Human laws are of little avail when they come in conflict with the higher law, and with human sympathies....

... Its general route was virtually approved by its adoption by the great corpora-

53

tion now known as the C., B. and Q.R.R. connecting the central metropolis with the southwest and west. Its track was more flexible; deviating sometimes this way, and sometimes the other, as circumstance required, the main circumstance being the safety of the freight....

... Upon the line of which we write, or the small section of it coming within our immediate notice, Quincy and vicinity was the main depot upon the border; Mendon, Augusta, Plymouth, Macomb, Galesburg, and other points beyond, prominent way-stations upon the line, with side tracks, or deflections, reaching Laharpe, Huntsville, and intermediate places, to be used as necessity required. These points are named as indicating the general course of the U.G.R.R. line, and not as fixing precisely the location of depots. These depots were peculiar in their character. While all was plain to the initiated, the Egyptians might about as well have hunted the lynchpins of their crippled chariots in the darkness and fog of their night march into the Red Sea, as for an outsider to attempt the search for freight at an U.G.R.R. depot....

A Fortunate Blunder

... It was often thought best to start out a train on the U.G.R.R. by daylight; in fact, day trains were less liable to suspicion, if conducted with due caution, than night trains, but the reception of a consignment by daylight was ordinarily extra-hazardous. We give an incident or two to show that sometimes this extra-risk, in reality, proved to be the only safeguard against detection and exposure. It was thought that important discoveries and captures might be made if a watch was kept upon the premises of Mr. W_____ , and for a considerable time his residence was under close scrutiny at night, without any knowledge of the fact on his part, the guard going on duty at dark, and off at daylight.

During this time a covered carriage from Mendon drove up to Mr. W_____ 's house one afternoon, say two hours before dark, containing the driver and a lady friend of his upon the front seat. Back of this, concealed under the cover, was a negro woman and two children of about seven and twelve years respectively. These Mr. W_____ was expected to care for and forward. He was surprised that any driver in his senses should bring a consignment of negroes to his place in daylight, exposed as it was to public observation; and with a pretty sharp reproof, and warning not to repeat such an act of supposed imprudence, the driver was dismissed. No hesitation in meeting an emergency was allowable with the true U.G.R.R. man, and Mr. W. was ready to make the best of this. The colored woman and children were promptly placed in the garret over the kitchen, duly cared for, and at the earliest favorable opportunity sent in care of a trusty conductor to Macomb.

Lost—Stepping "Down and Out"

On another occasion, three negro men, well armed with rifles, who had started out upon the trip, determined not to be taken back alive, had arrived at Augusta. From there they started, one night, piloted by a young man of the Augusta U.G. force, for the house of Mr. W. at Plymouth. For greater safety they went on foot, keeping away from the road, and under cover of the woods and underbrush. In the darkness of the night they lost their way and wandered about all night in a fruitless effort to reach their destination. Daylight revealed his bearings to the guide, and an hour later the party reached Mr. W_____'s, a weary, forlorn company. This party was taken to the woods, concealed and cared for three days, before it was thought prudent to attempt another stage in their journey. Mr. X_____ undertook to conduct them to Macomb. That station, like this, was widely scattered, having places for the reception of U.G. freight at various points and distances from town. To one of the more distant of these Mr. X_____ directed his course. When near his destination, in passing through a strip of woods, he saw some men in the road, some distance ahead, that he at once suspected of being on the lookout for just such freight as he carried. Giving the negroes a hint, they quickly and quietly stepped "down and out" in the rear, and took to the woods, apparently undiscovered. His wagon then presenting no appearance of concealed freight, X_____ drove on, passed the men, and reported the situation to the proper party at the depot. By means of a concerted signal system, the negroes were readily found, when wanted, duly cared for, and properly forwarded....

True Manhood

We give another incident showing how a true manhood rises above all petty considerations of politics or personal self-interest, and recognizes the rights of man without regard to the color of his skin. It had been well if more of his political associates could have learned the lesson he taught — that free men were under no *moral* obligation to lower themselves to the plane of blood-hounds and engage in hunting down negroes like wild beasts.

In all the incidents given we have withheld the names of the living, and of those engaged in any transactions that might be considered questionable in their character; but as he has passed beyond the reach of praise or censure, by friend or foe, we take pleasure in associating the name of Mr. C. H. Cuyler, deceased, with a little transaction in the U.G.R.R line, alike honorable to himself and a common humanity. Being a prominent democrat, Mr. Cuyler was well known here as having no sympathy with the U.G.R.R business. He had received a circular describing two runaway negroes and offering a reward of $100 each for their apprehension. While this was in his office, two negroes came to his house one night inquiring the way to the house of a prominent U.G. agent. Mr. Cuyler recognized them at once as the men described in the circular. He told them it would be difficult to direct them so that they could find their way to the place, in the dark; "but," said he, "boys! the best thing you can do is, to come in, get what supper you want, then go and sleep in my barn, come in early in the morning, get your breakfast, and then I will show you which way to go." They acted on his advice, and went on their way in the morning in safety. "Two hundred dollars thrown away!" some negro hunter will exclaim. Aye! indeed!! But Mr. Charles H. Cuyler's manhood was not to be measured by any such paltry standard.

A Lively Load and Lively Time

Mr. Y_____ called at the house of Mr. W_____ on his way home from a three day trip to Quincy, and found that a company of six negroes had just arrived, that were to be sent on their way to freedom. There was a man and his wife, with two children, and a young man, all under the leadership of a negro called Charley, who had been over the line half a dozen times or more. He had become well known to the regular agents of the route. His various trips to and from the Missouri had been made for the purpose of getting his wife away; failing in which, he would gather up such friends as he could and pilot them to freedom.

Mr. Y_____ detailed himself for the service of taking the party to Macomb, to start next morning, making a day trip. The party of six were stowed as well as possible at full length on the bottom of the wagon and covered closely with sacks of straw. These were so light that they showed a decided tendency to jolt out of place, and thus perhaps to make unwelcome revelations on the road. To remedy this a rope was drawn down tightly over the sacks and fastened at the ends of the wagon. This kept things to place, and all went well until near the end of the journey. Here Mr. Y_____ became doubtful as the proper road to take, took the wrong one, and passed three young men getting out logs in a piece of woods through which his way led him. He did not dare to stop and inquire the way of them, for fear they might pry into the nature of his load too closely. As he drove on he thought there was a striking family likeness in the young men, to the man he was looking for. He went on, however, until he came to a cabin a little off the road, where he thought it safer to inquire. As he went in he confronted a man that he recognized only too well as one he cared little to meet on such a mission. But it was a cold, snowy day, and his face was so concealed by his wrappings that he was not recognized by the occupant of the cabin, who gave him the information sought. Mr. Y_____ found that the had gone too far, had to retrace his way to the woods and there turn off. Here again he came upon the young men who had been delayed with their load by getting "stalled" in a deep rut. Better satisfied now as to their identity, he inquired the way of them. Guessing his mission readily, they made free inquiries about his load, which were answered as freely. Finding "Charley" was in the company, one of the young men determined to frighten him, or at least have a joke at his expense. Calling his name in stern tones, he told him that he knew he had passed over the line several times in safety; "but," said he, "I have caught you at last; you are now my prisoner." Charley, still in concealment with the others under the sacks, recognized the voice of an old acquaintance, did not turn white with fear, but enjoyed the pleasantry.

Soon all were safely housed at Mr._____'s. After supper "all hands" gathered in the parlor, where for a time there was a free intermingling of story, song and mirth; after which an old violin was produced and "operated" upon by some one of the company while negroes "let themselves out" into a regular old-fashioned plantation "hoe down," which lasted until all were ready to retire with aching sides from excess of fun. This evening's entertainment is noted as a particularly bright spot in U.G.R.R. experience —*brightened with genuine negro polish.*

"Charlie" or "Charley" reappears several times in pre–Civil War stories as a fugitive who had escaped from slavery in Missouri. He was said to have then traveled back and forth through western Illinois, crossing into Missouri, in order to help other slaves seek freedom:

A Pair of Photographs

We ought not to forget what slavery was, nor what it did. To refresh our memory let us look at a photograph or two.

One day a genteel looking young man of somewhat dark complexion came to Mr.

Y____'s and conversed with him some time before he was suspected of being a fugitive. When asked if this was his position, he frankly admitted it.

On his way over he had met Mrs. Y____ and another lady, and inquired of them the way. From his appearance and genteel address they had no suspicion of his being a runaway slave. While stopping here Mr. Y____ took him, one day, to the house of a friend. They staid for dinner, and during the meal the subject of caste came up, in the discussion of which Mr. Y____ remarked to the host, that he was then entertaining a negro slave at his table. The host was greatly surprised, and could be scarcely convinced of the fact. It was deemed entirely safe, by the U.G. agents, for this fugitive to travel openly by daylight, and he had done so from Quincy, and continued his journey from here in the same way, stopping with friends on the route (as occasion required), to whom he was directed from place to place.

This young man was his *master's son* by a slave mother. He grew up active, intelligent and trusty. He had for some time been in sole charge of his father-master's business, a position of considerable trust and responsibility, in which he proved himself trustworthy and fully competent. He had a "legitimate" brother, the two bearing a strong family resemblance, about the only difference being a very slight tinge in the color of the slave brother's skin.

The legitimate brother was a profligate, a spendthrift, and a tyrant; a constant source of vexation and trouble to his father, and who was yet allowed by him to tyrannize over and abuse his slave brother until life was almost a burden. This abuse was in his estimation, "forbearance ceased to be a virtue," and relief was sought in a successful flight. No moralizing in this case is necessary.

Let us look now for a moment on a photograph No. 2. An old man, from fifty to sixty years of age, had made his way, somehow, from forty miles below New Orleans to Quincy. He had had a fearful experience of the rigors of slave life in the far south, and was now making his escape there from. At Quincy he providentially stumbled into a sawmill on the river bank, to sleep. This, he found out in some way, belonged to the very man, of all others in Quincy, that he wanted to see — the principal U.G. agent there. He was soon put upon the line and sent forward, arriving safely upon Round Prairie, and was placed in care of Mr. Y____. Here, out in a clump of underbrush, he stripped off his shirt to exhibit to his host a rare specimen of workmanship done in human flesh, by such cunning malignity as could only be born of slavery, aided by the prince of darkness.

A cat — not the sailor's instrument of torture, known as the "cat-o'-nine-tails," a sort of whip — but a living cat with its four sharp sets of fearful claws, had been taken by the cruel overseer, by its tail and neck, and dragged backwards down the man's back resenting such treatment as only a cat could by setting its claws as firmly as possible into the quivering flesh. This operation was continued until no space was left upon his back for it further application. These wounds had festered, leaving a series of deep, close furrows, plainly legible in lines of living flesh covering the whole back. Across these were an irregular series of heavy welts raised by the overseer's lash.

We have no taste, dear reader, for the exhibition of such pictures; but historic truth demands that we present them as having been exhibited already, in this nineteenth century, on Round Prairie, in the free State of Illinois.

This account, strongly suggests that after No. 2, the old man, arrived in Quincy, he was fortunate to have found his way to the sawmill of John Vandorn. He was the

UGRR "agent" mentioned in chapter 2 as a person who had helped large numbers of runaways escape:

A Grand Rally and Hunt

Perhaps the most exciting incident that has ever occurred in the history of the U.G.R.R. in Round Prairie, and at the same time the most dramatic in its details, occurred in the fall of 1857. A professional writer of sensational stories might easily work up the material furnished by this incident into a novel of respectable size. Our aim in giving its details, shall be, as it has been in all the incidents found in this book, to give an exact and faithful narrative of the facts as obtained from the best sources of information open to us. We may say further here, once and for all, that the facts of every anecdote found upon these pages, unless otherwise specified, have been furnished us by parties who were active participants in the scenes described, or who were otherwise thoroughly conversant with the facts stated. We deem this statement due to the facts, many of which "are stranger than fiction."

Late one Saturday night, or, rather, perhaps early Sunday morning, a covered wagon stopped at the house of Mr. X_____, located at a point on Round Prairie that we shall not designate. The driver aroused Mr. X_____ and called him out to inform him that he had a consignment of negroes that he wished to place in his care. Under ordinary circumstances the charge would have been readily accepted; but at this time Mr. X_____ had in his employ an Irishman who could have found no greater pleasure than to get scent of a trail that might lead to the capture of a runaway "nager." For this reason it was thought imprudent for Mr. X_____ to receive the freight. The driver was informed of the peculiar situation and advised to take his cargo to the house of Mr. Y_____. In the mean time the Irishman, awakened by the slight disturbance below, looked out, saw the wagon, and was sharp enough to take in the situation at a glance. In his eagerness he rushed out, without stopping to consider the propriety of his appearance in company in his very limited night apparel. He approached the driver in a very familiar way, and tried to convince him that, being himself a sound "abolitionist," there would be no harm in admitting him to confidence, and allowing him to share in the management of the case. The driver, duly forewarned, paid no attention to his blarney and drove off, hoping thus to get rid of his too familiar attentions.

But the Irishman determined to track the game to its hiding place, and then arrange for its capture. Not daring to lose the time necessary to add to his wearing apparel, he followed as he was, keeping far enough from the wagon to escape observation, yet near enough to be sure of its destination. The distance to Y_____'s house was not great, and the Irishman was rejoiced to see the wagon stop there, and the living cargo unload and approach the house. So well satisfied was he now, that the game was safe, that he hastened home to add somewhat to his dress, and then notify some of the nearest neighbors, who were as eager for such game as himself, and secure their assistance in its capture.

No attempt to pass the negroes on, or to change their quarters, was expected until the coming night; and being the Sabbath, no legal steps could be taken at once for their arrest. A quiet outlook may have been kept over the premises during the day to guard against any flank movement by Mr. Y_____ against surprise and the capture of the game.

III. Hancock County

The Sabbath hours furnished abundant time for the Irishman to consult with his friends, make the necessary plans, and secure all the assistance he might need. It was deemed prudent to place a strong guard around the premises at night to prevent the possibility of an escapade. At an early hour on Sunday evening armed men arrived in sufficient numbers to carry out the plan. As night drew on, the crowd increased. A neighbor on his way to prayer meeting, purposed passing Mr. Y_____'s house that evening as it was nearer than by the road, and when near the place, was ordered to halt by a little cluster of men not far from the point at which it appeared he was attempting to pass the picket line of the guard. Failing to comprehend the situation, or not recognizing their authority, he passed on. The order was repeated in more emphatic tones, but not regarded. The sharp report of a gun close upon the order, demanded consideration. The neighbor halted, turned his course, abandoned his peaceful mission to the house of prayer, and returned home for his gun, remarking to a friend that, "if shooting was the game, it had at least two sides to it." On his way back he notified other neighbors of the situation, some of whom proceeded with him to Mr. Y_____'s. Here things began to look serious; some of the family were alarmed and frightened at the supposed, or, possibly, real danger.

With the hope of getting rid of the annoyance more speedily, Mr. Y_____ approached some of the leaders, and offered them the privilege of making their contemplated search at once, without legal warrant. But they were in no mood to take advice from Mr. Y_____ or his friends. Having a sure thing of it, they were going about its execution in their own way. Changing front, Y_____ then told them they were trespassing upon his premises without authority of law, disturbing his family, breaking the peace — in brief, that they were *rioters,* and that unless they promptly dispersed and left his premises, he should take speedy measures to have them arrested as such. Scorning his threat, as they had his previous advice, they told him that he was their prisoner, and would not be allowed to leave the premises. With the aid of a friend, however, who led his horse out of the lines at one point, while he passed out at another, Mr. Y_____ was soon on his way to the office of a justice of the peace in a distant part of the township. The friend who had aided Y_____ in getting out of the lines, did not add greatly to the good nature of the crowd, by pointing to the receding form of the horseman, and taunting them with their inefficiency as a guard, as they had allowed their "prisoner" to escape. This was of small consequence to them, however, as compared with the game still in "the bush."

The hours of the Sabbath finally passed away , and the curtain of midnight fell upon the scene, to rise again with the early dawn upon another exciting act in the passing drama. The wild Irish leader had gone, at the first opportunity after the Sabbath had passed, to the office of a justice of the peace near at hand, for a warrant to search the house, and arrest the negroes. This document is worthy of record here, as showing the *legal status of men* with a black skin, at that time; also as defining a crime now obsolete in this country, and as containing a classification of "property" that already seems strange, and will seem more so as the years go by. The substance of the warrant is reproduced here from memory, by one who copied it from the docket soon after it was issued, and who preserved it for years as a memento of the occasion, and is thought to be substantially, if not really, verbatim. It reads as follows, except names and dates: viz., "M_____ W_____ come, and on his oath declares that a larceny has been committed at the County of Schuyler, State of Illinois, and that the goods stolen, to wit: three negroes are supposed to be concealed in the house of J.B.Y_____.

"To all constables, etc., greeting:

"You are hereby commanded to search in the daytime, the house of said J.B.Y_____, and if any of the said goods be found, the same are to be seized and brought before me.

"(Signed), A. B_____, J.P."

Armed with this document, the Irishman returned to the field of action, to await with his comrades the coming of the morning, and of the officer who had been secured to execute the warrant. During this interim, an interesting little episode occurred that deserves notice.

Questioning the fact, that the Irishman had a search warrant, the friends of Mr. Y_____ demanded to see and read if for their own satisfaction. This was refused on the plea that they wanted possession of the paper for the purpose of destroying it. Protesting against this charge, and claiming good intentions, and to be acting in good faith, the demand was renewed, but again refused. The demand was then made that the Irishman, or some of his friends, should read it aloud, as they certainly had a right to be satisfied as the fact of his having the authority claimed. This proposition was assented to, a light procured, and some one selected to do the reading. The one chosen, however, proved a failure in this scholastic art. With all the legal clearness and precision of the document, the reader failed to make anything intelligible out of it. After further parley, it was agreed that, the Irishman holding the document, a friend of Y_____'s might approach, take hold of one corner of the paper, and looking over at the Irishman's side, read it. When nearly through, suspicions of foul play came into the Irishman's head again, and jerking away the paper, he blew out the light, brought down his gun, and ordered the party to stand back. Sharp words ensued upon this abrupt termination of the affair, but nobody was hurt, and the episode had helped to pass away the tedious hours of night.

Morning came, and with it the officer, to whom was committed the responsibility of maintaining, by his personal service or sacrifice, if need be, the majesty of the law. The constable, accompanied by the Irishman, armed with revolvers and huge knives, proceeded to search the house. They were afforded the fullest opportunity to make thorough work of it. With extreme caution they went over the house, in constant dread of having their heads broken by the clubs of the burly negroes whom they expected would suddenly spring upon them from their concealment.

Thus the search went on, from cellar to garret; every room, closet, nook or cranny, that was supposed to afford space for the concealment of a human being, was thoroughly explored, but not a *curly head* could be found.

The case began to look hopeless. The mystery was beyond comprehension. That the negroes had been fairly tracked to the place designated, there was no more doubt than there was of the existence of the Irishman who saw them there with his own eyes. That there had been time enough to spirit them away during his brief absence from the place, or that any attempt to move them on to another point that night, would be made, were deemed too improbable for consideration. So the mystery deepened. The negro hunters were foiled, bitterly disappointed and chop-fallen at the miserable failure of their search.

To add to their chagrin, the friends of Mr. Y_____ now began to ridicule them for their inefficiency as hunters. Old logs and boards were turned over about the premises, exposing rat holes that they were urged to look into. All sorts of suggestions were made to tantalize them, and urge their search into various improbable places of concealment. This storm of ridicule they were now in no mood to meet or resent.

To make their discomfiture complete, as they were about to abandon the search and leave the field , a new actor appeared on the stage, in the person of an officer armed with a warrant for the arrest of the Irishman and several of his most prominent followers, on a charge of riot. To the execution of this writ all submitted quietly but one young man, who swore he "wouldn't go." The officer ordered a posse to seize the rebellious young man, tie him, and load him into the wagon with the other prisoners. Two stout men sprang forward to execute the mandate, when the young man "came down" with such grace as he could command, and climbed into the wagon. All were taken before a Justice of the Peace some miles distant, examined, and bound over for their appearance at court. The final result of the case was, that after various dilatory proceedings, delaying it from term to term, it was thrown out of court in consequence of an error that had crept into the date of an important paper, placing the event a year from the time of its actual occurrence. How this error happened, is one of the legal mysteries of the case, supposed to be understood only by the profession. Its explanation we do not attempt.

An interesting side scene occurred that Sunday night, while the great drama was on the boards, that has a place in our story, and is of permanent interest to a considerable circle of friends.

A near friend of Mr. Y_____ was seen making hurried movements about the neighborhood, in the darkness, under cover of night, suggestive of active preparation for some pressing emergency. Any such action on the part of Mr. Y_____'s friends at this stage of affairs, was thought to be decidedly suspicious, and as indicating some shrewd, bold flank movement for the escape of the negroes from the snare so surely closing in upon them. A close watch was kept upon this man's movements, with the earnest expectation that a clue might thus be obtained to important revelations. Nor was this expectation disappointed, *except in the nature of the revelation.*

No runaway negroes were found, no "larceny" discovered, nor "stolen goods" unearthed; but a certain promising young man, who is sometimes seen upon our streets, dates his *birthday* (?) back to that eventful Sunday night: viz., November 8th, 1857.

The sequel to this story furnishes an important act in the drama; and the events we now relate will probably furnish many of the actors in the scene their first knowledge of the reasons why they failed in their search for the negroes.

Mr. Y_____ knew that he was a "marked man," and that his premises were sometimes watched, and peculiarly liable to search if any suspicious circumstance should point that way. Extreme caution was therefore necessary on his part.

The three negroes were received by Mr. Y_____ precisely as the Irishman had stated, but were not taken into the house, nor concealed on the premises, but led around in rear of the house and down to lower ground, a short distance away, that would hide the party from observation in the opposite direction, and then taken to the house of Mr. Z_____, a near neighbor who at that time was not so much under the ban of suspicion as Mr. Y_____. This movement was executed with so much celerity that Mr. Y_____ was safely at home again before the Irishman's counter movement was carried out.

Mr. Z_____ received the negroes, put them in his garret, supplied them with food for the day, and as the time approached, went about the usual preparations for going to church. There was at this time a lady visitor in his family, who would have objected strongly to being an original party to any such "underground" proceedings as now surrounded her. Knowing, as he did, that her views were directly opposite his own upon this subject, Z_____ did not hesitate to explain the situation to her, so far as necessary; and relying safely on her honor as a lady, and her obligations as a guest, left her alone in charge of the house, and virtually on guard over the negroes, while he and his family went to church as usual.

Apprehensive that a failure of the search at Y_____'s might lead to the search of other premises near by, it was deemed prudent to get the negroes further from the scene on Sunday night, before the search should be made at Y_____'s. Accordingly Mr. X_____ and Mr. Z_____ went with them after night across lots, to a place in the neighborhood about two miles away, where it was thought they would be safe. After getting there, upon consultation it was thought best to take them out of the neighborhood altogether. In accordance with this decision, X_____ and Z_____ took the negroes on horseback, struck off upon a side track directly away from the main line, placed them in safe quarters ten miles away, near Huntsville, and were back upon the scene of the excitement in the early morning, to join in the sport made at the expense of the discomforted negro-hunters.[4]

Among the most important figures involved with the Round Prairie Underground Railroad were Abraham and Isaac Pettijohn in Huntsville and Nathan Burton in Birmingham. The Pettijohns and Burton are known to have operated in extreme western Schuyler County and were almost certainly three of the primary "agents" described in the foregoing account.

T. H. Gregg's *History of Hancock County, Illinois*, mentions two areas in that county where UGRR "agents" functioned. In addition to the Round Prairie operation there was one in LaHarpe, in the county's northeastern section. Gregg was not reluctant to identify L. C. Maynard as a station operator and important leader in that community. Maynard was also identified as a LaHarpe "keeper" by his niece, Professor Lucy Maynard Salmon of Vassar College, in a letter she wrote to Wilbur Siebert.[5] According to Gregg's county history:

> Mr. Maynard is (was) not only one of the early pioneers who has by his energy and labor made this country what it is, socially, morally, and financially, but he is honored and respected by everyone for his strict honesty and his enterprise in things pertaining to the benefit of his fellow men, for all of which his purse and heart were ever open. He was an abolitionist before the war; his house was known among the officers of the Underground Railroad as a station, and many black men, no doubt, today remember with grateful hearts and memories the helping hand to freedom that was extended to them from this station....
>
> On Mr. Maynard's arrival in this county, there was no Congregational Church at this place; in the summer of 1836 a company was collected for the purpose of organizing a church at this house, a log cabin. Rev. Asa Turner, of Quincy, officiated on the occasion.[6]

In the November 17, 1893, issue of Hancock County's *LaHarper* there appeared a long story written shortly after the death of L. C. Maynard. The story identified his home as a "depot" one mile east of LaHarpe and also named "Jos. Hindman, Dr. Richardson, and others" as helping "fleeing slaves." The newspaper account indicated that Maynard was LaHarpe's first merchant and that he was an "abolitionist when there were few to espouse the cause of slave people." The story concluded by saying:

> Never did man, bond or free, ask alms of Deacon Maynard, but what his wants were supplied, and the ever returning wants of suffering humanity made a constant draft upon his time and means. It was not an uncommon thing to see the Deacon distributing a load of fruit or vegetables among the widows and poor of the town. His business integrity and moral standing were never questioned....
>
> ... He was a solid landmark amid the waves of faction, the storms of passion and the conflicts of error.

Underground Railroad operator L. C. Maynard was one of Hancock County's most dedicated agents. He was also one of the earliest and most highly respected settlers in the county.

But when T. H. Gregg discussed Round Prairie, where other Underground Railroad activity existed in Hancock County, he chose, like E. H. Young, not to reveal his sources. Instead, he referred to the information as having come from "one of these conductors":

> These conductors wore no insignia of office, but knew each other as if by intuition. They were generally intelligent and sharp-witted men, could tell a white sheep from a black one on the darkest night, and would make their way through a dense forest or trackless prairie, with no better guide than the north star or the moss on the sides of trees....
>
> ... One of these conductors who resided, and yet does, in a south-eastern township, furnishes us with the following as part of his experience in that kind of railroading, which we give as nearly as we can in his own words:
>
> "In the winter of 1843–4 I commenced my first experience in this country, having previously acted as conductor in Northern Ohio for ten years. I met father in town.

PHOTOGRAPH BY THE AUTHOR.

L. C. Maynard harbored runaway slaves in this house, one mile east of LaHarpe in Hancock County.

He asked me to come up to his house after dinner, which I did. Went to the barn, and climbed up over the girt-beam, and found two colored men. I asked them if they were steering for Canada. They said, 'Yes, Sah!' I told them it was a cold, desolate country. The oldest one replied that he knew it, as this was his seventh trip from Missouri there as pilot. This time he came back for his wife. He said, 'I could not get her, so I have brought my youngest brother.'

"I was interested in his case at once, and forwarded them to the next station. To show that he got through all right, I was in Detroit in November of 1848, and stepped into a barber's shop to get shaved. I asked the barber if he knew anything about Benjamin and James Penney. He said 'No." I saw by their looks that they did. So I said, 'Boys, you needn't be afraid of me; I am an old stager; I helped those boys along on their trip.' The barber then told me that Benjamin, the eldest one, caught a severe cold while on that trip, and died of consumption the next summer; the younger, James, is at school in Chatham, getting a good education. Hearing this, I felt fully paid for my trouble in helping them to escape from slavery.

"The next December I was wakened by a rap on the door about two o'clock at night. I opened it, and found three square-built black men, with a friend of mine from Adams County. I took them in, and while my wife was preparing breakfast, they showed me their passes to go where they chose from Christmas until New Years. I asked the boys if they were not taking a rather enlarged view of those passes.

They thought perhaps they were. Before sunrise they were guided on to the next station in safety. The next I heard of them they were in Farmington, Fulton County, at Deacon B_____'s.[7] The deacon took a copy of their passes in a memorandum book. Within a week, three slave-hunters came along. They inquired of a drayman if he had heard of any runaway slaves. He told them he had not seen any, but if any had been there, Deacon B_____ would probably know about them. They went over to the deacon's, and inquired of him. He told them: 'Yes, there were three boys stayed here a few nights ago.' By referring to the memorandum it was proven that they were the owners of the runaways, their names being on the passes.

"This happened about dark, and the deacon kindly invited them to stay all night with him, which two of them did, the other one returning to the hotel. During the evening, the three daughters of the deacon entertained the strangers with songs and music on the melodeon. One of the girls was quite fleshy. The evening passed very pleasantly, and in the morning the strangers offered to pay for their lodging, which the deacon refused,

PHOTOGRAPH BY THE AUTHOR.

Big bluestem prairie grass dominated the landscape of McDonough County before the Civil War. The tall grass helped to shield freedom seekers who passed through Western Illinois.

saying that the black boys stayed without paying, and they were welcome to the same, adding, that should they return that way, he would like them to stop and tell him what luck they had. On their way to town they met the third gentleman, who had spent the night in town. They, of course, stopped to talk of how they had been entertained, not thinking they were overheard by the deacon's hired man, who happened to be behind the hedge. The two said to the one, 'If these are the kind of men that are helping our boys to escape, there is no use in hunting them any more, and I feel rather ashamed of the business, anyway. I believe if I should meet Jerry on the street, I should tell him to go ahead.' They all started back to Missouri.

"At that time there were slaves at every house, in every kitchen, dining rooms, and barn, about home. These men, of course, often told of their experience in hunting the slaves in Illinois, and were as often overheard, until, by their own story, they described the country so well, even to the deacon's daughters, that many of the blacks determined to undertake the trip for themselves....

... "At another time I was going to Quincy with a load of cheese, probably in 1852. Between Bear Creek and Mendon, I met a covered carriage with the curtains down. As it passed me I recognized the near horse as having stayed at my place but a short time before, and suspected what might be inside. I said, 'Hold on; I want to see what you have got.' The driver never saw me in the day-time but knew my voice and stopped. His passengers were badly scared. He said he was steering for my house, but now should go to Rev. K's.[8] I told him K. had gone to Galesburg. So he struck for Round Prairie and stopped. Part of the load was a colored woman with a little boy, two years old. Before the next morning she gave birth to another boy. Physicians in the country were all pro-slavery; but there were mothers in Israel willing to minister to her wants. She remained there a few days and then moved on to Canada.

"These are but a few of the many instances in which we lent our aid to the U.G.R.R., and which we never regretted."[9]

IV

McDonough County—Traveling through Tall Grass Prairies

The flight to freedom moved out of stops in Round Prairie and LaHarpe in Hancock County into McDonough County. The cluster of hideouts in this county were located in or close to Macomb[1] and Bushnell, as well as in the southeastern part of that county, close to Industry. This county included or bordered the three largest tall grass prairie ranges in western Illinois; the Carthage Prairie, the Bushnell Prairie, and the Hancock Prairie.

In 1922 D. N. Blazer wrote an article entitled "The History of the Underground Railroad of McDonough County, Illinois." He seemed to have been particularly interested in getting the story straight, so we find efforts on his part to clarify some past accounts that he felt were incorrect. He explains that he did not intend "to assemble anything like a chronological account of the events that transpired in those troubled times." Instead he limited his observations "to incidents related to me by my father (James) and mother, coupled with much valuable information secured from the children of Andrew and Harmon Allison, who like the Blazers were ardent abolitionists, and a part of the underground system." He further hoped "that this account, which is as accurate and complete as it is in my power to give at this late date, may assist you in gaining an idea of the strife and animosities that existed in the decade ending in 1860." The following is from Blazer's article:

> All underground railroads started on the line of some free state that bordered on a slave state. The road that extended through McDonough county started at Quincy, which was station No. 1, receiving negroes from across the Mississippi river in Missouri. Station No. 2 was down at Round Prairie in Hancock county, at the Pettyjohn or Burton home. Station No. 3, in McDonough county, was generally at the home of some one of the Blazers down on Camp Creek in Industry township, or at the home of Uncle Billy Allison, or one of his sons[2] up on Troublesome Creek. Part

67

of them lived in Chalmers and others in Scotland township. Station No. 4 was at the home of Henry Dobbins in Fulton county, from whence cargoes of negroes were dispatched to Galesburg, Princeton and on to Canada, the terminus of all underground railroads. It is interesting to recall that the Princeton station was in charge of the Lovejoy family, which played such an important part in the early abolition movement.

At the time when the quarrel between the abolitionists and adherents of slavery was becoming most bitter, proponents of emancipation engaged an orator to speak afternoon and night at Old Camp Creek church, then located about a mile and a half southeast of Ebenezer church and a like distance southwest of the present Camp Creek church. Antagonists served notice that the speaker would not be permitted to talk, and when the afternoon meeting hour drew near there was an organized gang present bent on breaking up the meeting and probably doing violence to the orator. These men were armed and acting in a threatening manner.

The atmosphere was tense with excitement. Bloodshed was feared.

There were men and women present, who, while not in sympathy with any argument that could be delivered against slavery, were governed by cooler judgments, and they prevailed upon the gang not to start any trouble. "Let him speak; we'd like to hear what he has to say," was the admonition that calmed the armed band.

The address was an impassioned speech depicting the negro in chains, cowed to the dust under the whip of the master, sold and bartered like cattle and torn asunder mother from child, father from son — the negro, though black by no fault of his own, born in the image of his Creator and entitled to life, liberty and happiness no less than his white brother.

The orator held his audience well, but only for the moment. Animosities were too bitter to be wiped out with a single flash of oratorical genius; hatred of the negro as a free and equal being was too deeply imbedded. When the address was finished and the more inflammable minds descended to the level of everyday thinking, these hatreds and animosities again came to the surface, and there was a general determination that the speaker had said enough for one day. A council of the abolitionists was held, and both men and women debated whether or not it would be advisable to permit the speaker to go through with his evening program. It was finally decided that in order to avoid probable bloodshed, the evening session should be called off.

In 1852 the abolitionists had a candidate for president in John P. Hale. The adherents of slavery declared there should not be an abolitionist vote cast in McDonough county. In those days there were a number of voting places in the county and any resident could go where he chose to vote, but there was no secret ballot then. When you went to the polls you gave the clerk your name, who wrote it down, called through the list of offices to be filled and you told him your choice, which was registered. The voting place in Macomb that year was James M. Campbell's store on the west side of the square and north of West Jackson street, known for years as Cambell's Corner.

Now the abolitionists were just as defiant as their opponents and sent word back to them that they would vote at 10 o'clock in Macomb. The records show there were nine votes cast for Hale. The archives in the attic of your court house have been thoroughly searched for the names of the nine men but they are not to be found. George, Andrew and Harmon Allison and Charles, John and James Blazer made up six of the nine men, but I am not positive as to the other three.

I am indebted to the late Alex. McClain for the information that the nine men met in the Court House yard. By lot they decided their places in the line, and then marched across to Campbell's Corner, single file, each with his gun on his shoulder. There were many men of the opposition there with guns and many who were there just to see what would happen. Of course, the vast majority of them, as now, felt that every man should have the right to vote his own sentiments, and probably that spirit had much to do with preventing bloodshed....

... One of the early experiences of the Blazers, told to me by my father, occurred in the early 'forties. One evening there was a party of several men gathered across the ravine back of my grandmother Blazer's house, better known in late years as the Butcher place. They all carried guns and the Blazer men went into the house to get their weapons but my grandmother said, "No, do not take any guns, we will just go over and see what they want." They went but by the time they got there the men had disappeared. On their way back the boys discovered that their mother carried a meat ax under her apron.

When my cousin, Jennie Blazer Watson, was a little tot and just beginning to talk, a neighbor man, who had very curly hair, came to my grandmother's. Jennie toddled up to him and said, "You have curly hair all over your head, just like little Maggie." Well, Maggie was a little black girl, who with her mother, previously had gone through on their way to Canada.

A child's prattle could not be used as evidence in court so nothing came of it except to cause more talk and more discussion of the fugitive slave law, for the Missouri Compromise and the Dred Scott decision were ably and fluently discussed at that time by school children and men who could neither read nor write.

The following account is about "Charlie," the same fugitive slave, discussed in the previous chapter. This incredibly bold ex-slave was probably the most remarkable fugitive known to UGRR "conductors" inside the Military Tract. This account reveals that UGRR "agents" in Fulton County were also aware of his daring exploits.

The most interesting story connected with any negro that passed through the underground railroad of McDonough County was woven around Charlie, a very light colored buck, with a sharp nose. He probably was a quadroon, or quarter-blood and was the property of a man by the name of Busch, whose plantation lay back some miles from the Missouri river. It was customary with the planters when the wheat was threshed to go to town and stay while negro boys hauled it to market. Charlie and two others were hauling the Busch wheat. When "teaed up" one night Busch and the other planters were discussing recent escapes of slaves from Missouri, when Busch turned banteringly to Charlie and asked him why he didn't try running away just for a little excitement. When Charlie went to his quarters that night he was thinking, and before he went to sleep he had it all figured out how he was going to make a break for Yankeedom.

Next morning Charlie was up early and on their way the boys scolded him for driving so hard. When they reached home Charlie, who was the boss when his master was not around, put the boys to loading the wagons with wheat for the next day's trip to the river. Charlie told the boys he was going to a dance across the way and went to an old mammy and asked for some bacon and pone. She gave it to him but said, "Nigger what you up to? You know you would not need any bacon or pone if you were going to a nigger dance. You are up to some deviltry." Charlie struck out a foot, but not a word did he tell his wife for he said he knew it would break her heart. He had nearly forty-eight hours start, for the boys had to drive to the river and the master go back home to secure dogs and organize for the chase. When the pursuers reached the big river Charlie was housed securely with the Van Dorns and John Brown in Quincy.

The Balzers gave Charlie the credit of being the smartest negro that ever passed over the McDonough county route. After reaching Canada Charlie got some Pennsylvania Presbyterians interested in trying to get his wife and two children to Canada. They sent an old Presbyterian minister through, who arranged with Busch for their freedom for $800. The preacher went back and raised the money but when he returned with the cash Busch had raised to $1200. He went back to Pennsylvania, secured the $1200 but Busch had concluded he must have $1500. This Charlie would not agree to, determining to go back, steal them, and take them to Canada. He made several trips. Twice he succeeded in getting his wife and children and making a start. After the first attempt Busch had the mother and two children sleep in the loft above his and his wife's bedroom, which was reached by a ladder and a scuttle hole, but Charlie climbed to the top of the cabin, removed the clapboards and succeeded in getting nearly to the Illinois side of the Mississippi with his loved ones when the chase was so close it was evident they were going to be captured. On the advice of his wife Charlie jumped in to the river and escaped in the dark.

A few days later he was at the Balzers on his way to Canada. Charlie by this time knew the road and did not require any conductor. Lodging and something to eat were his only needs and he always had a new and interesting experience to relate. One is worth a place here.

Charlie was on his way to Missouri and left Dobbins, the Fulton county station, for the Balzers, but he had not gone far when a fog arose and Charlie lost his way. He wandered around nearly all night, finally gave up and lay down to sleep. When he awoke it was daylight and two men were standing over him. They ordered him to get up, which he did, but Charlie jerked a big dirk knife and made a slash at one of them. Charlie escaped and arrived at my father's early that night. They fed him but decided he had better strike out for the next station immediately. Charlie said he cut the fellow's clothing but did not think he was hurt much. The fact that one of them carried an ox whip suggested that the men from whom Charlie escaped had been plowing prairie and were at the time of the encounter looking for their cattle which had been unyoked and turned loose to graze during the night. This guess proved to be true, for later one of the ploughmen was found laid up from a slight wound such as might have been caused by a knife. However, the ploughman did not mention any set-to with the fugitive negro, declaring that he had accidentally fallen against a ploughshare. Perhaps they thought it would not be of any credit to them to acknowledge that a negro was too much for two of them.

Charlie did not succeed in stealing his wife and children but on the other hand they finally captured Charlie and sent him to the hemp[3] works in Tennessee.[4] There was only one place worse that you could send a negro and that was the indigo[5] works in Florida. There he would lose his finger nails inside of two years and be a dead nigger in five years. But Charlie was too smart for them to keep him any place unless they kept him chained. A few months later, just at the opening of the Civil War, Charlie crossed the Ohio River near Cincinnati and went up through Ohio.

He told the Ohio people of his wonderful experiences, which they doubted, but he gave them the address of Henry Dobbins. They wrote to him and he verified Charlie's story.

After the emancipation of the slaves Charlie's wife and two children reached Canada, the Canaan of all negroes.

It frequently happened that families were divided on the slave question. The Chase family and an incident directly connected with the underground railway is worth a place in this article. A conductor from the station in Hancock county started to bring a darkey to the Allison station. A fog, which was very common at that time, rose and he found he was lost. After driving for some time he came to a house and called the man out and asked the road to Macomb and found he was just out south of town. He knew Rev. James Chase lived close to Macomb and was an abolitionist, so he inquired the way to Chase's.

He was told it was just a little way over to the Chase home and was directed to the Harvey Chase place, which stood just this side of Kill Jordan, now within the city limits of Macomb, where the Archie Fisher home stands. Now it happened that Harvey Chase, who had been reared as an abolitionist the same as James, had changed and was on the other side of the question.

When he called Mr. Chase out and informed him of his mission he was told that he was wanting James Chase and was directed to his home, which was on the farm east of the county farm.

When the abolitionists asked Harvey Chase why he did not call an officer and have the darkey sent back to his master he explained by saying, "the stranger came to him in good faith and he, as a gentleman, was honor bound to keep the faith." But his brother, James, had a different explanation. He said "brother Harvey knew slavery was wrong and while he talked in favor of it he did not believe in it." The Chase brothers were gentlemen of honor.

The last cargo of negroes passed over the underground railway in McDonough county in 1860. This last cargo was not only the largest but the most valuable that ever passed over our route, and the only negro ever captured in this county was taken from this cargo. They were all big husky fellows, picked with a view to strength and endurance and were bought up for the hemp works of Tennessee. They were brought into a river town and were to be delivered the next morning when the master would get his money but that night they all escaped and reached Quincy, this was in June. The prize was a big one; $500 per head was the sum offered for their capture.

The cargo of negroes had been out to Round Prairie two or three times and back-tracked to Quincy until things would quiet down, but was finally delivered to us by Pettyjohn of the Huntsville country one morning before daylight in September, 1860.

I was aroused and told to go to my uncle's to inform him of the arrival of the negroes. I rapped gently on the window of Uncle John's bedroom. He signaled with a light tapping on the pane to let me know that he understood. I returned home, and by the time I had reached there the negroes had been stowed away, each in a shock of corn, and supplied with food and water. I am not sure at this late date whether there were eleven or twelve negroes in the cargo, as the shipments were then called. Clark's history [most likely S. J. Clarke's *History of McDonough County, Illinois*] incorrectly reports the number as five.

The Underground Railroad in Western Illinois

When Pettyjohn delivered the negroes at our home he started on his return trip immediately.

Just after daylight on a hill west of Middletown, or Fandon, he passed a man on horseback. At some distance Pettyjohn looked back and saw that the other traveler had stopped and was looking over the conductor and his empty train. Pettyjohn at once knew that he was suspicious. The man on horseback was not one of those that took part in hunts for runaway slaves, but as afterwards told to my father, he happened to meet and mention the matter to Dave Chrisman who was the leader of the slavery-sympathizers in McDonough county. Clark's History reports that the driver got lost and left his team and wagon in a gully near Dave Chrisman's house, and in that way it was learned that the cargo had arrived at the Blazers. That was Dave Chrisman's story, and it was generally believed. There was no means of knowing that it was not true and Mr. Clark was justified in writing it as the abolitionists would not give the historian any facts. At the time this history was written the negroes had long since been free and the abolitionists were only too glad to dismiss the old strifes from their thoughts. Dave Chrisman was a bluffer and invented the story of finding the team near his house thinking it would add to his notoriety.

I recall very well that while the dozen negroes sat and sweat in the corn shocks, for it was a hot September day, my father and John Blazer flailed buckwheat just south of the John Balzer house and they had company all day long. Dave Chrisman was the first visitor. He had been the rounds and notified his followers and made arrangements which were to be carried out that night. No one stayed very long but one visitor was not any more than gone when another rode up and would sit on his horse out in the road and talked for a time. All carried rifles, which was not unusual those times for there was still considerable game in the country. But the visitors were not the only people who had guns for two rifles stood inside the fence near where the two men flailed and talked to their neighbors while I sat on the fence. I listened and watched and reported who was coming. The sober, quiet, determined men knew that trouble was ahead of them and when by themselves talked over their plans for the coming night when the valuable cargo must be delivered to the next station.

You may think it strange but each insisted that they should be in charge of the negroes when they started on the perilous trip and each had a good reason why he should go but John had the best argument. It was his turn and my father, when the time came, started up the prairie just after dark with a wagon load of grain covered with a tarpaulin. Before he had gone a half mile some twenty-five or thirty horsemen rode up, all carrying guns, and rode along for a mile or more and visited, when they dropped back and held a short consultation, and four came back, caught up with him, and rode away. My father went on to Bernadotte to mill and did not know the fate of the darkies until he returned home the next day.

Now John and the colored boys had swung off toward the timber and then went straight east up the prairie until even with the Dickie Craig farm. When they started to the timber they had to cross a new plank fence which had been built just long the south side of the Craig land. Just as John and the negroes got on to the fence Chrisman and his men, who had been lying in the shadow of the fence, raised up.

John Blazer said to the negroes, "Run boys for the timber." They did as told and all got away but one, which Chrisman hit over the head with a gun.

Chrisman, accompanied by one or two of the leaders, took the negro to Macomb

72

where he was held in jail until the owner came and claimed his property. But Chrisman, as was often the case, then failed to get his reward, as the owner said he had lost his man's work, and spent so much money trying to get him back that he could not afford to pay anything.

Ten or twelve men, comprising the balance of the party that, together with Chrisman, had captured the negro, came back that night and threw clubs and rocks on our house and shouted and yelled. My mother went to the door which had no lock, and stood with an ax in her hand, ready to protect her home and children.

Threats that my father and uncle would be indicted by the next grand jury, that they had been caught red handed in transporting negroes and would have an opportunity to serve time at Alton, was not a pleasant greeting to their families. This did not go direct to the ears of my father and uncle. Even Dave Chrisman was too gentlemanly to discuss the question with the Blazers or Allisons. Those were trying times but do not conclude that this condition existed all over the country. It was much worse in the neighborhoods where there was an underground station. Now, I do not believe any one who was not intimate with conditions, can realize just what it meant to a family to be in such strife and turmoil.[6]

S. J. Clarke's *History of McDonough County, Illinois*, recounts a story obviously told to the author by someone who Clarke chose not to identify. The story is about a fugitive slave who realized he was being taken south by his Missouri owner to be sold. The slave, Caesar, decided to leave the Mississippi steamer he was on in order to strike out for freedom. He was afforded the opportunity to escape because his owner had hired him out to the boat's captain to pay for the slave's passage. Clarke's account ends as follows:

When the boat landed, Caesar was sent with other deck hands to load it with wood. He moved off as if with the intention of doing the work, and when out of sight of his companions, he started off on a run. His presence at first was not missed, and when the fact was discovered, the boat could not be delayed that his capture might be effected. Steering directly north, Caesar in due time found himself in the vicinity of Upper Alton.[7] While passing along the road he heard behind him a couple of horsemen in full gallop, and supposing they were after him, it was his first thought to run, but fearing this would excite their apprehension, if they were not in search of him, he quietly stepped to one side, and began plucking the plums from a tree by the roadside. Luckily the horsemen paid no attention to him, even if they observed him. He continued on his way, and soon another horseman came galloping up behind. As before he could not escape without observation, and the horseman soon overtook him and quietly asked:

"Going north?"

"Yes, sah, am traveling that way."

"Well, then get on this horse and travel until you come to a certain house [describing it] there hitch your horse, go in, and you will be cared for."

Although he did not know whether he was a friend or foe, Caesar concluded to trust him and take his advice. Mounting the horse he proceeded on the way until he reached the designated place where he stopped, and on going in, without a word being spoken, he was shown a large upper room and told to remain there until called for. Food was provided him, and when night came he was conducted on his way. He was now on the line of the famous Underground railway, and in due time passed through this county (McDonough) on his way to Canada.

Some months after, he returned over the line to secure, if possible, his wife. Arriving in the vicinity of Hannibal he learned that she had been sold and removed to some unknown place, and all efforts to learn of her whereabouts were unavailing, and he never saw or heard from her.[8]

When fugitive slaves left McDonough County, UGRR routes moved them toward freedom north, northeast, or east. Straight north would have taken them through Warren County and the town of Roseville. William and Mary Dilly, who were operators running a safe house for fugitives in that community, were closely connected to Underground Railroad operators in Galesburg. The Roseville Congregational Church was dedicated in 1851 and Knox College's abolitionist president, Jonathan Blanchard, came down from Galesburg to officiate at the ceremony. In the mid–1850s, J. A. R. Rogers, a radical antislavery advocate from Oberlin College in Ohio, served the Roseville Congregationalists as their minister. Runaway "cargo" would be sent from there through Monmouth or angled on byways through southeast Warren County into southwest Knox County, and then on into Galesburg. The northeast route went directly into Galesburg, and the east route took them to the maze of hiding places located in Fulton County. Fugitives would now have been in the heart of the grasslands, and no matter which of the three courses they took, the prairie landscape helped to keep them out of sight. Runaway slaves who left the Mississippi River north of Quincy, or east of Keokuk and Fort Madison, Iowa, would have found uninterrupted stretches of prairie grass from the river all the way to Monmouth and Galesburg. The land gradually sloped upward into Warren and Knox counties, forming the high prairie watershed between the Mississippi and Illinois rivers. It is estimated that four-fifths of Knox County's entire landscape was taken up by prairie grass in the 1850s.[9]

In many cases, "agents" worked together in order to protect themselves against surprise visits from unwanted parties of slave catchers, regional bounty hunters, or officers of the law. If three or more operators were available to help escapees at the same time, scouts could be posted. One "brakeman" would be positioned a few miles in front of a wagon and the other was placed a safe distance behind. If trouble was detected at either end of the route, the wagon driver and "cargo" could be warned. These tactics also could have been deployed when fugitives were not being transported, in order to confuse slave chasers.

If runaways and operators were afforded the opportunity to make emergency drop-off plans before leaving one station and traveling to the next, a tremendous advantage was gained by the conspirators. There are accounts of "carriers" leaving fugitives in cornfields, by timber groves, or close to streams, only to return later to pick up the "cargo" after the danger had passed. Through prearranged signals like commonly mimicked bird calls (owls, cardinals, and crows), the distinct drumming sound of a prairie chicken, or the bark and whine of a prairie wolf, the parties involved would know when wayfarers could safely emerge from their hiding places in order to resume the trip north. In some cases fugitives were left intentionally by a conductor and instructed to follow a creek bed or angle across a stretch of prairie grass. In

BRENDA PATTERSON, BG PATTERSON GRAPHICS.

Untold numbers of fugitive slaves made their way to freedom alone, without ever receiving help from Underground Railroad operators.

such cases, UGRR agents would have traveled the next leg of the journey alone and reconnected with escapees at a safer location. Even in cases where secreted passengers were unexpectedly interrupted by slave catchers, it was possible to lay plans ahead of time if the escapees knew how to reestablish contact with agents. Once into western Illinois, the percentage of fugitives who ultimately made it to safety seems very high. Most of those who chronicled the Underground Railroad inside the three rivers triangle tell of but few "passengers" actually captured and returned to slavery. The edge invariably went against the bounty hunter, who was likely to have been unfamiliar with local geography.

In 1845, the Missouri Legislature passed a new law that seemed to take notice of the fact that Illinois was becoming an increasingly popular place for fugitives to cross into during their flight from slavery. The law provided that Missouri's treasurer was to pay for the publication of the state's runaway slave legislation in two Illinois newspapers. This statute stipulated that if a fugitive slave 20 years or older was captured beyond Missouri's borders and handed over to either a sheriff or slave owner, a slave tracker would receive $100. If a runaway slave under 20 years of age was captured, the reward was $50. But if the fugitive was caught inside Missouri, the slave tracker was paid only $25.[10]

V

Fulton County—
Cluster of "Depots"

A fugitive fortunate enough to make it into Fulton County encountered a cluster of hiding places for runaways. Escapees not only moved into the county from the west but they also arrived from points south and from the east and southeast after leaving the Illinois River. Some locations, like the village of Midway and Harlan's barn, disappeared long ago. But, other small communities that provided safe havens still exist, like Bernadotte (Francis Overton/operator), Cuba (Dan Heller and Henry Berry/operators), Fiatt (E. L. Boynton/operator), Smithfield (Jesse and James Fate/operators), and Table Grove (Thomas Berry/operator). In the midst of these little towns was another small village, Ipava, where John C. Dobbins was a regionally known "keeper." Clarke's previously cited *History of McDonough County, Illinois* includes a story about Dobbins's very young son helping out a runaway slave:

> A little son of Mr. Dobbins, about eight or nine years old, near Ipava, Fulton county, while a number of negroes were hid in father's barn, was sent regularly to carry them their food. On one occasion his mother had prepared the negroes' dinner, and placing it upon a tray, started her little boy with it to the barn. As he opened the door on the porch he observed three or four neighboring women. To either go forward or return would excite their suspicions, and quick as thought he began whistling for the dogs. His mother hearing him, and divining his reason, called out to him, "Don't throw that out to the dogs, bring it back here; that's good." The boy quickly returned, and the unwelcome visitors never suspected anything wrong.[1]

The larger Fulton County towns of Lewiston, which was the county seat,[2] along with Canton,[3] and particularly Farmington[4] were "honeycombed" with UGRR "shepherds." A story that appeared in the *Canton Weekly Register* on December 15, 1910, reported that the town's UGRR residents met in Lyman Walker's home about once a month. The group recited a verse in unison when each meeting began:

77

Come all ye true friends of the nation;
attend to humanity's call;
come aid the poor slaves liberation;
and roll on the temperance ball.

Farmington's most renowned UGRR agent was Luther Birge, a carpenter, who constructed a tunnel on his property in order to help slaves escape. Tunnels and other subterranean hiding places often figured in favorite myths retold after the Civil War, but we know that Birge actually made one. Birge was indicted by a grand jury three times, but was never convicted. He was said to have sometimes "painted" fugitives with whitewash to help disguise them, and there were other stories told about his having enticed slave trackers to drink doctored coffee or cider that induced sleep so that fugitives would have more time to get away.

COURTESY OF *THE FARMINGTON SHOPPER*,
FARMINGTON SHOPPER PRESS.

Luther Birge was a Fulton County Underground Railroad agent who was said to delay slave trackers' pursuit of fugitive slaves by giving them doped drinks that put them to sleep.

In 1899, Harvey Lee Ross wrote a book about his family history entitled *The Early Pioneers and Pioneer Events of the State of Illinois*. His father, Ossian M. Ross, who founded Lewiston, was one of the first men in Fulton County to commit his time and energy to the antislavery cause. This included the time he spent fighting against the effort, in 1824, to make Illinois a slave state. The following are accounts found in Harvey Ross's book about the work of his father and Peter Cartwright:

When Peter Cartwright came from Kentucky to Sangamon County in 1823 and bought a farm seven miles west of Springfield, he found the people greatly agitated (as I have said in a former letter) over the question whether Illinois should be a slave or free state. An election to settle the question was called for the first Monday in August, 1824. He had left Kentucky to get away from slavery, and it was natural, with his combative disposition, that he should go into the battle for freedom with all his soul and might. He thoroughly canvassed the counties of Sangamon and Morgan,

Luther Birge's house in Farmington was a place where many freedom seekers were given aid. Escapees were sent from his house northwest to Galesburg, due north to Stark County, or northeast to Brimfield and Princeville in Peoria County.

making speeches against slavery in all the churches and schoolhouses, or wherever he could get an audience.

At that time there were but thirty counties in the state, and Sangamon and Morgan were the two northern counties on the east side of the Illinois river. Pike and Fulton were the only counties on the west side of the river. Fulton was the extreme northern county, taking in Fort Clark (now Peoria) and Galena and Chicago.

There was at that time in Fulton county a man who perhaps did as much to defeat slavery as did Mr. Cartwright or any other man in Illinois. His name was Ossian M. Ross. He thoroughly canvassed the counties of Fulton and Pike. He was a Quaker, and the Quakers were bitterly opposed to human slavery. He went into the conflict with all his might, and never ceased until the votes were counted and the battle of freedom won. I believe there was more credit due him and Peter Cartwright for carrying the state against slavery than any other two men in Illinois. Following is the vote on that question. The vote of Morgan, Sangamon, Pike and Fulton will show how well they succeeded.

The Vote on Slavery

	For	Against
Alexander	75	51
Bond	63	240
Clark	32	116
Crawford	134	262
Edgar	3	234
Edwards	186	371
Fayette	125	121
Franklin	170	113
Fulton	5	60
Gallatin	596	133
Greene	134	405
Hamilton	173	86
Jackson	180	93
Jefferson	90	43
Johnson	74	74
Lawrence	158	261
Madison	351	58
Marion	45	53
Montgomery	74	99
Monroe	171	196
Morgan	43	555
Pike	23	261
Pope	275	124
Randolph	357	184
Sangamon	153	722
St. Clair	427	543
Union	213	240
Washington	112	173
Wayne	189	111
White	355	326
Total	4950	6822
Majority against slavery		1872

... In the early settlement of Illinois the southern part of the state was settled first, and mainly by people from the slave states. These people brought with them their slave laws, slave prejudices, and many of them also brought their slaves. They found that many of the staple products of the South, such as hemp, tobacco and cotton, could be raised in southern Illinois, and they believed that these products could not be profitably raised without slave labor. There was another condition that influenced the people to favor slavery: About that time a tremendous emigration was pouring through southern Illinois into Missouri from Virginia and Kentucky. In the fall of the year every great road was crowded with these movers in long trains of teams, and with their negroes, and with plenty of money. They were the wealthiest and best educated emigrants from the slave states. The early settlers of Illinois saw it all with great envy for Missouri's good fortune. The lordly emigrant as he passed along with his droves of negroes and piles of money took malicious delight in adding to the unrest by pretending to regret the short sighted policy of Illinois which excluded him by declaring against the institution of slavery. This gave the people of southern Illinois a strong desire to hold another election, hoping that slavery might be voted in.

And so the agitation was kept up from year to year. The same infamous old "black laws" were still on the statute book, and many negroes were held in slavery, especially in the southern counties along the Ohio and Mississippi rivers. They were hemmed in by slave states, Kentucky on the southeast and Missouri on the west. So the sentiment was strong for slavery. There were but few men in the legislature who dared oppose these bad laws or slavery. It would have been a very unpopular if not dangerous step. Then there was great fear of being called an "abolitionist," the most odious epithet that in those times could be applied to a man.[5]

The victory at the polls in 1824 that defeated efforts to make Illinois a slave state was accomplished through a combination of people who believed human bondage was inhumane and immoral and others who were not opposed to slavery on principle. In the latter group were people who were openly prejudiced toward blacks and who did not want them living in Illinois, but who had no problem at all with slavery's existence in the south. They did not want to see either slavery or black migration take hold in the Prairie State.[6]

On October 1, 1838, Farmington hosted the First Annual Meeting of the Illinois Anti-Slavery Society.[7] This collection of 99 delegates and kindred spirits from across the state included Owen Lovejoy,[8] George Washington Gale, Edward Beecher, and Quincy's Dr. David Nelson. The most prominent figure in attendance, however, was Putnam County's Benjamin Lundy, whose reputation as a giant in the antislavery struggle in the eastern United States was well-known to those assembled at the Fulton County gathering. The society agreed to support Lundy's effort to revive the publication of his newspaper *Genius of Universal Emancipation* in Illinois, originally published in Philadelphia and by then out of print.

The Underground Railroad has often been referred to, in many locales across the northern United States, as a loosely organized band of agents made up of people not that familiar, or only vaguely familiar, with one another along UGRR routes. The proceedings of the Illinois Anti-Slavery Society's first anniversary meeting in Farmington, make clear that, in western Illinois at least, the foregoing description is simply not true. Most of the people who gathered together that fall in Fulton County were to remain committed to the cause and to each other for over two more decades. The key figures, from Adams County to Bureau County, started putting together the pieces of a resistance movement very early on. One of the most significant pieces of business transacted at the 1838 meeting was the selection of the Reverend Chauncey Cook to be a traveling agent for the society. There can be no doubt about the fact that these freedom fighters knew each other very well from the beginning of the Illinois antislavery crusade. Their friendship, loyalty, and common commitment extended a network across the Mississippi River to southeastern Iowa, where their comrade, Asa Turner, was doing the same kind of work. He, in turn, knew exactly where to send enslaved blacks courageous enough to risk running away. Turner was listed as the "Iowa Territory" representative at the Farmington meeting. Further, it seems not to have been an accident that Owen Lovejoy, shortly after the Farmington meeting adjourned, found his way to Princeton, Illinois, at what could be considered just the right junction point on the western Illinois UGRR.

Here is part of what Lundy recorded in his newspaper about the Farmington meeting. It appeared in the rebirth of *The Genius of Universal Emancipation*, which was published in February 1839, five months before Lundy died:

First Anniversary of the Illinois Anti-Slavery Society Monday, October 1, 1838

A number of the members and friends of the Illinois Anti-Slavery Society being met, according to the invitation of the Farmington Anti-Slavery Society, in the Presbyterian Church, in anticipation of the annual meeting of the State Society—it was recorded that a meeting, preparatory to the anniversary, be now organized, for the purpose of forming a roll of members now present.

Charles W. Hunter, a Vice-President of the society, was requested to take the chair, and Owen Lovejoy and Thomas Tippincott were appointed secretaries....

Tuesday Morning, 8 O'clock

The Illinois Anti-Slavery Society met, agreeable to notice and was called to order by the President Elihu Wolcott. Commenced with sermon of prayer, after which, on motion, it was resolved, that a committee of five be appointed, to present business for the action of the society. The following were the committee: John Waters, Jeremiah Porter, Thomas Galt, Edward Beecher and J. J. Mitner....

Report of the Executive Committee of the Illinois Anti-Slavery Society

The momentous and thrilling events of the past year, connected with the operation of this society, are doubtless fresh in the recollection of its members, and such have been the difficulties and embarrassments that have resulted therefrom, the Executive Committee has been able to direct little in fulfillment of the duties of its appointment. It will be remembered that in the very commencement of its existence, the society was exposed to a storm of popular fury, which did not cease until the life of one of the champions of our cause—the lamented E. P. Lovejoy—was sacrificed on the bloody altar of prejudice and oppression—and at the same time his free and independent press, dedicated to piety and philanthropy, was doomed to destruction, in order to satiate the full spirit of persecution and lawless violence....

... In the month of April, last, the Rev. Mr. Beecher and the Rev. Hale were commissioned to procure funds for the re-establishment of the Alton Observer. But, efforts failed; and for the present the enterprise has been abandoned....

... Notwithstanding the temporary success of the enemies of freedom, law and order, in the state, — when principles of liberty were scoffed at and reviled — when the constitutions and laws of government were trampled in the dust — when an American citizen suffered martyrdom to appease the brutal rage of mobocratic violence — and although many, who had partially embraced our cause, shrunk back in the hour of trial, and even some who had been active in promoting the great and good work of philanthropy, were induced to pause, for the moment: still, in casting our eyes around, we behold much that is calculated to cheer our hearts and invigorate our hopes for the future success of our efforts; the eventual triumph of our principles; and the final accomplishment of our objectives.

While we are fain to acknowledge that we cannot enumerate many recent instances of public advancement of this important reformation, within the limits of our state — yet we are happy to learn that some new associations have been organized, and strong symptoms of revival are manifest in various places. But we hazard nothing in saying that the alarming events of the past year have produced an important change in the sentiments of many individuals. A portion of the people have been roused, and awakened throughout the land. The bloody tragedy at Alton had unmasked the gory fiend of American oppression and we are enabled to view this horrible system in its malignancy of aspect and characteristic vileness. Thousands of our citizens, who lately believed they had "nothing to do with the subject of slavery," now begin to discover their error. They have found at least, that slavery has something to do with them, and their interests....

... When justice is beheld triumphant, the fetters of the slave broken in atoms and the elements of wrath hushed into silence and those who were the first, the loudest, and the most vindictive in opposing this righteous measure are seen cordially giving it the sanction of the approbation; we say, when all these circumstances are taken under review, we have the most undeniable evidence of the feasibility of our undertaking, and the certain assurance of eventual success, in [illegible] we continue the advocacy of our cause with tireless energy and unflinching perseverance.

In conclusion, we commence to our brethren, in this state a careful inspection of passing events, as they are unfolded to public view, and a renewal of effort to promote the glorious cause of our association. The evidence that our cause is just cannot be gained by the honest and upright heart. That our doctrines are sound, and our measures practicable, safe and necessary, we have proof both ample and conclusive. Let us, then, buckle our armor, and re-commence active operations, in this great moral warfare. The conflict between the friends and enemies of this cause, is between virtue and vice, mercy and cruelty, Christianity and paganism, liberty and slavery....

... The Committee appointed to recommend a course respecting a paper reported — that, in existing circumstances, it seems to them expedient to unite in recommending and sustaining the Genius of Universal Emancipation to be published by Benjamin Lundy.

They will therefore recommend the following resolution.

Resolved that this society, for the present year, will patronize the Genius of Universal Emancipation to be published at Hennepin by Benjamin Lundy, and that they adopt it as their organ of communication.

The following resolution was offered and adopted....

... The committee on funds made the following report, which was adopted; viz. that two-thousand dollars will be necessary to meet the expenses of the society the ensuing year; and the committee would recommend that subscriptions be now received of the members of the society, for raising the above sum; that it be the duty of the general agent to solicit funds for the same object; and that the auxiliary societies take up the collection for the same purpose and forward the sum to the treas-

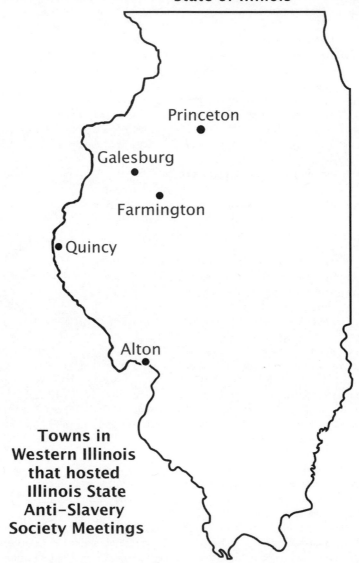

State of Illinois

Princeton

Galesburg

Farmington

Quincy

Alton

Towns in Western Illinois that hosted Illinois State Anti-Slavery Society Meetings

urer of the state society and the receipts of it be acknowledged in the Genius of Universal Emancipation....

... Resolved; that the Illinois State Anti-Slavery Society hold its next anniversary at Quincy, Adams County, on the fourth Wednesday of September, 1839, at 9 o'clock, am....

... Resolved, that the thanks of the society be tendered to the citizens of Farmington, for their kindness and benevolence, in their gratuitous accommodations offered to its members.

The business, before the meeting having now been disposed of, it was, on motion, resolved to adjourn.[9]

The bonded network was getting organized. The following year, the Illinois State Anti-Slavery Society met in Quincy, Nelson's city; the year after in Owen Lovejoy's community, Princeton; and in 1841, they gathered in Galesburg, Gale's town. The society's members became familiar with one another at their gatherings and forged friendships that contributed to the operational structure and success of the western Illinois Underground Railroad. The Illinois antislavery crusaders learned some valuable lessons about strategy and tactics following their society's first meeting in Alton only weeks before Elijah P. Lovejoy was killed there in 1837. In the future, the society decided to pull back from gathering in southern Illinois and meet instead within the more protective cocoon of the three rivers triangle. These ardent abolitionists knew that if they met in small western Illinois towns, it would be highly unlikely that proslavery troublemakers would break up their assemblages. The communities of Farmington, Princeton, and Galesburg were not that far from Missouri, and Quincy bordered the slave state. By gathering annually in this region for their state conventions, these abolitionists sent a clear signal — the counties of west central Illinois were filled with people who opposed slavery; many of them were well-known with each other; and a good number of them would help carry fugitives to freedom.

In 1916, the *Canton Daily Ledger* published the recollections of Julia Wright, whose father, John Wright, had lived only a few miles from Canton and was a Fulton County representative at the 1838 Anti-Slavery Society's meeting in Farmington. Her story shows the dramatic impact Harriett Beecher Stowe's *Uncle Tom's Cabin* had on an impressionable young girl:

I have so often been asked for my recollections of this peculiar railway system that I now attempt hesitatingly to give a few of them as they come to me. But before proceeding we are prone to notice that this is an age of many and various kinds of highways.

In Caesar's time the old Roman military roads linked together many of the real estate possessions and provinces, but our American roads are not by any means like the solid, substantial Roman highways. A national highway was at one time completed as far as the Mississippi River, but there stopped, leaving us to flounder through mud or sand to some depth, causing much complaint of the weather, or against the road commissioner. But when as a people we began to seek pleasure on these highways, then man called for a better road. What a boon was the steel rail and the iron horse, and what automobilist does not welcome the late Lincoln Highway, from the east to the west coast, so well named after the honored man who did so much for his country and made us a nation.

But the highway I am to consider, was not made for the general public. It was laid for a people without a home, without a country, without education. It was to aid the black man, who in those days, if he had a family, never knew when or where they would be separated and sold to the highest bidder, as we would sell grain or stock.

When the oppression became so great we can readily see why he sought to find a land of freedom. That land was Canada, but there was always the problem of how to get there without being recaptured and placed under greater oppression. The Underground Railway sprung up as if by magic to help him.

This railway was traveled only by night. The road was our common rough, muddy highway with no street lights. Usually the railway system was in operation only in the dark of the moon. The engine was the common farm horse; the passenger coach, the famous farm wagon, while the conductors were the large-hearted men who loved their home and friends and who fully believed in "Equal rights to all men." But it did require some character and heroism to meet the opposition in sentiment in those days, and rendering assistance to the black man in getting across the country to freedom was fraught with danger and might mean imprisonment for life, if not death, as a result.

My early home was only one and one-half miles northwest of Canton on the well known farm of Deacon Royal Wright, afterwards known as the John M. Wright estate. It was there my six brothers and I spent our childhood, remaining until all were mature, and it was there I first became interested in the dark people.

While lying in my little trundle bed next door to the dining room, where were grandfather, father, mother, aunt, and the hired help if they cared to be present, I have raptly listened as one or another read aloud from that old New York publication, the "Christian Era," the story of Uncle Tom's Cabin, as written by Harriet B. Stowe....

... I couldn't sleep, so great was my interest in Eliza, Topsy, Uncle Tom and Eva and I would take my little chair and sit at mother's knee to listen, though often admonished to "go back to bed." I learned later that the book was finished in grandfather's room and I only learned through mother what became of Uncle Tom and Eva, and later, when I read it myself.

As I grew older I was given a room over grandfather's where the chimney warmed it with the aid of the stovepipe which passed up through the floor but I didn't understand why it was that frequently I found myself back in the trundle bed next morning until one day mother said, "Would you like to see a real, black baby?" She took me upstairs to my own room where were the mother, father, grandmother, aunt, and boy, and the most cunning, plump, black-eyed, curly-haired baby. Then I saw why I had to be taken at night from one room to another, as mine was the only room that was warm and was a safe place for them during the day. There were no furnaces then.

The old darky grandmother was quite lame with rheumatism, and when asked how she got away, she said, "Our master was after us, so they buried me by a log, covered me with leaves and left my nose alone exposed so I could breathe. Then at night they came for me."

It was then I learned my father and one good neighbor many nights helped those dark people on by their teams as far as Farmington. It was a bitter cold night that the family I referred to was taken northward, so they placed plenty of hay in the wagon and covered them up, afterwards placing sacks of bran over all so that if they were followed they would suppose they were returning from the Ellisville flour mill.

It was seldom the colored people stayed in the house and often the hay loft or corn crib was the resort. One night two strong men slept by the kitchen stove as they had come in a damp, cold rain. The question arose as to how they were to be fed without our hired help suspecting them. I have known mother to send the maid elsewhere while she herself prepared a good meal, placing it in a milk bucket and father distributing it.

One night two or three were brought to father. A tap on the window and the spoken words "A friend" was the warning. We had company, but they were cared for and the next night he couldn't get started as soon as he wished and he directed the men to walk on across a narrow strip of woods and get into a corn field directly east going into the second corn row. They were both armed and very strong men, so father took my oldest brother with him into the wagon.

As father and brother approached the corn field the men, who had expected them from another direction, were ready to shoot, when he gave the password—"A friend."

"Ah, Massa, how glad we are we didn't shoot; your voice saved you," they cried out in unison. These men had taken their master's horses to make their escape from the south and turned them loose when they felt safe. They were asked, "Didn't you know that was stealing?" They answered, "No, sah, we done paid for them more than once, by working...."

... The line extending through this county was one of the many which converged at Chicago. Once reaching Chicago the slaves were practically free from capture as they were usually placed on great vessels which, without stopping at intermediate ports could land the fugitives on Canadian soil.

Most of the fugitives helped through Fulton County came from Quincy station, though the mass of the community there was against anything which savored of abolition. One of the main leaders in Quincy was a Dr. David Nelson, who established a "Mission Institute" after being driven from Palmyra, Mo., where he had established Marion College.

At the Institute Dr. Nelson disseminated his anti-slavery views while educating young men as missionaries, but finally the institution was burned by enemies from Missouri.

Dr. Richard Eells, according to the Historical Encyclopedia of Illinois, was an aid of Nelson and was indicted. He was prosecuted before Stephen A. Douglas, then a judge of the circuit court, and fined for aiding a fugitive to escape, and then judgment against him was finally confirmed by the Supreme Court after his death in 1852, ten years after the original indictment.

Prominent men in all walks of life were known to give aid to operators of the railroad. Lawyers of national reputation as Thaddeus Stevens, Rutherford B. Hayes, Richard H. Dana, Salmon P. Chase, and others gave their service to the railroad without fee, defending either the operators or their human freight. Wealthy men over the country contributed thousands to the cause.

The Underground Railroad in Western Illinois

A significant fact is that many of the operators all over the country were deacons, and such was the case in Fulton County, as for instance there were Deacon Jones of Canton and Deacon Birge of Farmington.

One of the best posted men today on the operation of the Underground Railroad is W.H. Driggs, a veteran, who as a youngster personally knew several of the station masters. In fact his father, Chauncey Driggs, was one of them. Interviewed today Mr. Driggs told the following story:

"Of course I was just a small boy then and a great deal of what father told me of the happenings of the time I have forgotten, but from what he told me in later years, I think Deacon Nathan Jones was the president and Lyman Walker was the secretary and treasurer of that peculiar railroad system. The laymen were Henry Andrews, father of George B. Andrews, who recently moved to California; Chency Jones, brother of Nathan Jones and father of Mrs. B. E. Eyerly, now deceased; John Wright, father of Miss Julia Wright of Canton and Isaac Swan, grandfather of Frank Fulton of near Canton.

"All the men I named were prominent in Fulton County. They were not ashamed of what part they took in helping the refugees but necessarily because of the sentiment in some sections their operations were secret....

"...I don't know how often the members of the Fulton County system had a meeting, and a great deal of other matters never became known for their meetings were more secret than any regularly organized secret society that I know of. The members had the universal password, 'Friend,' and the affairs of the system were never under any consideration discussed when 'strangers' were present.

"The greatest activity of the railroad was during the early forties. While the system was in operation almost until the time of the war, there was little activity in this section after '55. In the early forties it was no strange sight to see detectives in Canton and other towns in Fulton county looking for runaway slaves. There seemed to be more detectives than there possibly could have been slaves transported through here.

"I never heard of a detective ever making a capture in this section despite the large number forever passing through here. Many a house was searched and certain homes were watched for night after night but so carefully did the operators of the railroad plan and execute that there was only one instance I recall which came near resulting in capture, and this incident had a tragic ending.

"It occurred one night in the spring of 1843. A slave had been brought to the south side of Spoon River to one of the underground agents, who was a squatter in a patch of woods, near where Ipava now stands. The squatter kept the slave in safety that day and the next night the agent started to Canton via the Bernadotte bridge.*

"Detectives for the slave owner were on the scent and one of them was watching at the other side of the bridge, having seen the wagon start toward the bridge. He hid behind a large tree and when the wagon passed he sprang into the wagon as quick as lightning, but the fugitive, a powerful negro, who was ever on the alert, had a great ugly knife in his grasp.

The covered bridge at Bernadotte is usually said to have been built in 1844. Here a bridge is said to have been in existence in the spring of 1843. Assuming that the generally given date is correct, and excluding a typographical error, then Miss Wright must have been in error by several years, or else another, less pretentious bridge must have spanned the river at that time.

"The detective not only failed in his attempt to handcuff the runaway slave but paid the forfeit of his life in the attempt. The negro, in slashing at his pursuer, had nearly severed the man's head from his body.

"The agent, who had no hand whatever in the killing, realized at once his bad predicament and though greatly disturbed, set about to dispose of the dead man, for he knew even in Fulton County there would be many questions to answer should he be found with the corpse and the darky also.

"Finally, on suggestion of the slave he took a large sack he had in his conveyance — a heavy farm wagon — and placed a great rock in it, then tied the sack to the man's body. In a few seconds sack and all disappeared in the waters of Spoon River. The agent continued his journey to Canton where the slave was taken care of and the next night was helped northward."[10]

Francis Overton and his wife, Sarah, were operators of the UGRR near Bernadotte. Here the Spoon River, a particularly desirable water course for escapees, flowing south from London Mills and Ellisville, turns sharply to the east before emptying into the Illinois River. The Overton's daughter, Harriett, who was an excellent handler of horses, once rescued her father from a proslavery mob that was attacking him by riding into the melee and passing a lead pipe to him for protection. In 1914, Harriet's brother, Luther, wrote a series of articles that appeared in the *Table Grove Herald*. The following selections are taken from these stories:

The following recollections of the principles and workings of the Underground Railroad reach back to a period about the year 1844. The station was located on the east side of Spoon River, two miles north of Bernadotte, on a farm known as the Overton farm, having been settled on by said family, and title obtained from the government about the year 1832. A few years later partly because of its out-of-the-way location, but more than that because of strong convictions that God in His merciful decree never intended one human being with a living soul to be kept in bondage as chattel property, the above farm was designated as a station.

My first remembrance was a young man, black as the African ever became, dropped off one night. Being young and very active, he was seen by a neighbor, and that interfered with moving him on time, which was always after night. My father had neighbors who formerly had slaves in the family. He well knew what would come, and at dusk that night he sent a trusty man with a negro boy one mile down Spoon River through the woods and placed him in a neighbor's straw stack, with strict orders never to move until they came for him, and as expected, when dark came we were waiting. Men began to gather with lanterns and guns, and one good old neighbor came in our house with a gun which looked a little exciting. He made common inquiry in regard to the family, and after looking very carefully all over the little log cabin he departed. In the time he made his friendly visit others were pulling our straw stack down and some were searching our corn field, and next it was plain everything had been thoroughly searched. Again, a large burly negro had to be moved and suspicion was aroused when he took a very bad-looking knife from his boot, made it very sharp and said: "I will never be taken alive." Not daring to start from the station with a team, my mother piloted him nearly a mile by a side road on foot, and alone, until they could connect with a conductor on the way.

When they met the word was "Who's there?" and the answer was, "A Friend." Many times when a boy my father would say, "Get the team together and hitch to the wagon; in the night I will go to mill." Henry Berry was running a mill at Cuba and it was quite convenient to start in the night in order to get our grinding done and get home the next day. Said Berry had the password — Friend — and no conductor was afraid to call at his mill with an African grist at any time of night. There was one family near Table Grove, two near Ipava, and near the Elrod school house, two others in or about Bernadotte and one and one-half miles south of Smithfield, all of which were well acquainted with the Underground stations, and could give or take the sign of the U. R. R.[11]

As the Underground Railroad system continued north out of Fulton County on trails and byways, and along and across the Spoon River into Knox, western Peoria, Stark and Marshall counties, there were scores of UGRR "keepers" who were well acquainted with each other. Those seeking escape from legalized oppression who made it this far had passed into much safer territory than farther south, but they were still quite vulnerable to being captured.

VI

Peoria County — Danger in the City of Peoria

The city of Peoria, site of one of the state's oldest settlements,[1] is located on the Illinois River in eastern Peoria County. This river town was overwhelmingly unsympathetic to the antislavery movement and in February 1843, a mob there prevented William T. Allan, yet another of Weld's "Seventy" in western Illinois, from organizing an antislavery society. Peoria shared characteristics common to most river cities in the great middle west. While there were religious leaders, established churches, and a good number of educated men and women, they were countered in these towns by an element that included swindlers, con men, ruffians, and other port-city types, many of whom did not care for abolitionists. There was also a more respectable group in the community opposed to the establishment of an antislavery society in Peoria. They passed the following resolution shortly before rioters attacked the Reverend Allan and his abolitionist friends:

> Resolved to oppose by force, if necessary, the organization of any antislavery society in Peoria. The reasons were given as follows: The doctrines advocated by members of said society, are in direct conflict with the laws and constitution of the United States, and their ultimate, if not direct, tendency is to produce discord and disunion between the Federal States of this Union, with no possibility of a benefit resulting to those in whose favor their sympathies seem to be enlisted, and the organization of such society in the town of Peoria would only tend to disparage and disgrace us as a community, and create domestic and personal difficulties and disorders.[2]

In May of 1846, well-known Illinois antislavery crusaders Jonathan Blanchard, Ichabod Codding, Levi Spencer, and Nehemiah West all happened to be in Peoria when another mob again violently stopped the abolitionists from meeting. By the time the violence was played out, Spencer was badly injured.

However, a small but committed group of people in Peoria did support aboli-

91

tionism. The aforementioned Spencer, brother-in-law of Galesburg abolitionist Nehemiah West, who had long served the antislavery effort throughout Illinois, moved to Peoria in the late 1840s, and stood firm for the cause until his death there in 1853. Likewise, Lois and Moses Pettingil were other equally well-known activists in the river city. One of the fiercest opponents of Peoria's proslavery faction was Mary Brown Davis, who moved there in 1837. She lived in Peoria for 12 years until, following her husband Samuel's[3] death, she moved to Galesburg. During most of the time she lived in Peoria, she wrote numerous newspaper articles condemning the evils of slavery and the deprivations blacks endured in the north. In the December 14, 1847, edition of the *Western Citizen*, Mrs. Davis wrote a piece that described the positive treatment Negroes received in Galesburg, comparing it to the hostility they faced in Peoria. Davis is a good example of someone who was clearly an abolitionist, who stood by her antislavery convictions and in the early 1840s seemed willing to help fugitives escape. Ultimately, she lost her enthusiasm for the personalities and illegal activity associated with the Underground Railroad. She wrote the following in the *Western Citizen* on August 12, 1842:

> I believe that the simultaneous abolition of slavery in the different states is not only entirely practicable, but perfectly consistent with the safety, happiness, and prosperity of the inhabitants of these states.
>
> Who can look at the progress of good order, morality, and religion in those islands where the system of immediate emancipation has been adopted, and remain skeptical with regard to this fact? What has been done in the West India Islands can be done in our own country, and must be done at no distant day.

She ends the same article by saying:

> To this cause, I propose, by grace of God, to devote my powers; my time, as far as practicable; my prayers; my all; and in this cause I hope and I believe the "Western Citizen" will become a powerful and valuable auxiliary. M.B.D.[4]

But by the mid–1850s, she refused to stand with those who overtly violated the law. She continued to deplore the Fugitive Slave Law of 1850, but had no sympathy with those abolitionists who flew in the face of law and order. In 1854, she wrote, "when intrigue and self-promotion are the ruling motives I say *away with it*."[5]

It was in the western part of Peoria County that antislavery forces were concentrated. In Elmwood, Harkness Grove, Rochester, Brimfield, and Princeville and on farms close to those settlements, the UGRR was moving "freight." Eli Wilson was a particularly active Underground Railroad "agent" in this area. As a young man, he had developed a strong opposition to slavery, and his house in Trivoli Township[6] was known as an underground "depot." In Princeville, a graduate of the Harvard Medical College, Dr. Charles Cutter, conspired to help escapees.[7] In Brimfield, the Reverend J. E. Roy, pastor of the Congregational Church, along with Virgil Huey and

William J. Phelps's barn in Peoria County was a signal station. When a lighted lantern was shining through the cross-shaped opening in the eastern gable, it was a signal to Underground operators that it was safe to usher fugitive slaves northward.

his son, J. D., helped moved runaways along freedom's highway. Roy, a Knox College graduate, was well known to Jonathan Blanchard, the school's president, who had helped the Brimfield Congregationalists stay organized by occasionally coming to their village to preach. In 1854, a Congregational Church was built and dedicated by the residents of Brimfield and the parishioners selected Roy as their minister.[8] Roy was considered a "violent abolitionist" and many of his sermons vehemently attacked the evils of slavery.[9] On one occasion, a party of 11 escaped slaves, who had fled from Palmyra, Missouri, passed through the Brimfield "station." This group included "a crippled woman whom the others carried in a sheet, tied at the corners and suspended on a pole."[10]

One of the most openly engaged Underground Railroad operators in Peoria County was Edwin R. Brown, "the sage of Elmwood." The *Peoria Daily Transcript* published his obituary on August 10, 1896, which noted "he took to the stump and identified himself with the cause of emancipation ... he moved to Elmwood in 1856 and took part in the same work ... many a fugitive slave seeking the North Star and liberty was received, housed and sheltered by Mr. Brown." In 1906, the *Elmwood Gazette* featured a short article about the area's Underground Railroad activity that was attributed to H. B., who seemed to have been particularly well-informed about the subject:

The Underground Railroad

...EDITOR GAZETTE: It can be said that while Peoria city has an unenviable record in the days previous to the civil war in regard to the antislavery struggle; that the towns in the west part of the country did much help on the cause of emancipation. For there was a well equipped underground rail road running through Elmwood, Milbrook and Brimfield, with Fount Watkins of Elmwood, Virgil Huey of Brimfield, and Mr. Wyckoff of Rochester [Elmore] as volunteer station agents and conductors on the same. The road started at the Nelson school or college, near Quincy, and practically ended at Princeton, for at this point the road was brought to the surface and the fugitive slaves were sent on to Canada above ground. It took the courage of real conviction of earnest men to espouse the cause of the slave in those days. The laws of the nation and the state were all against them, and nine tenths of the people were either indifferent to or hotly opposed to anything like aid to the "damned nigger." The people seemed to believe that a man had no legal or moral right to be born black, and if he was foolish enough to commit that stupid error that he must suffer the consequences. Among the incidents which the brave Watkins gave me, I recall one or two to show the best [of] what was done by him and his fellow abolitionists in this unlawful work. He said that at one time a scared fugitive came to him saying that the slave catchers were hot on his trail and that he wanted to get on. Fountain immediately saddled horses, one with a side saddle, dressed the man in garments belonging to his wife, and, though meeting some people who would have called a halt on him if they had suspected that he was helping a man to liberty, he made his way safely to Mr. Wyckoffs' at Rochester [Elmore].

At another time while taking a fugitive to Brimfield he stopped for a rest at Mr. Wilcox's home, and while there a neighbor with his family drove into the yard for a short visit. As this neighbor was intensely, pro-slavery and he threatened the "slave stealers" with the full limit of the law, which was $1,000 fine and a years' imprisonment, if he caught them at their work, they were in a dread of fear, but Mr. Wilcox said "here, put him in our bed," and he was stowed away in quick time and was completely covered over so as not to be seen. When the wraps of the visiting ladies were taken off Mrs. Wilcox laid them on the bed as was her custom. But this came near being her undoing for the hidden fugitive fell asleep and began to snore, and Fountain had to get busy telling them yarns and laughing at them with noise enough to wake the dead. And after the visitors had gone, he hurried on in double quick time to the Brimfield station. At another time the good Deacon Berg of Farmington, came up with three runaways, and as they were valuable men the country about had been aroused, and one man living north west of Elmwood had disclosed his purpose to catch the "nigger stealers" this time at all hazards.

Deacon Berg, who was as good in invention as he was fearless in the work, said that they would throw him off the track in good style. So they packed the Fugitives in a wagon and sent them away of the road north to Princeton while the two well known underground men took the road leading by this man's house, feeling that they might possibly meet him on the way but did not. As they passed his house he hailed them and told them to drive in. But they made no reply and whipped up their horses and took the road west to Galesburg. The good farmer hurriedly hitched up and loading in all the help at hand gave chase. As they were a half a mile ahead they had made five miles or more when overtaken; and Fountain said it was worth all the labor to see the disgust and wrath of this law-abiding man, when he uncovered a bunch of hay instead of the three thousand dollar colored prizes he was sure of. Bidding the swearing man a cheerful good bye they drove on, circling back home when out of sights. H.B.[11]

Courtesy of *The Farmington Shopper*, Farmington Shopper Press.

Fountain Watkins, known as the laughing abolitionist, used highly imaginative ruses while conducting fugitive slaves through Peoria County.

Further confirmation of the city of Peoria's antipathy toward blacks came from the most famous former slave in the United States, Frederick Douglass.[12] In order to deliver a speech in Elmwood, Douglass took the Peoria and Oquawka Railroad west from Peoria, where he clearly enjoyed seeing his "friend" Edwin Brown. The renowned lecturer, however, later wrote about his "dread" when considering his return trip to Peoria on a frigid winter night:

> A dozen years ago, or more, on one of the frostiest and coldest nights I ever experienced, I delivered a lecture in the town of Elmwood, Illinois, twenty miles distant from Peoria. It was one of those bleak and flinty nights, when prairie winds pierce like needles, and a step on the snow sounds like a file on the steel teeth of a saw. My next appointment after Elmwood was on Monday night, and in order to reach it in time, it was necessary to go to Peoria the night previous, so as to take an early

morning train, and I could only accomplish this by leaving Elmwood after my lecture at midnight, for there was no Sunday train. So a little before the hour at which my train was expected at Elmwood, I started for the station with my friend Mr. Brown, the gentleman who had kindly entertained me during my stay. On the way I said to him, "I am going to Peoria with something like a real dread of the place. I expect to be compelled to walk the streets of that city all night to keep from freezing." I told him "that the last time I was there I could obtain no shelter at any hotel, and that I feared I should meet a similar exclusion to-night." Mr. Brown was visibly affected by the statement, and for some time was silent. At last, as if suddenly discovering a way out of a painful situation, he said, "I know a man in Peoria, should the hotels be closed against you there, who would gladly open his doors to you — a man who will receive you at any hour of the night, and in any weather, and that man is Robert J. Ingersoll."[13] Why," said I, "it would not do to disturb a family at such a time as I shall arrive there, on a night so cold as this." "No matter about the hour," he said; "neither he nor his family would be happy if they thought you were shelterless on such a night. I know Mr. Ingersoll, and that he will be glad to welcome you at midnight or at cock-crow." I became much interested by this description of Mr. Ingersoll. Fortunately I had no occasion for disturbing him or his family. I found quarters at the best hotel in the city for the night. In the morning I resolved to know more of this now famous and noted "infidel." I gave him an early call, for I was not so abundant in cash as to refuse hospitality in a strange city when on a mission of "good will to men." The experiment worked admirably. Mr. Ingersoll was at home, and if I have ever met a man with real living human sunshine in his face, and honest, manly kindness in his voice, I met one who possessed these qualities that morning. I received a welcome from Mr. Ingersoll and his family which would have been a cordial to the bruised heart of any proscribed and storm-beaten stranger, and one which I can never forget or fail to appreciate. Perhaps there were Christian ministers and Christian families in Peoria at that time by whom I might have been received in the same gracious manner. In charity I am bound to say there probably were such ministers and such families, but I am equally bound to say that in my former visits to this place I had failed to find them. Incidents of this character have greatly tended to liberalize my views as to the value of creeds in estimating the character of men. They have brought me to the conclusion that genuine goodness is the same, whether found inside or outside the church, and that to be an "infidel" no more proves a man to be selfish, mean, and wicked, than to be evangelical proves him to be honest, just, and humane.[14]

In 1936, the childhood reminisces of Jennie Bartholomew were printed in the *Elmwood Gazette*. Jennie Bartholomew Scott was then 78 years old and living in Kansas City, Missouri. She recalled her father's involvement with the Underground Railroad and his difficult decision not to leave the family in order to join the Union army during the Civil War. She wrote the story, she explained, at the urging of her children, who remembered listening to tales she told them when they were youngsters:

> There was a small stream of water with timber each side of it just east of Elmwood. I think it was called the Kickapoo. There was no stream or spring near our farm. The land was all under cultivation and very productive. Very few wild flowers were

to be found. The farmers raised wheat, corn, oats, clover and some raised broom corn. One year Father raised a big crop of broom corn and had men come and make brooms on the farm. He built a long shed, put machinery in it and it was interesting to see the different kinds of brooms they would turn out. They made some just the right size for me to sweep with. I can just remember when they harvested the wheat with a cradle. But it was not long before the reapers came. I do not know why, but Father hauled wheat and all kinds of grain to Peoria. The railroad had come to Elmwood before I was born, yet Father often took his grain to Peoria for market. One time he was going to drive in with a load of wheat, so he took me with him for company. It was twenty-five miles. We went to the Peoria House, the first hotel I can remember. We stayed all night and it was all a wonderful experience for me. It has lingered in my mind as one of the happiest trips of my life. The river, the boats, the long bridge, the tall bluffs and the big city filled me to running over with awe. I was not old enough to read of such things and didn't know they existed. I had much to tell Mother when I got home.

Mine was a very happy childhood. Well cared for, with jolly good parents, brothers and sisters, and a big supply of cousins to play with. If I needed anything I did not realize it. Nothing pleased me better than to sit on the spring seat of the lumber wagon by Father with a load of grain or hogs, it did not matter which. Our lives were full of sunshine, Father was [illegible] and generous, and our home life was full of love. I was getting old enough so I liked to sit on Father's knee and listen to the conversations that were being carried on by the grown ups. Often Grandfather would come to talk things over and I heard them talk of war and soldiers fighting battles. I heard them talk a great deal about Mr. Lincoln, the President of the United States, but I was too young to realize the meaning of it all at that time. I did understand when my father would drive off after dark that he would bring negroes home and put them in the cellar and then next night he would take them to some other house where they could hide through the day, and so on until they would reach Canada. I did know that we must not tell anybody they were there. Sometimes he would let me sit on the stairs when he would take their dinners to them. When I was older grown I learned that it was called the under-ground railway. That in the Northern states there was an organized system of aiding slaves to freedom. The houses of those engaged in the work were called stations. During the day the slaves were secreted in these stations then hurried on at night until Canada was reached....

... I was very much in love with my father and when I thought about it, I had great fear that he would have to go to war. I was too young to be very patriotic. I did not want him to be examined and I felt terrible when one day he told us he had passed the examination. His hands were so full that he had put off volunteering and toward the last of the war he was drafted for service. When I heard that he had to go I was broken hearted. I went to the barn, got up in the hay mow to cry my sorrow out all by myself. Finally I was missed and in the family search Father heard me sobbing. He came up the hay mow stairway and took me in his arms and told me not to cry any more, he was not going to leave me. Then he told me how he and Grandfather had talked it all over and decided it was not his duty to go, but he must stay at home because of the many responsibilities. There was the great-grandmother, his aged parents, the little twins and all the rest. This would be too great a responsibility for Mother. They would hire a man to take his place in the war. They got a substitute to go for $1000. Child as I was I keenly remember to this day how happy we all were and how happy he made me and how I hung on to him when he carried me down from the hay mow and up to the house to tell Mother all about it.[15]

The clearly written, warmly recalled, and often ironic words of Stanley Du Bois must be among the most remarkable ever put down about life in western Illinois before the end of the Civil War. He wrote so well one can't help but wonder if he might have been a professional author. Du Bois' words revealed the grandeur of the native countryside as well as the values, aspirations, and vision of the pioneers who settled the region. He evoked beautifully a bygone era, vividly rekindling it for us to see. The following selections are taken from three pieces he wrote for the *Elmwood Gazette* in April of 1907:

BOYS OF ELMWOOD

Story of Early Times in Elmwood
by Mr. Stanley Du Bois

... At the time which this story began Elmwood, Peoria county, Il. , was a village of about eight hundred inhabitants. It was set down at the edge of a prairie, lovely for location. For miles and miles, north and west, to a world round horizon, those prairies in summer time were covered with a kaleidoscopic carpet of agricultural verdure, or blossomed brilliantly with a wealth of wild flowers and grasses.

These prairies were dotted here and there with the modest, plain and mostly poor little farm houses and farm buildings of the pioneers; buds of a future harvest of wealth, comfort and high civilization, which is not now surpassed anywhere in the United States.

In the long summer days the heat wavered and glimmered over these seemingly petrified billows of land with an intensity that brought to the grasses, wild hay and farm products, a sweetness and luxuriance that was marvelous. To the south and east of the village was a belt of heavy timber, along the edge of which ran a little stream called the Kickapoo creek. This insignificant stream curved along, now in forest, now in meadow, with no other seeming purposes than to delay as long as possible its junction with the muddy Illinois river some twenty-five or thirty miles away. It was far enough from the village so that it could not be an every day delight to the boys, but still, it was near enough that on Saturday or holiday, and during the long summer vacation, there are few clear days indeed, but that a stroll along its banks would reveal groups of boys in swimming, or here or there a solitary fisher, with a willow pole, seated on the bank ,or on a log, with a can of worms beside him, silent and absorbed in watching his bobble, happy if he but got bites, and in ecstasy of joy if only from out some fortunately found hold he caught a string of chubs, cat fish or shiners. Sometime after a heavy summer rain, its banks would overflow, and the yellow torrent would sweep along, laden with small brush....

... The forest seemed to have been created for the special delight of the boys. There were plum thickets, where in the spring time there were a prefect cloud of white blossoms on the trees. There, too, were the crab apple blooms with their

98

exquisite coloring and delicate perfume. The great white dogwood flowers; the locust tree who[se] perfume was plain a mile away, and in the dark thickets along the unfinished railway banks there was to be had a wealth of raspberry and black-berry blossoms just for the gathering.

The very earth, too, yielded us beauty and fragrance and was carpeted from early spring beginning with the shy little thing we call "Spring Beauty" lifting its brave head through a mat of cold, sodden leaves, on till the heat of summer, when we plucked "Johnny-jump-ups." May apple blossoms with their sweet, strong odor, clear along till late autumn when we gather[d] yellow rosin weed, the plumy golden rod, asters and fringed gentians. All these were [illegible] for our lads far above the price of rubies.

I much doubt if there was a boy in the place who knew the botanical name of a thing they saw, but we had some sort of a name for each and everything that grew, and I am sure we enjoyed their beauty if we were not book wise.

But the greatest sight of all was the gorgeous painting of the entire foliage of the forest after [unreadable] autumn frosts. It was a wealth, an extravagance of color, so rich, so profuse, and so blended that it seemed to the boys as they stood on some overlooking height, that go where they might and see what they might, they never again could behold anything half so beautiful....

Our village was largely settled by families from the New England states. The names of the principal ones had a flavor of Massachusetts, Connecticut, the granite hills and the Mayflower. Among them were these of Phelps, Winthrop, Truax, Blakesley, Parsall, Bartholomew, Kellogg, Cope, and plain Smith, Thompson, Jones and Brown. They brought with them their love of freedom, education and the church, so, soon after a church had been organized a school house was built.

It was a plain little frame structure, cheerless and comfortless, unpainted without and poorly furnished within. But it was a school house in the largest sense of that much meaning word. Within its walls were taught lessons of knowledge and moral-ity to boys and girls who as home builders and nation builders have stood to the front.

In the dark days of the civil war, whose portentous cloud even then hung over our peaceful village, from that school house there went forth heroes whose names stand clear and bright on their country's banner of honor; some lie in unmarked, unknown graves, none the less honored and mourned by parents and friends, whose heads are now gray, or who have long since joined them in the Land of Peace.

That was a typical New England school. There was no attempt made to teach anything but what was deeply thought to be needful in the active, busy life which was before the boys and girls gathered there.

The teacher was a versatile genius, and from A B C through elementary algebra was perfectly at home. He was selected quite as much on account of his physical abil-ity as for his ability to teach what was in the books. There were no namby-pamby notions about corporal punishment in that community in those days. If a pupil was habitually truant, or misbehaved, or failed to learn the lesson, or for any reason which seemed to him good, and we children sometimes thought for no reason at all, he thought punishment was needed, he proceeded to administer it at once, and sometimes what the big rebellious boys, and girls, too, on occasion, he needed all the power with which he was possessed in order to maintain his authority....

... Being not so very far removed by time and place from the frontier, the sports of us boys partook much of the nature of half civilized young savages. There was only one negro family in the place, that of a Mr. Cross. He gained a precarious livelihood by keeping a barber shop on Saturdays, sawing wood and doing heavy chores for any who would employ him at other times. He was of huge size and possessed prodigious strength. He was in great demand at hog killing time, barn raisings and the like where his strength stood him in good stead. Though the majority of the people of Elmwood were strong Abolitionists, I fear that Cross had rather a lonesome time of it, for he had no associates at all. To my shame I say it, we boys did all in our power to make the life of his daughter a burden to her, by singing ribald doggerel, directed against negroes in general and herself in particular, and we would chase her and throw clods at her, as near her home as we dared to go, for, miserable cowards that we were, we stood in wholesome fear of her big black father. I can remember that I thought, more than once, in a hazy sort of way that the theory and practice of the Abolitionists of Elmwood were somehow not in accord. Just outside the village was a station of what was known as the "Underground Railroad," a route by which run away slaves from the south were sent along on their way to Canada and freedom. It was known to a few of us boys, but we were never expected to speak of it to anybody, and rarely ever did. Helen Cross came to school with the rest of us and got along as well as the [unreadable], which was not saying any great things. Our community was not rich and no doubt they gave us the best education they could afford, they gave it freely, and when they were able added to the regular work of the teacher from the stores of their own knowledge. I am sure there was not a boy or girl in the place who had not some sort of education, as much as could well be given, and I think I am perfectly correct in saying that there was not for miles around anyone who could not read and write....

... The boys of Elmwood thought and cared but little about politics, only as it was a source of amusement to them.

At the time of which this is told, there were two great political parties in the country, the Democrats and the Republicans, known as the pro-slave people, and the Abolitionists, or the Lincoln and Douglas partisans. As a matter of fact, there were others as well, but they did not count at all in the estimation of the boys and really for anybody else around there. Each party was doing its best to make political converts, each organization had its political clubs, which marched up and down the streets, unknowingly training for those terribly serious marches in the war which was fast following their peaceful evolutions in the little prairie town in Illinois.

To us boys the "wide awakes" of the Republicans were fellows of immense importance, and when they with their tin torches and oil cloth capes, in flaming ranks trailed over the town in serpentine lengths of fire, we boys ran alongside and shouted ourselves hoarse for Lincoln and Hamlin.

There were not enough "ever readies" to make much of a company, they were the Democrats, so when the Democrats wanted a torch light procession in Elmwood, they came up from Farmington, over the mound from Yates City and from the benighted region 'round about Trivoli Center. Them we made faces at, at a safe distance, and once in a while, when certain we wouldn't get caught at it some brave boy would throw into the ranks a clod of dirt, or a corn cob, or if he could, a rotten egg, but he must be a bold fellow indeed who would dare do that.

After the election of Mr. Lincoln there was no more of political turmoil to interest us boys.

I well remember one day several weeks after the election. My father had been down town, at dinner time he came back, and there was a look of great trouble on his face. He sat down to the table, and after asking a longer and more fervent blessing than usual, we all began to eat; he soon laid down his knife and fork, and with tear brimming eyes and a voice choked with emotion he said: "Wife, they have fired on Fort Sumter." There was no more dinner for us that day. We adjourned to the spare room and there on bended knees our father prayed the God of nations would temper the wrath of man in this crisis as to bring about everything to His honor and glory [unreadable]. We boys did not know as much as our elders about the awfulness of war and we were full of joy in the security of seeing the çoming pomp and circumstance of war little appreciating the suffering of those in Charleston that day inflicted on the people of this fair land, both south and north.

For a few days all was quiet, and then a perfect volcano of patriotism burst forth. It was nothing everywhere but war, war, war, and to us boys was as though all gotten up for our special pleasure.

At the first call made by President Lincoln for volunteers our village had a company ready, but it was not accepted. Soon there came another call, and what with fifes and drums, and drilling in evolutions and with all sorts of firearms, from old flint lock muskets to shot guns and squirrel rifles and little or no attempt made a uniforms, except it might be caps. There was enthusiasm and patriotism bubbling over at white heat. Party lines were forgotten in the general trouble, and really so anxious were the many volunteers to get into service that one company from our town, not finding an immediate place in an Illinois regiment went into the Eighth Missouri.

We boys organized a company of our own, and with wooden guns drilled the best we knew how, according to Upton's Tactics, fought imaginary rebels, had our little camp made of boards, begged from Bill Kellogg in which we slept occasionally and unconsciously imbibed a large portion of the patriotism and military [unreadable] of the times. Of course of real war we neither saw nor knew anything; its destructions and hardships were far from us; but, when after the battle of Shiloh some of our well known and loved friends were reported among the killed, then it began to seem a little more real. When Private O'Donnell came back from the battle of Ft. Donelson with his finger shot off, why we boys fairly worshipped him; and before his finger was entirely healed he had raised another company, was elected captain and was off again for the front.

I said that of hardships we had none, but may be some would think different now. Muslin rose to such a price, and was so scarce, that our mothers used flour sacks to make our shirts out of and sometimes the brand wasn't washed out, either, but little cared we. We ate more corn bread and less wheat, but we had plenty of it and never went hungry; we went barefooted later in autumn and earlier in spring, but that made no hardship to a healthy boy.

I remember that the older people were sadly put to it for coffee. It got to be so expensive that few could afford to drink it; it went to a dollar and half a pound. Substitutes, such as rye, sweet potato, chicory and some other wretched take places were used with more or less dissatisfaction, usually more. We boys were not expected to drink coffee, so we felt small loss on that score. Really, we did not miss much fun if war's grim skeleton did occasion[ally] stalk through our village. Soldiers in uniform came and went, many went and never came back again.

There was a camp at Peoria, twenty-five miles away, where the 77th Illinois regiment was organized and from whence it went to the front....

The Knox County Courthouse in Knoxville is the building where legal proceedings were heard in the Susan Van Allen Richardson case.

> ... We were joyful in victory, depressed in defeat and after the long, weary struggle had been fought out to an end and to victory, [unreadable] loomed our soldiers back with more hearty cheers or should have been gladder that the war was over than the boys of Elmwood.
>
> The struggle left but few scars, as our villagers were too nearly of one mind in regard to the cause and conduct of it. In those years the mutations of time and circumstance had placed on a pedastal a few, who previously were no [illegible], and abased some who had thought themselves much, but all agreed as it were, that they had enough of fighting and universal peace and brotherhood was the order of the day in the little town.[16]
>
> Stanley Du Bois

Real security awaited runaways who followed the routes out of Peoria, Fulton, and McDonough counties through Knox County and into Galesburg. It was first necessary, however, to slip past proslavery elements that surrounded this Yankee town. Freedom seekers were still very much at risk if seen by the enemies of the Underground operation even this far north. Fugitives had the option of moving on three lines north from southwestern Peoria and northern Fulton counties. One route went toward

S. G. Wright and W. W. Webster in Stark County, with hideouts along the way in Rochester (now Elmore) in northwest Peoria County. A second line went northeast, passing through the "Huey Station" in Brimfield and then headed to Lawn Prairie in Marshall County, where Deacon Nathaniel Smith was an "operator."[17] The next stop on this second course was most likely the small town of Putnam in western Putnam County. Most Underground Railroad activity in Putnam County, however, took place east of the Illinois River in Hennepin, Granville, and Magnolia. The third track took "freight" into Galesburg, with lines running through the Knox County townships of Salem, Elba, Maquon, Chestnut, and Haw Creek. Runaways, would then be moved through the village of Knoxville, where stations also existed, and finally to George Washington Gale's safe town.

The cluster or web pattern of "stations" was prevalent in this part of Illinois. One explanation of this model of success seems to have been that "operators" knew that safe havens established reasonably close to each other served as escape valves. If the heat got to be too hot at one "station," the pressure could be eased by directing fugitives to another hideout relatively close by. As the chain of western Illinois "depots" were knitted together over time, the close proximity of optional stops helped to increase the odds that escaping slaves would reach freedom.

VII

Knox County — Sanctuary in the College Town

Runaway slaves, antislavery crusaders and slave catchers alike knew that once fugitives entered Galesburg in western Knox County they were virtually safe from capture. Galesburg's early settlers, like many in the middle west, first built their homes close to forest groves. They wanted to be close to a supply of wood; they feared prairie fires and desired protection from wind; and erroneously assumed that prairies were unfertile. After a brief time in Log City, on the edge of Henderson Grove, these settlers ventured onto the prairie itself to build their town and abolitionist college.

Wilbur Siebert, in his highly regarded book, *The Underground Railroad from Slavery to Freedom*,[1] referred to Galesburg as "probably the principal underground station in Illinois." No other town in Illinois had more escape routes converge at one point than did this antislavery community. Verna Cooley's 1917 article in the Illinois Historical Society's journal says:

> Galesburg, perhaps due to the pride of later generations which led them to preserve the experiences and exploits of their predecessors who were prominent in the community, stands out as probably the principal Underground Railroad Station in Illinois. This prominence is also due to the evidence of cooperation between the residents of Galesburg and the surrounding neighborhood.... Galesburg, which was founded in 1837, by Presbyterians and Congregationalists who united to form one religious society under the name of the Presbyterian Church of Galesburg[2] as a result of intense antislavery sentiment, was a place where the fugitive was sure of a refuge. George Davis,[3] Nehemiah West, Neely, Blanchard, and Samuel Hitchcock were willing not only to shelter the fugitive but to pilot him onward by way of Andover [Henry County] and Ontario [Knox County] to Stark County, where they were received by Wycoff, S.G. Wright, and W.W. Webster.[4]

Grace Humphrey's *Centennial History of Illinois*, published in 1917, identified Chicago as the "great railroad center in Illinois" for fugitives, but she went so far as to describe Galesburg as a place where "a runaway slave was safe on the streets."[5] Indeed, there are numerous verifiable accounts of the Old First Church belfry in Galesburg being used as a hideout for fugitive slaves. A photograph of the church is one of only a few site photographs shown in Siebert's notable 1898 work on the Underground Railroad. A letter sent to Siebert by one of Galesburg's most eminent citizens and educators, George Churchill, recalled that "the Old First Church of Galesburg ... was [used] as a sort of Railway Station in which passengers were not easily seen by curious people who had no right to know them."[6] Booker T. Washington, in a speech delivered in early 1900 in Galesburg, made reference to how pleased he was to give a lecture "on the spot where once stood one of the garret stations of the old underground railroad."[7] In addition, several houses and barns at the edges of Galesburg were used to harbor runaways as well. But, as was always true of these western Illinois communities, mixed among those helping the fugitives were some individuals not sympathetic to the Underground movement. When the previously discussed abolitionist zealot John Cross moved into Knox County, he settled, perhaps intentionally, close to the residence of Jacob Kightlinger, a justice of the peace. Kightlinger put down this account in Charles C. Chapman's *History of Knox County, Illinois*, published in 1878:

> About the year 1839 or 1840, Rev. Mr. John Cross came into the township of Elba, Knox county. He was a Presbyterian preacher, and an abolitionist at that. He told me to come and hear him preach, and the next Sunday I took my wife and family, and went, and he preached a very good sermon. I had no objections to his preaching. After the services we started for home. We got into the wagon, and seeing that Mr. Cross was afoot, I said, "Mr. Cross, you can ride in my wagon if you choose." So he got in, and we started. Very soon he commenced running down the laws of Illinois, saying they were *black*, and he would not obey them. He said he would harbor, feed, and convey off negroes in defiance of the *black laws* of Illinois. I then said, "Mr. Cross, do not let me see you violate the law." "Why, sir, what would you do?" "I would take you up for violating the law." "That, sir, is just what I want to find. Some one that has the fortitude to take me up."
>
> So that week a load of negroes passed my house, and was conveyed to Mr. Cross' house by a man named Wilson. I, with five or six neighbors, went after Wilson, and we met him coming back empty. I asked him where his negroes were. He would not tell; so we went to Mr. Cross' house, and found the negroes in a lot of corn. We took the negroes to Mr. Palmer, the constable, and told him to give them a good dinner, and I said I would pay for it. Mrs. Cross had dinner cooking for them. It was corn in the ear and potatoes with the skins on, all boiling together in one pot. I said they should have a better dinner than that, for I fed my hogs in that way, on that kind of feed.
>
> Mr. Cross had gone down South after some negroes that day, and he was afraid that I would take the negroes from him; so he sent a spy to my house — a Mr. Thomas, of Farmington. He came to my house about midnight, and wanted to know the way to Spoon river bridge, about five miles off. Said I, "You appear to be

The Spoon River, shown here at London Mills in southern Knox County, was a natural escape route used by fugitive slaves heading northward inside the Military Tract.

in a hurry." "Yes," said he. "Well, sir, what is your business?" He said he did not tell his business to every person. "Well, sir, you will tell it to me, or you shall not leave here to-night," and I picked up my rifle. I saw he got some scared, and then he was ready to tell me his business. He said he was in search of some negroes. I said, "Have you lost some negroes?" "Yes." "Can you describe them?" "Yes." "Well, go at it." He commenced, and described them perfectly. Said I, "Do you own those negroes?" He said he had an interest in them, so I took him to be the owner of said negroes. I said, "I will put your horse up, and in the morning I will tell you where your negroes are." I set my rifle up and walked out, and I heard a wagon down at the bridge. Said I, "Do you know what wagon that is?" He said it was the Rev. Mr. Cross. "Ho, ho! You are a spy and an infernal scoundrel!" cried I. He jumped on his horse, and went to Mr. Cross, and told him that I would take his new load of negroes from him. So Mr. Cross put the negroes in Wilson's wagon, and he drove up empty. Another man and I were mounted on horses at my gate, when Mr. Cross drove up. I called three times, "Is that you, Mr. Cross?" But instead of answering, he put whip to his horses, and they ran, and I after them about a mile and a half. I called to a man that lived there, named McLaughlin, to stop Cross. I said, "Shoot the horses if he won't stop, for he has stolen something," but he did not shoot. There was another man further on, however, who with a pole struck down both horses.

The next day Mr. Cross went to Galesburg and swore out a warrant against me, and I went to Galesburg before an abolition squire, and he fined me $100. I then took an appeal to the Circuit Court. When all the evidence was given in, the judge (Douglas) threw it out of court — no cause for action. I then went into the grand jury room, sent for witnesses, and Cross was indicted, and three bills found against him for stealing negroes. He was put in jail. Afterwards the abolitionists of Galesburg bailed him out. This is all true.

Jacob Kightlinger[8]

In the summer of 1838, Galesburg's founder, George Washington Gale, traveled to Farmington with his friend and fellow abolitionist, Charles Gilbert, to deliver a Fourth of July speech to the town's antislavery advocates.[9] The occasion also gave him the opportunity to cement relations with antislavery sympathizers in that region, one of whom was Farmington's Jeremiah Porter, who had previously lived and been active in antislavery work in Peoria. The Reverend Porter's impression of Gale's part in the day's festivities appeared shortly thereafter in a letter he wrote to the *Peoria Register and Northwestern Gazetteer*. His description is quite the opposite of what one usually associates with a festive Independence Day atmosphere, for there were no parades, bands, or frivolity. To the contrary, Porter found the mood "sabbath still." Those gathered in the Presbyterian Church were there for the serious business of addressing "means for the liberation of the millions of colored slaves."[10] The following are excerpts from Gale's remarks that day:

The clanking chains of more than two million of our countrymen proclaim to the world that the principles to which our venerable fathers pledged their dearest interests are trifled with ... when the sacred principles of liberty are fast fading from the minds of multitudes, when the freedom of debate is stifled in the halls of legislation; when ecclesiastical courts inflict their highest censure upon those who plead for impartial liberty and who remonstrate against the enslaving by their brethren of those whom Christ has made free, when our temples dedicated to freedom are maliciously burnt down, in spite of constitutional guarantees, and the rulers of the land are winking at their enormities; when the press that dares to plead for the oppressed is broken and cast into the street, and the blood of those who gave voice to the press mingled on the ground with its scattered types, with the entire impunity of the assassins ... at such time it is proper to wake up the spirit of our fathers to reassert the principles of liberty, and with trumpet lung proclaim them through the land till every tyrant trembles upon his seat, and every minion in his train flies terror stricken at the sound, and the walls and ramparts of slavery like those of Jericho fall to the ground.[11]

Porter said in the letter that Gale then discussed the relevance of "the issue" to the Declaration of Independence. The Declaration of Independence was a popular text for abolitionist ministers who used it to connect Christian principles to secular ideas of what was the right course to follow regarding slavery. They could emphasize phrases like "all men are created equal" and that people are "endowed by their Creator with certain unalienable rights ... life, liberty and the pursuit of happiness." There were those in the Fourth of July audience in Farmington who interpreted the logic of Gale's remarks to strongly suggest, that until the laws were changed, it was their duty to help fugitives escape. The framers had made a mistake by letting slavery exist when the U.S. Constitution was originally written; the right thing to do, argued ministers like Gale, was to change the law and give slaves their freedom immediately:[12]

> The speaker then gave a lucid exposition of the principles of the declaration of independence. Then, that existing slavery violated all those principles; and finally, the duty of our countrymen in relation to it. I may not trespass upon your readers by following through his argument, but will present briefly his views under the last head.
>
> We must not let it alone, for that would have no more influence in removing this evil than it had in removing intemperance. No politician, no statesman, no philanthropist ever thought a national sin could be thus removed. The physician does not thus heal diseases. What then can we do:
>
> 1. The Christian must pray for its removal.
> 2. He must bear testimony against the sin.
> 3. The church must treat it as they do other sins.
> 4. The patriot must make this subject of paramount importance. The legislator must see that the laws are right on the subject; and the elector must see to it that his vote is given for the many who will truly represent his wishes.
> 5. Light must be diffused on the subject. This will bring men to feel and act right on this matter.

The speaker then sustained his remarks by reading some facts of delightful interest from a volume recently published in New York, entitled "Emancipation in the West Indies," written by Messrs. Thome & Kimball, the former a native of Kentucky and formerly himself a slave-holder. In this volume the authors show that the experiment of immediate emancipation has been tried on the island of Antigua with the most perfect success, even beyond the sanguine hopes of his most ardent friends. In a population of 39,000, 30,000 were slaves and 2,500 free persons of color. *But in one day these were all made free*, and are now happily working the same plantations for wages where they once worked without pay and *under the lash*; and the island never enjoyed half the prosperity, quiet and peace before emancipation, that it now has. The governor, members of the council, lawyers, physicians, planters and overseers, have given their written testimony to these facts which are now published with their names. These had their fears of insurrection, massacre and every species of misery if liberty were once given to such a multitude; but those fears have given place now to the most perfect confidence in the safety, justice and utility of immediate emancipation.[13]

Though the Susan Van Allen Richardson story related in the first chapter rightfully deserves to be recalled as the single most memorable UGRR affair in Knox County, another tale was also well remembered and retold. It involved a runaway that "Aunt Sukey" herself helped while she lived in Galesburg.[14] This account is an excellent example of how blacks knew very well that they had to look out for each other constantly, no matter where they were. Bill Casey's story is one of many Underground Railroad accounts included in Chapman's Knox County history. Chapman chronicles stories easily verified by other contemporary and post–Civil War accounts:

> Bill Casey was another passenger over the Underground Railroad, but so closely pursued that he left the main line and worked his way as far as Galesburg himself. That city was well known among the negroes, and a runaway slave was considered as free from capture when within its limits as if in Canada. Being settled by Eastern people, who not only had no sympathy with slavery, but held for it a righteous indignation, and whose citizens would any time violate an inhumane and unjust law to help a fugitive slave, Galesburg was known throughout the country as the strongest kind of an abolitionist place. Here the weary, hunted slaves could find a refuge, some comfort, and a host of sympathizing friends.
>
> Bill Casey reached Galesburg Saturday night, and going to the residence of the colored lady, Susan Richardson, whose coming to the county is related above, he was admitted and kindly cared for. He was a miserable and affecting human being to look upon, having neither shoes nor hat and almost naked, with feet bleeding and swollen, and body bruised, besides being almost in a starving state, having had nothing with which to appease his hunger for several days. With five companions he had started from Missouri. They were pursued, and two or three of the number had been shot, and the others captured, and only by the rapidity of his flight through the woods with heavy undergrowth had he escaped. Sunday morning came, and "Aunt Sukey" locked her house and with her family as usual went to church, leaving Casey at her home. She knew, as she told us, "who to tell." Accordingly she soon made known to members of the Underground Railroad that a fugitive was at her

house. They immediately visited him, and found him in a needy condition, and that he must have a pair of shoes before he could go farther, as well as some clothing. So Messrs. Neeley, West and Blanchard began to prepare him for the journey. Of course he could not be taken to the store and have his shoes fitted there, but they had to bring them to him. His feet were so badly swollen that it was necessary for them to make three or four trips before they could find shoes that would fit or he could wear. After everything was fully arranged, Casey was put in charge of a conductor on the Underground Railroad and conveyed to the next station. In a year or two he returned to Galesburg and engaged in cutting timber northwest of town.

One day two men, evidently "Southern Gentlemen," rode up to the Galesburg hotel. There they met a young negro boy, Charley Love, of whom they inquired of Bill Casey. Although small, Charlie was well posted, and of course "never heard of such a fellow." However, as soon as possible he ran and gave the alarm, and immediately a fleet-footed horse with noble rider was off for the woods where Casey was at work. The two strangers referred to were on the hunt for Casey, and after some inquiries learned his whereabouts and started for him, but Charlie Love had saved him, for he was warned in time and escaped capture.[15]

Charlie Love grew up and remained in Galesburg, making his living by operating his own barber shop.

The Blanchard referred to above, was, the previously mentioned second president of Knox College, John Blanchard. He was a striking figure; handsome, with flashing eyes and a confident air. Blanchard was well connected to some of the nation's leading antislavery politicians, including Thaddeus Stevens and Salmon P. Chase. During his years as the president of Knox, the school flourished and Blanchard helped keep its antislavery zeal alive.

The third selection from Chapman's Knox County history discusses Galesburg's safe havens in general, the Ontario station to the North, and the work of Samuel Hitchcock who was, most likely, the area's most active agent. Hitchcock's widowed mother had moved to Galesburg during the early days of its settlement, and when she became the second wife of Sylvanus Ferris, Samuel remained on the family property and continued to work the rich prairie soil. By 1850, he and his wife, Catharine, both 32 years of age, were well-established farmers raising their three children just outside of Galesburg. He lived in a strategically advantageous spot about halfway between Galesburg and Henderson Grove, where numerous possible hideouts existed in the large maze of timber:

> Galesburg, from the very starting of the colony to the time of the war, was noted as the principal depot of the Underground Railroad in Western Illinois, if not in the whole State. The refugees were from Missouri, and most of them would first stop at a Quaker[16] settlement in southeastern Iowa, where friends would keep them and bring them on at night to Galesburg. Here George Davis, Samuel Hitchcock, Nehemiah West and others would promote their welfare as far toward Canada as Stark county or Ontario in this county. A Mr. Hizer, one of the Iowa Quakers,

Galesburg Underground Railroad operators successfully hid fugitive slaves inside Old Colony Church. Wilbur Siebert, in his classic book about the Underground Railroad published in 1898, and Booker T. Washington, in a speech he delivered in 1900, identified the church as a place in which freedom seekers had been concealed.

called on Mr. Davis in this city only two years ago, surprising him with an unexpected but very pleasurable visit, and the gentlemen refreshed their memories concerning a certain colored man whom they had helped through over thirty years previously. Mr. Davis, was accompanied by Rev. R. C. Dunn in taking the refugee to Mr. Wyckoff's in the southern part of Stark county. In 1858 a colored man was taken through here to Canada, who shortly afterward found his way back to Missouri and started with nine other slaves for the land of freedom, but reached Galesburg with only five or six. With these it is presumed he got safely through to Canada.

There was a negro man, who stopped at Nehemiah West's on his way to freedom. He formerly lived in luxury, being the favored coachman of an eminent gentleman, but who, through misfortune, failed and consequently all his property was sold....

... Another one, a cook, stopped at the same place. He was a fine intelligent fellow, but not unlike all others, he was continually on the watch, thinking every footstep he heard was made by his master. Mrs. West says they would run and hide the moment they heard the slightest evidence of some one approaching. This cook was anxious to help prepare the meals. He was sent to the well, just a few feet from the house, to peel some potatoes, but becoming nervous he would start, even at the fall of a leaf. Finally being unable to endure the torture of fear any longer, he begged to come into the house and work, which request was granted him....

... Four negroes were hidden, and kept one day in the cupola of the First Church, of Galesburg, and when night came they were hurried on their journey....

... There is no telling how many fugitive slaves were helped through this region of the country, no one thinking at the time what important history he was making for future generations to write up. The number, however, was quite large, for often business was quite brisk over the road.[17]

ONTARIO STATION

The depot of the Underground Railroad in Ontario township was at the residence of C. F. Camp, Hod Powell, conductor. Passengers for one train consisted of four well dressed negroes, who were evidently rather intelligent. They arrived on the evening train from Galesburg in care of Conductor Neeley. After a partial night's lodging, and a sumptuous meal, Conductor Powell, with his lad, looking as if he were going to mill, started for Andover Station, the next on the route. One of the above four returned South three different times for his family. He was so closely watched that he failed each time to rescue his loved ones. On the third trip he found they had been sold and sent farther south.[18]

The reference above to "one of the four" strongly suggests the possibility that this was the previously mentioned fugitive "Charlie." If so, this would have been yet another county in western Illinois where he was familiar to Underground Railroad "agents."

In 1855, another important individual who joined the Ontario station conspirators was Erastus Child and his arrival in western Illinois was preceded by his work with Hiram Wilson at the southern border of Ontario, Canada. Wilson was very well-known there for giving aid to fugitive slaves who were fortunate to escape from the United States. As a result, Child was well aware of what newly arrived freedom seekers required in Canada and he also would have been savvy about what they would need to know in order to escape safely. He was no stranger to many of the people of Ontario Township, for Child had grown up as one of them in New York State before finally joining them in western Illinois. After leaving New York, he worked for a time with the antislavery crusade in Ohio before going to Canada:

HITCHCOCK STATION

Samuel Hitchcock's farm, three miles northwest of Galesburg, was a prominent station of the Underground Railroad for ten years. Many a time he secreted six or more of the fugitive slaves in his hay mow, or in the back rooms of the house. He usually carried them to the next station in Ontario township, fifteen miles distant, starting at 9 or 10 o'clock in the evening. On one occasion, which happened to be Commencement day of Knox College, and a very warm June morning, a gentleman from Warren county, Mr. Dilley by name, drove up, in company with one Mr. Parker and hailed Mr. Hitchcock. "All right!" Mr. Hitchcock exclaimed. "All right," was again the response, when the load of straw began to present signs of life and one by one crawled out the brunettes, until three women, one man and three children, seven in all, were safely landed at Mr. Hitchcock's. They were kept and secreted until opportunity offered to forward them to the next station.[19]

Population records suggest that Galesburg must have seemed a particularly welcome community to both free blacks and fugitives. In 1849, 16 blacks were recorded as living in Galesburg. By the end of the 1850s, that number had increased more than fivefold. In 1857, the *Galesburg Free Democrat* reported that George Washington Gale celebrated a "Negro Festival on his premises" honoring the anniversary of the emancipation of slaves in the West Indies. "Colored people" were in attendance from Galesburg, as well as surrounding communities. When John Brown was executed for his attack on Harper's Ferry, Galesburg blacks felt sufficiently safe from harassment and ridicule to hold a tribute to Brown with a prominent white politician, Clark Carr, as one of the speakers. It seems highly unlikely that blacks in this part of the country would have found many other communities so openly willing to embrace important issues to African Americans.

Among those men who enlisted for military service in the most famous black regiment in the Union army, the 54th Massachusetts, were 12 African American soldiers from Galesburg. Forty-year-old brick layer and plasterer Joseph H. Barquet, who lived in a small brick house close to city hall, was credited with having organized the Galesburg men to join him and enlist in this unit, which took heavy casualties at the battle of Fort Fischer in July 1863.[20]

There is little information to be found about the life of blacks in Galesburg before and during the Civil War era but the following partial account was included in Albert J. Perry's *History of Knox County, Illinois*, published in 1912. It was written by Louis A Carter, a fugitive slave, who arrived in Galesburg in 1863:

> Thomas Richardson[21] was also among the early colored people of Galesburg. He and his first wife, were about the second arrivals in Galesburg of the colored people. Mr. Richardson became a prominent and useful citizen of Knox county. His home was on the corner of West and Ferris streets where the Galesburg Electric Light and Power company's plant now stands. The property passed out of the hands of the Richardsons a few years ago. Mr. Richardson was well known as a good farmer and a very capable teamster. He had eight children, four sons and four daughters and all grew to manhood and womanhood. The boys were Tilford, Samuel, Benjamin and Richard; the daughters, Angeline, Janet, Clarissa, and Prodine. Farming was the

principal occupation of the sons. They were well known in the city and county for years. Samuel owned property in the northwest corner of section nine, Galesburg township. As far as known, all of the first family of children are dead. Some of the grandchildren are living. Alfred Richardson still resides in this city. He has been a trusted night watchman of the Chicago, Burlington & Quincy Railroad company for many years, and his devotion to duty has given him an enviable reputation. It is said of him that he is known to the tramps who swarm in this part of the state as a man who permits no lounging about the company's buildings or yard. He has served several terms on the police force of the city with equal credit.

The Searles family was one of the largest of the early colored families. The old gentleman, Mr. Francis Searles, was born in Steward county, Georgia, March 8, 1772. He was a white man. His wife, Mrs. Polly Searles, as born in the same county and state and was a colored woman. They left their native state in the year 1847 and came to Galesburg where they made their home until he died, in 1875. For a time they lived on South Chambers street. He bought the old Chappell farm situated one mile northwest of Galesburg, where he was living at the time of his death. His wife followed him a few years after. Their family consisted of three sons and six daughters and they all reached mature ages, and they stood well among their people. James Matteson Searles, the oldest son, was an expert in well-digging and laying sewer. His son George W. Searles was a graduate of Knox college. John Adams Searles, the youngest son, moved to Kansas and settled upon a farm belonging to one of his sisters, where he died last year. The other brother died in 1880. The daughters were Mary Ann, Jane Gensey, Betsey, Sarah, Charlotte and Martha....

... Rev. Levi Henderson was the first negro minister of Galesburg. He came in an early day and his home was about No. 423 West Tompkins street. Rev. Henderson built the first colored church in Galesburg, known as Allen Chapel on East Tompkins street. Rev. Henderson was a very devout man. The writer of this article, at that time a runaway slave boy, had the pleasure of living with him in July, 1863. He died in the '70s and his wife followed him a few years later.

Rev. McGill and his wife, Rachel, were a very venerable couple. Mr. McGill was one of the early pastors of Allen chapel. He was a retired minister of the denomination. He was the father of seven children, two sons and five daughters. One of the daughters is living in Iowa. His son, Isaiah McGill, was well known in Galesburg for many years. He followed the trade of brick mason and plasterer. His son, Hiram McGill, is not living in this city and follows the trade of his father Isaiah.

Many families came from the south during and after the war, which increased the colored population of Galesburg and Knox county very materially. Aaron Welcome and his wife, Sarah, came in 1862. He was a farmer and also followed the carpenter's trade. In 1863 he, with William Webster, John Davis and several others, enlisted in the Union army of the war of the rebellion....

... Among those who came to Galesburg about this time were William Stewart and wife, Levi Johnson and wife (the wife being a sister of the Gashes), Isaac Green and wife, Mrs. Melissa Alexander (later Mrs. Warren, who became a successful nurse), Jesse Hazel and wife, Henry Will and wife and William Davis. Isaac Green died December 11, 1911, at the age of 76 years. He raised a large family. Jesse Hazel was a soldier in the war of the rebellion, was taken prisoner and confined in Libby prison for nine months. He is still a conspicuous figure on our streets. William Davis was also a soldier and a capable plasterer and mason.

Mr. Metcalf moved to Oneida in the spring of 1866 and I hired out to Wm. Stephenson for three months. The remainder of the summer I worked for Henry Leffingwell at Ontario. He was a brother of Dr. Leffingwell of St. Mary's school, Knoxville.

About the middle of August, 1866, I met Mr. S. H. Ferris who lived in Galesburg. He owned a farm at Woodhull. I finally bound myself to him until I would be twenty-one years of age. I was to have board, clothing, three months' schooling each year, one dollar a month to buy collars, ties, take my girl to shows and buggy riding, and one hundred dollars at the end of my service. I had to figure some to make ends meet. When I became twenty-one I had overdrawn $2.35 of my monthly dues, so that was taken off of my hundred dollars. I took a horse instead of the money. A year later I sold the horse to a Mr. David Cutter for $75. I finally had to take two months' board for pay. That was living high—five years' work for two months' board. All together I obtained twenty-two months' schooling, against nine years' schooling that the average boy gets today. All of my four boys received that or more.

I worked nine months for Mr. Ferris after I was twenty-one. The last of November, 1871, I went to work for Mr. Henry Hitchcock, superintendent of the "Burlington" at Galesburg. I worked for him five years, then went into the grocery store of Greene & Dore, June 12, 1876. I remained with that store through five changes of proprietors, covering a period of seventeen and one fourth years. From that house I took up employment with the D. C. Raymond & Son, for whom I have worked over eighteen years, making over thirty-five years in the grocery business.

In 1878, June 18th, I was married to Miss Emily Louisa Alexander, daughter of Mrs. Melissa Alexander, a widow, who came from Palmyra in the fall of 1864. They were the slaves of Walker Loutham of Palmyra in the fall of 1864. Her brothers, Ralph and John, came with them. Ralph Alexander was one of the first mail carriers in Galesburg, appointed by Hon. Clark E. Carr while he was postmaster. To our union six children were born, four sons and two daughters, Eugene, Estelle, Lewis, Jr., Eva, Clarence and Harold. At this writing all are living and in good health. The oldest is thirty-two, the youngest eighteen. We purchased our home at 186 West South Street from Hon. T. J. Hale in 1881 and are living in the same house at the present time. I have always endeavored to lend my influence to every cause that seemed good to me, and to work as far as possible for the improvement of the moral tone of the city, and I am pleased to add that my wife has always been an active associate and worker in all efforts of this kind.[22]

In 1887 George Davis, who was treasurer of Knox College for 15 years, addressed a gathering celebrating the 50th anniversary of the establishment of the Congregational Church in Galesburg. He spoke among other things, about what originally brought him to the community, the construction of the church, and the close friends he had made after moving to Galesburg. The following is a partial account of what Davis said that evening about his involvement in the Galesburg Underground Railroad.

My induction as an underground railroad conductor was peculiar.... One beautiful October afternoon a covered wagon drove into the yard. Two quakers[23] from Iowa got out and informed us they were directed here as a station on the underground railroad. Here was a pretty fix. I was a Whig of hitherto unblemished coon-skin notoriety. How could I run away a nigger if his peril was ever so great. Wife mildly suggested that under the circumstances it was my duty; but I thought I would try something else first. So I came up to the village for help, but the men were almost all away to Cherry Grove[24] attending an anti-slavery debate. Dr. Gale, and Father Haines, and John Mitchell of Monmouth, were having a meeting in the C.P. church. Well, I was in a quandary till Father Holyoke suggested a way out of the trouble. "Brother George," he said, "there is only one way to do this. If, as you say, one of your teams is unfit for the jaunt, take my chestnut mare in welcome and help the poor man to liberty." "Well," said I, "in for a penny, in for a pound; here goes." I found Richard Dunn and made the thing known to him. He was ready and willing and we started. My intention was to overtake Sherman Williams, father of the Hon. E.P. Williams, our legal adviser, who had started that morning with a load of wool for Chicago; but we failed in that and went for Toulon, delivering the fugitive to Mr. Wyckoff, father of the Rev. Mr. Wyckoff, and grandfather of the beautiful twin sisters that are such a credit to the dominie and his good wife, and such an honor to the old First Church. That was my first trip, but not the last by a good many.[25]

Forty-five years after Charles Ferris Gettemy graduated from Knox College, he wrote *A Memoir of Silvanus Ferris 1773–1861 and a Genealogy of His Descendants*. Gettemy grew up in Galesburg, where his mother, Mary Ellen Ferris Gettemy, was the principal of Galesburg High School for 25 years. His grandfather, William Mead Ferris,[26] was the son of Silvanus Ferris who was second only to George Washington Gale for having helped to start and then stabilize the Yankee colony. William Ferris was a UGRR "conductor," but of quite a different personality from nearly all the others in the college town. The following selections reveal just how out of step Gettemy's grandfather "Uncle Billy" Ferris was from the pious citizens of the prairie village:

> William Mead's [Ferris] home property in Galesburg consisted of what was called in my early boyhood a "10-acre lot," extending on Academy from West Main Street, northerly to North Street. This may have been included in a tract of four so-called "10-acre lots" containing in all 37 acres more or less, which he had bought of the college in 1845 for $894....
>
> ... The original deed whose text is transcribed is on a printed form which was used for many years by the college, perhaps indeed until all the college lands were sold, being based upon a resolution passed by the Trustees of the College, Feb. 10, 1838, "that all deeds for lands in this township given by this board have a clause attached to the same prohibiting the manufacture and sale of intoxicating drinks." But this resolution appears to have been subsequently modified so as to apply only to village property and not to farms. Now William Mead Ferris laid out the northerly part of his home property in an apple orchard and the southerly part in pasture and a vineyard in which he produced for many years abundant harvests of grapes which he made into port wine and sold; if this land was a part of his farm, which lay outside the village precincts, the prohibition against the making of liquor upon it did not, of course, apply, but if it was a village lot, as I think it was, the various churches in the town, which bought the wine for sacramental purposes, and which constituted his principal market, were apparently willing to wink at the sale

for the worthy purpose for which the wine was intended; at any rate, there is no record of William Mead Ferris being prosecuted or his lands made forfeit because of his manufacture and sale of intoxicants, — whether for use as a beverage or merely for medicinal or sacramental purposes....

... Also, though the demand for wine for personal use was probably never large in the earlier years of the community, my grandfather apparently had no scruples against supplying it, and I still have some of the "Port Wine" labels he used on his bottles. I have too a vivid recollection of him in his later years, sitting up until late o'nights with some of his old cronies in an old house which stood in the rear of the family dwelling, guzzling this product of his own manufacture and consuming vast quantities of raw oysters which he had shipped to him in tins by the case from Baltimore, — a habit which grieved my good grandmother greatly. The house in which this riotous conduct occurred was much larger than the dwelling, and was commonly known as the "cheese-house," for here William Mead made cheese in the early days from milk produced from a herd of cattle consisting at one time of as many as 50 head, and here he had his wine press, and in the cellar there were great barrels of port, covered in my boyhood with mold and cobwebs. There was also a carpenter shop, and on the second floor numerous bed rooms fully furnished as lodgings for the hired help.

William Mead was a man of varied occupations and of a character which made him a well-known figure to everybody in town, so that he acquired the familiar sobriquet of "Uncle Billy...."

... And he somewhere got hold of a recipe for making a marvelous gastronomic novelty that had a wonderfully delicious appeal in the cultivation of an appetite for cooling sweets in the hot summer months, the popularity of which, once established, has never waned with the American public; and thereupon the store windows of all the restaurants and eating places in town were adorned with glass painted signs, — blue letters on a yellow background, — admonishing everybody to "EAT UNCLE BILLY'S ICE CREAM." In these various manners he made apparently his chief living. I do not think he ever personally farmed the section of land given him by his father, nor obtained any substantial return from it, though he speculated quite actively in Military Tract land warrants; but, like most speculators, whether in land or grain or stocks on the exchanges, he had in the end nothing to show for these activities, and when he died, his material possessions, measured in terms of money value, were negligible.

William Mead was an ardent anti-slavery man, who, as I always understood as a boy, had many times secreted fugitive slaves in the hay mows of the old barn on his home place (reputed to have been the largest barn in the county), and Galesburg being a well-known "station" on the "Underground Railway" between the south and Canada; and at night he would place the negro runaways under straw in a box-wagon and send them along to the next station at Princeton, northeasterly from Galesburg, whence they would be forwarded by other sympathetic conspirators until finally they got out of the country. But ten years after the close of the Civil War he was to welcome into his family a rosy-cheeked girl of 19, Sally Estill, from the blue-grass state, whose father had been the owner of a large plantation and many slaves before the war, as the bride of his son and namesake, William Mead, Jr., but the sectional feelings and prejudices which were then still rife throughout both North and South were quickly dissipated in the case of this particular Kentucky belle, who

117

speedily found a warm place in the hearts of all the Ferrises, and, for that matter, all the other Galesburg abolitionists, and where she still abides (1934), cherished by all of us of the succeeding generations for her innate charm and genuine goodness of character, as "Aunt Goodie."[27]

In 1883, Jeriah Bonham, an early 19th-century Illinois editor and publisher, published *Fifty Years' Recollections with Observations and Reflections on Historical Events*. He devoted one section of his book to Nehemiah West and an enthusiastic endorsement of West's work for the antislavery and Underground Railroad causes. Bonham, in 1839, had passed through "a primitive" Galesburg at the very beginning of its existence when he was a young man traveling toward the Mississippi River and Iowa. He remembered the town as a "city of the plains in embryo." Bonham included in his sketch of West the following description of this significant "pioneer of the place":

> He was an Old Line Abolitionist when that was a term of reproach, not a title of honor as it is now. His home was a station on the Underground Railroad and he was one of its most efficient conductors. Many a load of frightened fugitives did he carry to the next station, the home of Owen Lovejoy, in Princeton. The fall before he died he was the anti-slavery candidate for the legislature, and then the acceptance of such a nomination meant ostracism and mob violence. He was secretary of the first anti-slavery convention known in this part of the state, held in an "upper chamber" over Curtenius & Griswold's store, in Peoria, while a pro-slavery mob raged through the streets. The house in which Mr. West and others of that Spartan band spent that night was attacked by the mob and his brother-in-law, Rev. Levi Spencer, seriously injured. Mr. West's little daughter, who witnessed these exciting scenes with her father, lived to see the leader of this mob, who then stood over her with a club, the captain of a "Wide Awake" company which paraded the streets of Galesburg in honor of Abraham Lincoln.
>
> Thus we see Mr. West was identified with the grand movements which so largely shaped the history of Illinois in its early days. He battled bravely "for free speech, free labor and free men...."

> "He stood four square to every wind that blew."[28]

Information about Susan Van Allen Richardson's life after she started living in Galesburg is sketchy and partial. However the following obituary found in the *Galesburg Republican Register*, June 20, 1904, summarizes the remarkable life of "Aunt Sukey":

Was Called to Her Reward
One of the Founders of the A.M.E. Church
Died Last Thursday in Chicago

Mrs. Susan Van Allen Richardson, a resident of this city for nearly sixty years, died Thursday afternoon at 4 o'clock at the home of her daughter, Mrs. Mary Fleming, at No. 2923 Dearborn Street, Chicago. The cause of her death being old age. The remains were brought to this city Sunday morning and taken to the undertaking parlors of Horton Foley. The remains were accompanied here by the daughter, Mrs.

Fleming, and the grandchildren, George W. Fleming and Miss Susan Estella Fleming.

Mrs. Richardson was born June 6, 1810, in Virginia, of slave parents. She was brought to Sparta, Ill. when a young child and as slaves could not be kept in this State, was adopted by the family that brought her here. She came to Galesburg about the year 1843, and in 1845, was married to Harry Van Allen. She was married the second time to Thomas Richardson, about 1856.

She was a lady highly respected by all who knew her and was one of the charter members of the A.M.E. church of this city, and it was greatly through her efforts that the church was founded. She made Galesburg her home until the past four years and since then has been living with relatives at different places. For the past two years she has been living with her daughter in Chicago.

To mourn her death she leaves her daughter, Mrs. Fleming of Chicago, and a son, Owen Van Allen of Kansas City, besides other numerous relatives and friends.

The funeral services were held this afternoon at 2:30 o'clock at the A.M.E. church and were largely attended. In charge was Rev. Mr. Ferribee, and assisted by Rev. Mr. Douglas, pastor of the Second Baptist church. The singing was by the regular church choir. On the casket were numerous floral sprays from the relatives and friends.

The pallbearers were Isaiah McGill, Jesse Hazel, George Fletcher, William Davis, Richard Worthington, and Mr. Casen.

The burial was in Hope cemetery.[29]

Recorded incidents involving slave trackers searching inside the city of Galesburg reveal two very different strategies for thwarting them; the first was direct confrontation and the second was deception.

R. C. Edgerton was a physician who practiced medicine in Altona in northern Knox County, and as a young man living in Galesburg, he helped fugitives seeking freedom. On one occasion in 1844, Edgerton gave a meal to Missouri runaways who had reached Galesburg and later he ushered them to a grove of trees outside of town. Shortly thereafter, the fugitives' owners arrived at Edgerton's door with a posse and bloodhounds. The pursuers threatened Edgerton and ordered him to help chase down the escapees but he refused. Instead, in an example of confrontation strategy, Edgerton sought the aid of some young companions in town and they, in turn, demanded that the outnumbered slave trackers leave Galesburg, which they did immediately.

Julia Wells moved to Galesburg with her family in the mid–1840s following her husband's death in Henry County. Wells immediately was befriended by Jonathan Blanchard, George Davis, and John West and became active in the operation of the Galesburg UGRR. She once hid a fugitive slave in the garret of her house. One day, Wells disguised a runaway she was harboring in her family's cast-off clothing, which included an old wide-brimmed straw hat. She put the fugitive to work hoeing the family garden behind the house and, in an example of deception strategy, warned him to always work with his back facing the street so he wouldn't be recognized. The runaway was in plain sight but was never discovered, even when slave hunters passed by the house. He was later moved safely out of town.[30]

When Ernest Elmo Calkins wrote his history of Galesburg, he looked back over the community's first two decades and concluded that the town's "fanatical abolitionists" had not chosen an easy course to follow compared to other Illinois communities. The settlement's strict restrictions on people's personal behavior and amusements on Sundays, as well as it's strong support of the temperance movement, undoubtedly also set it apart. But, most importantly, the open presence of "operators of the Underground Railroad" in the town meant that all the people of Galesburg necessarily "incurred dislike, expense, and personal danger." Had the town not been so dedicated to such an "extreme protest of slavery … it could have got on with less friction."[31]

Fugitive slaves had good reason to believe that the "promised land" might truly be reached when conductors sent them out of the Galesburg sanctuary. One heavily used route moved "cargo" northeast from Galesburg and Knoxville into Stark County. The other line headed directly north to the "station" of Hod Powell and C. F. Camp in northern Knox County, where it split in two directions. One of these courses continued due north to layovers in Andover and Cambridge in Henry County and then proceeded to Geneseo. The other route took fugitives east toward the Knox County/Stark County line. If this route was taken, UGRR "conductors" could take advantage of looking back from "Pilot Knob," one of the highest places inside the Military Tract. Here stood an elevated growth of virgin timber that could hide fugitives while, at the same time, offer them and their benefactors a dramatic view of the surrounding prairie. Anyone chasing down runaway slaves in this area would be visible from this natural lookout point.

VIII

Stark County—
The Minister's Diary

Escaped slaves were on fairly safe ground by the time they arrived in Stark County. The county is one of the smallest in Illinois but the underground operators there were as well organized and in as close association with each other as those in the counties immediately south and west. In 1887 M. A. Leeson published *Documents and Biography Pertaining to the Settlement and Progress of Stark County, Illinois.* He indicated that his sources were drawn from authentic records, historical works, and newspapers. His book includes valuable information about the Underground Railroad in Stark County and surrounding counties sometimes referring to UGRR workers previously mentioned:

M.A. Fuller's historical address, delivered at the meeting of 1880, stands as one of the most elaborate portrayals of pioneer life ever given.

The underground railroad must not be overlooked. About the time Stark county was organized this line began to assume practical form in the neighborhood, and was patronized by a few passengers. A few years later the road grew in favor with refugee slaves, and ultimately became an important highway between the Sunny South and the bleak Canadas. Galesburg Station was one of the best organized on the line of the Underground Railroad. There Nehemiah West, George Davis, A. Neeley and Samuel Hitchcock were the permanent conductors on the division extending to Ontario, in Knox county, and through Stark county. In Ontario township the house of C. F. Camp was the depot, and Hod Powell conductor. Rev. John Cross, connected with the railroad in 1843, was charged with aiding in the escape of slaves, but before the trial he removed to Bureau county, where a deputy sheriff was sent to arrest him. Mr. Cross offered to go with out opposition, but there were no means at the disposal of the deputy to travel, so that his prisoner agreed to supply his own team. They started on Saturday, stayed with Oliver Whitaker at Osceola Grove next day, where the prisoner preached. On Monday they left *en route* for Knox county, where Mr. Cross defended himself....

The Underground Railroad in Western Illinois

... W.H. Adams, in one of his pioneer sketches published in the *Sentinel*, speaks of Fountain Watkins, "the laughing Abolitionist," and of his connection with the Underground Railroad, better known as the "Great Southern and Canadian Underground Railway." In his sketch he refers to Dave Frisby, the first school-teacher in the Elmwood district, ... Mrs. Watkins, wife of Fountain Watkins; Eli Wilson, an old abolitionist; Peter, a colored fugitive; George Pierce and John Dalton, anti-abolitionists; Elias Wycoff and Nehemiah Wycoff, well-known names in Stark county. One of Watkins' stories as told to Mr. Adams is as follows: "Some time late in the forties, Eli Wilson brought quite a likely young man to my place, who said he had been a waiter on a Mississippi river steamboat. He stayed with us for about a week, and played with the boys in the woods. Some of our kind of men at Farmington sent me word one evening to push the boy ahead, as hunters were on his track. It would not answer to start that night, as it would be certain to invite pursuit. I finally concluded to wait until morning, and studied out a plan how the old woman and me would go visiting the next day on horseback. As the fall winds were kinder hard on the 'wimin's' faces, it was not more than natural for her to have on a veil. So the next morning I saddled a gray team I owned, and had Peter put on one of my wife's dresses and veils, and helped him to mount the horse with the side-saddle just as though it was my wife. I mounted the other horse, and admonished Peter not to talk unless I spoke to him. We struck out, taking a road that led in the direction of the east side of the mound west of the town of Elmwood. The road across the Kickapoo bottoms was lined on each side with a dense growth of high weeds and brush. While in this place we saw a team coming toward us with George Pierce and John Dalton in the wagon. I had been told that Dalton had been blowing around that if ever he caught me 'running off a nigger,' he would arrest me. I pulled out to the right and Peter to the left to let the wagon pass. I said: 'Good morning, ha! ha!' and they said 'good morning.' We had not got more than a rod from them when I heard George say: 'I'll be d_____d if I don't believe "Fount" has got a nigger with him.' Here the road made a sharp turn, the ground was soft, and didn't we ply the bud and let the horses go until we reached the high ground at the mound. Here we pulled rein and looked back. Not a soul was in sight. I told Pete that it was twelve miles to the next timber, and we had to travel, as there was danger of them cusses following us. We reached the hazel brush south of Rochester [now Elmore], on Spoon river, where I hid Pete and started for town to find something to eat for the horses, the fugitive and myself. Meeting Dave Frisby, I did not pretend to notice him; but he recognized me and said, 'Hel[l]o, Fount; how do you do? Where are you going?' I replied: 'Just down here to find a girl; my wife is not very well.' Dave said: 'You don't want a girl; you have a runaway somewhere in the brush, and are now looking for something to eat. I know you, old fellow; you can't fool this child, Fount. How is the wife and babies, anyhow? I said: 'Dave, where have you been?' He replied that he was in business at Rochester, and, continuing, said: 'Say, Fount, you've got a fugitive hid somewhere; don't you deny it. Do you see that house over there? I board there with Elias Wycoff, brother to Negemiah [sic], of Stark county, both sound abolitionists.' I said: 'Dave, Wycoff may be all right, but you always said it was not right to help the slaves get away from their masters.' He replied: 'Fount, you know I always said slavery was wrong; then it is right to free them. Here is my hand.' I could tie to Dave.

"I turned about and went with Dave. Wycoff was not at home, but was expected shortly. The horses were cared for, Dave and I went out to the fugitive's retreat. I gave the signal and the woman stepped out. We introduced her to the family and Mr. Wycoff. Mr. Wycoff then came and was delighted to help any one out of bondage. Pete and I had supper, and afterwards I informed Wycoff that the lady wished to make some change in her dress. She was shown into room, I followed after and said, 'Pete, take off your dress.' Wycoff said, 'Is that a man?' I replied that it was, that he had on my wife's dress, and that I wished to take it home with me as dresses were not over plenty at my house. Peter slipped out of the dress and stood before us in a suit of broadcloth. All laughed, the women came, and seeing the joke, also laughed. I waited until late that night, bade Pete and his new friends adieu, and arrived home just before daylight. Ha! ha! ha! You don't hear the crack of the slave-driver's whip now-a-days. Ha! ha! ha!"[1]

In 1925 an article appeared in *West Jersey Harvest Home* written by James Delano, the son of W. W. Webster. The article discusses the Underground work of Webster, which was referred to by others who chronicled this period as well. When Webster built his farmhouse, he and his family left their original log cabin standing; he used the old structure to harbor fugitives for a number of years thereafter. Webster moved to Stark County in 1837 and settled in West Jersey. The countryside was in the midst of rolling prairie, skirted with belts of timber close to the Spoon River flowing just a few miles away to the south. This location came to be called Nigger Point. According to G. A. Clifford, in an article he wrote for the *Stark County News* on May 30, 1862, the "neighborhood acquired [the name] from its once having been reputed to be a station on the Underground Railroad." Clifford also indicated that several runaways "have shared the hospitality of the Point:"

> One of the best organized stations in the state of Illinois was the one at Galesburg, the route which lay through Peoria and Stark Counties.
>
> Among the early settlers of Stark County, who were strong abolitionists, were Rev. S. G. Wright, Elias and Nehemiah Wycoff and my father. They soon became identified with the Underground Railroad and furnished aid to many a runaway slave.
>
> There was an Underground Railroad station on the Webster farm. Only four families were living in that section of the country then. They were Nehemiah Wycoff, W. W. Webster, Rev. S. G. Wright and the Pratz family.
>
> The negroes brought to my father's farm always came from Farmington and below. Some people discourage taking care of runaway slaves, while others encourage it.
>
> One time my father was away with a negro and three or four men came on horseback to his place, supposedly to search for horse thieves, but in reality to look for runaway slaves. Mother told them that Father was away. This was on Thanksgiving Day. It was chilly and raw and the men were thinly clad. Mother invited them to stay for supper and told them to put their horses in the barn and feed them. They sat by the fire to warm and Mother decided she had no bread (an excuse to hold them there) and had to make biscuits. The men stayed until ten or eleven o'clock and then decided it was too late and would not try to keep up their search any longer.

Once we had eleven negroes to take care of. The men were kept outside and the women kept in the house. Sometimes a delegation would stay for several days and pick corn or help with the peaches; if it was in that season of the year.

One time a negro came and it was a busy season. No one could leave to take him away. The minister said to dress him in women's clothes and he could sit beside him in the buggy. In those days, women wore bonnets and veils to protect their complexions. So, they dressed the negro up and the minister drove with him to the next station.

A man working on a barn at Wycoff's had said that he could smell a negro half a mile away, but they drove close enough to him that day to touch him with the buggy whip and he was none the wiser, though very much put out about it when he heard of it afterwards. Negroes were usually taken from station to station at night.

One instance of a happening at Rochester, [now Elmore] was when a man by the name of Fountain Watkins, from Farmington, brought a negro from there, but was not acquainted in this part of the country and did not know where to leave him. He left the negro in a thicket of brush until he could inquire who the abolitionists were. He rolled up his sleeves and pretended he would fight any abolitionist if he could just get hold of him. That caused the people to talk freely and they told him just where the families were, when he had obtained all of the information he needed, he went to the brush and whistled for his negro, and then drove to Wycoff's with him.

Under the Fugitive Slave Law, it was the duty of every man who found a runaway to return him to the owner.

In later years, a negro was at my father's and in some way, people got word of it. One of the neighbors said he was going to catch my father. The weeds along the road were pretty high and there was a rail fence. He thought he would catch my father pretty easily in the road. When Father reached this place, he touched the horses lightly on the flanks with the whip so that just as this man went to grab them by the reins they lunged forward and he was knocked over to the side of the road.[2]

Samuel G. Wright arrived in western Illinois from New Hampshire in the early 1830s. After studying at the Lane Seminary in Cincinnati, Wright was made a missionary of the Knox Presbytery in the early 1840s. The Presbytery was chaired by George Washington Gale and Wright's first mission station was a short distance north of Galesburg in Henderson, where he began to write an extensive diary about his life; shortly thereafter he was assigned to western Stark County.[3] His years of recorded notes are fascinating to consider on many levels. The intriguing diary describes his temperance lectures, efforts to navigate muddy roads in the spring, accounts of harsh winter storms, troubling family illnesses, his duties officiating at baptisms and funerals, and the incredible distances he traveled in order to meet his obligations as a preacher. In 1844, for instance, Wright preached 181 sermons and traveled over 3,000 miles. Wright was a Knox College trustee and his log makes clear that his aggressive stance against the systematic oppression of American slaves was a difficult thing for many of his potential parishioners to accept. There must have been, therefore, a remarkable sense of satisfaction and accomplishment for Wright as he listened to the following resolution, which was passed by his Congregational Church membership in Toulon,[4] Illinois, on September 2, 1854:

> We also deem American Slavery wholly unjustifiable and at war with the plainest precepts of the New Testament. Therefore, we feel bound to set ourselves in all practical ways against it, and are resolved:
>
> 1. We will not knowingly allow any slave holder, or apologist for American Slavery, to occupy our pulpit or dispense to us the sacrament.
> 2. We will sustain no society or public print that we believe sanctions or apologizes for American Slavery.[5]

Wright had come among the pioneers of Stark County over a decade earlier and had slowly influenced many of them to change their minds about slavery. The resolution passed by Toulon's Congregationalists probably reflected the reaction nationally that year by many northerners, to the controversial Kansas-Nebraska Act.

Wright's entries in his diary about his involvement with the UGRR are invaluable proof of how active the liberty lines were in west central Illinois:

COURTESY OF *THE STARK COUNTY NEWS,* STARK COUNTRY COMMUNICATIONS

The Reverend Samuel G. Wright, who lived for years in Stark County, kept a diary with recorded entries of the various ways he helped fugitive slaves on their way to freedom.

> On the 21st of August 1840 by advice of George W. Gale I visited Hendersonville & Henderson Grove or rather Cr[own] Ridge, as they had made application to Br. Gale on the same week for preaching the time at least. I came to examine into the demand in order to know whether it were my duty to labor in this vicinity rather than to go to the north of the State, where Br. Bascom had invited me....
>
> ... May 16th [1842]—Last Monday I went to Farmington to attend the trial of Br. Birge[6] and his wife. I was appointed by him to assist in managing the case, returning Tuesday night.
>
> ... August 22nd [1842]—There is an effort to destroy the influence of this church by reporting that we are abolitionists, and have formed lines for helping runaways. Hence we are as bad as horse thieves.
>
> Many are highly prejudiced against us, and what the end will be, the Lord only knows. We are conscientiously engaged in doing to others as we would that they should do unto us; and if this will injure the cause of Christ we are deceived. True it

is very unpopular, and many that would otherwise attend the preached word and Sabbath school stay away.

... September 14th [1842]—Went to Henderson and Galesburg; made arrangements for a meeting at LaFayette; at Knoxville was hindered all the next day endeavoring to get relief for five colored persons who were that day imprisoned because they could not produce full evidence that they were free.[7]

The September 14th entry was undoubtedly a reference to the capture of Susan Richardson, her three children, and the slave woman Hannah described in the first chapter. This would have been only nine days after the fugitives were captured in Knox County.

Continuing with Wright's diary:

December 27th [1842]—In the providence of God several fugitive slaves, at different times, have found their way into our neighborhood, and although the laws of our state are exceedingly severe rendering one liable to a fine of $500 who shall feed or harbor a colored man who does not give undoubted evidence of his freedom, yet our brethren felt that the statutes of Heaven were to be regarded before those of men and did not hesitate to "feed the hungry...."

... February 6th [1843]—Last week had much severe cold weather; had to be at home most of the week; read "Horne's Introduction," &c. On Friday another fugitive from slavery came along, making twenty-one that have passed through this settlement on their way to Canada. To-day it is extremely cold, the ink freezes in my pen as I try to write beside the stove....

... May 20th [1843]—The grand jury found a bill against me, and my Elder, W.W. Webster, for harboring runaway slaves! Some excitement exists, but hope good will result. Many sympathize with us and with the oppressed, who had seldom thought on the subject before; and these wicked laws "to be hated need but to be seen." Rev. Owen Lovejoy, of Princeton is also indicted. We have not yet been taken by the sheriff, but probably shall be soon.

On June 25, 1874, the *Chicago Tribune* printed the following letter from J. E. Roy, the Underground Railroad "agent" in Brimfield mentioned in chapter 6.

AN INCIDENT FOR HARBORING FUGITIVE SLAVES

To the Editor of the Chicago Tribune:

Sir: As you are just now engaged in supplying your cabinet with specimens of a former age for the use of savans in coming times, will you allow me to furnish, as a contribution a copy of the bill of indictment found in 1843, by the People of Illinois against the Rev. Samuel G. Wright in Stark County, for the crime of harboring ten negro fugitives? Mr. Wright was one of the oldest, most respected, and most useful Congregational ministers in the state. Last week I met him at the General Association of Kansas, where he has now taken up his ministry. In that body he reported that Elijah P. Lovejoy invited him to join in the colonization scheme; and that, in reply, he furnished for Mr. Lovejoy's paper an article on Emancipation, which had some effect upon the proto-martyr's mind. Mr. Wright furnished me the copy which is herewith furnished.

Yours, J.E. Roy

VIII. Stark County

Of the May term of the Stark County Circuit Court, in the year of our Lord one thousand eight hundred and forty-three.

State of Illinois, Stark County,—The grand jurors chosen, selected, and sworn, in and for the County of Stark, in the name and by the authority of the people of the State of Illinois, upon their oaths present, that Samuel G. Wright, of the County of Stark and State of Illinois, on the eighteenth day of March, in the year of our Lord one thousand eight hundred and forty-three, at and within the County of Stark aforesaid, did harbor and secret a negro, whose name is unknown to the jurors aforesaid, the same negro being a slave, and owed by and doing service and labor to, a certain person in the State of Missouri, whose name to the jurors aforesaid is unknown, against the form of the statute in such case made and provided, and against the peace and dignity of the same people of the State of Illinois.

The Grand Jurors aforesaid, upon their oaths aforesaid, do further present, that Samuel G. Wright, of the County of Stark, and State of Illinois, on the twentieth day of March, in the year of our Lord, one thousand eight hundred forty-three did harbor a certain other negro, whose name to the jurors aforesaid is unknown, the same negro being a slave, and being the property of, and owing service and labor to a certain person in the State of Missouri, whose name to the jurors aforesaid is unknown, against the form of the statute in such case made and provided and against the peace and dignity of the same people of the State of Illinois.

The Grand Jurors aforesaid, upon their oaths aforesaid, do further present that Samuel G. Wright, of the County of Stark and the State of Illinois, between the first day of August in the year of our Lord one thousand eight hundred and forty-two, at and within the County of Stark aforesaid, did harbor eight other negros, whose names to the jurors aforesaid are unknown, the same negros being slaves, and owing services and labor to some person in the State of Missouri, whose name to the Grand Jurors aforesaid is unknown, and against the form of the statute in such case made and provided and against the peace and dignity of the same people of the State of Illinois.

> Weed,
> State's Attorney pro tem.

The document is thus endorsed:

The People vs. Samuel G. Wright—indictment for harboring slaves. A true bill. Samuel Camp, Foreman of the Grand Jury. Witnesses names and residence: Jonathan Pratz, Augustus A. Dusen, William E. Dusen, Nehemiah Wyekoff, of Stark County; George Wyekoff of Peoria County; Martha M. Cullison, Knox County.

Wright and Webster were never convicted, as the minister's later entry of October 23, 1843, noted. Twenty years after the Civil War ended, Wright wrote a letter to Dr. H. M. Hall in which he commented on this case. The letter also reflected Wright's feeling that, with slavery behind the nation, the victory for the temperance movement was still to be achieved:

Times have indeed greatly changed since William W. Webster and myself were indicted by the grand jury of liberty-loving Stark county for the crime of harboring and comforting some refugees from oppression. Ordinarily it is deemed necessary on the part of a grand jury to know something about the circumstances of a crime, but in the excitement of the masses in 1843 the grand jury found true bills against us — when they declared they knew neither the day the crime was committed, nor the name of the slave who was comforted, or of the name or residence of the master of the slave, save that he was a citizen of the state of Missouri. What progress society is making toward universal brotherhood.... May we see prohibition become a national institution, and party politicians become more interested in the good of the country than in the success of their respective parties.[8]

Continuing with Wright's diary:

May 22nd [1843] — Last week was at home most of the time; planted potatoes, corn, &c., visited families; hope some good was done. Saturday, went to the Emery settlement, but found so strong an antipathy against abolitionists that but few would hear me preach, so I went on, and on Sabbath morning preached at Toulon to a large congregation; most of the seats filled. Report said the Mormons meant to encounter me here and draw me into a debate, but all passed off quietly.

... August 14th [1843] — Last week worked three days at harvesting. Much sickness around. Our election took place, and I believe there were eleven liberty votes cast in the country; last year there were but two...!

... October 2nd [1843] — Last week wrote a report to A.H.M.S. Tuesday eve. Lect. On Slavery at Lafayette 2–½ hours, very attentive congregation....

... October 9th [1843] — Last week Mon. went to Princeton to carry Sister Pendleton & attend to trial of Mr. Lovejoy. Left, before it was concluded.... To day circuit court sits & my trial on indictment for harboring a slave comes on. Have no doubt good will result, hence feel little anxiety. Jesus reigns, let us rejoice & submit to his authority. Last week preached 6 times & rode 114 miles & ad. t sac. 1.

... October 23rd [1843] — Last week attended Court 2 days. As the States attorney would not prosecute the case we were dismissed. Mr. Lovejoy was acquitted after a long trial & he [the States attorney] would not try again....

... May 24th [1844] — Last week court sat; no complaints against "Nigger stealers" this time; court held but one day. Tuesday went to Mr. Rhodes' and to Lafayette to make arrangements for a convention and debate of Friday. Friday, went to Toulon to attend the convention; W. J. Fraser and Esq. Kinney debated with James H. Dickey and O. P. Lovejoy, upon the principles and practices of the liberty party. The debate held from 2 P.M., till 5, and from 7 till 3 A.M. No decision was taken either by judges or vote; but we think the negative established nothing. It rained hard all night and in the morning creeks were almost impassable. In crossing a little branch between Mr. Silliman's and Hugh Rhodes' the water was so deep that my wagon uncoupled, and the hind parts floated off, and I went out with the fore wheels, well wet.

... June 24th [1844] — Went to Knoxville as a witness for Rev. Mr. Cross,[9] in the case of the People *vs.* Cross for harboring slaves; at length a *nolle prosequi* was entered and I returned home. On Friday, went to Farmington to attend a convention for organizing a general association for the state. The constitution was changed in diverse places, and the confession of faith slightly altered; strong resolutions passed on the subject of slavery.

... July 2nd [1844] — Last week went to Lafayette and Toulon to hear the candidates for congress speak. After Mr. Cross, the liberty candidate had spoken, Colonel

VIII. Stark County

W. H. Henderson delivered himself of a speech against abolitionists in general, and ministers in particular. At Toulon also, he expressed the same sentiments, only was more personal. He warned the people against all sorts of abolitionists, said 'they would destroy the country; slavery was a great curse, but God would remove it without human instrumentality. Warned all not to hear abolition preachers; he would not hear one preach, sing or pray! Neither should his children go to our Sabbath school; warned the children not to believe what such preachers said; he would say to the gentleman whom he had in his eye, we don't want him, he can go back to the east where he came from; I never heard him, and never will. If he comes here let him talk to empty seats'....

... July 8th [1845]—Last Saturday went to Walnut Creek & when near Reynolds t[he] horse shook off his bridle, took fright & ran. By a kind province I was enabled to escape without serious injury. After running 20 rods, just as he was coming among logs, lumber etc. both tugs became unhitched at once & he ran off with t[he] harness only. Sab. Preached at Walnut Grove & P.M. Walnut Creek. Monday attended t[he] adjourned discussion of Anti-slavery principles at Toulon. The Court house was crowded & a great responsibility must rest on those who by misrepresentation and sophistry tried to avert & hide t[he] trust. There was a direct attempt on t[he] part of our [o]pponents to move upon popular prejudice put *positive assertion* with t[he] least show of proof for *sound argument*, especially toward t[he] close, when the positions they had taken in t[he] earlier part of t[he] debate were shown to be untenable. I think however much good was done. Facts not before known were brought before enquiring minds, & nothing was said by our opponents that could shake t[he] faith in the least of any one who had adopted anti-slavery principles, or even to pervert t[he] minds of those who were anxiously enquiring after t[he] truth. I never before reali[z]ed how perfectly weak in argument must be he who opposes t[he] Liberty party principles. A Demagague may harangue & excite a populace by false isms & perversions, [b]ut no one in t[he] field of fair argumentation can long hold up his head in opposition...I regret to be obliged to enter this field, others ought to do it; but if they will not, shall I be silent? Would it please God? Would conscience leave me at ease? I pray God to guide me in this matter, and if I misapprehend my duty, may I know it....

... February 2nd [1846]—Went to Lafayette; found a Methodist meeting which had continued for nineteen days with good success; a spirit of union seemed to prevail. I was invited to preach, which I did; then went to Toulon and Wyoming to arrange appointments; I am met by a good degree of cordiality, that shows prejudice has greatly abated. Sabbath at Toulon; the prospect is flattering as compared with former times....

... February 24th [1846]—My labors appear to be very acceptable at Lafayette by all classes who hear me, but they exceedingly regret that I am an *abolitionist. O when will their eyes be opened....*

...April 4th [1846]—Last week Sat. went to Toulon to attend a county Antislavery Meeting—Gave an address showing the duty of xians & ministers of the Gos. In ref. to political action on the subject of Slavery especially....

... April 15th [1846]—.... Tues. visited several families & in t eve. Gave an antislavery lecture at t Wall School house. Good audience compared with what we had a little more than a year ago. The cause has gained quite a foothold—At Osceola I have a hope that some good may be affected. The brethren seem to begin to feel that something must be done....

... June 6th [1846]—Since the last entry I have been at Canton (exchanged with Mr. Jones)[10] all around the county with Mr. Codding,[11] etc. The cause [abolitionism] is prosperous in the country. No mob violence in Peoria or Fulton counties. I trust much good done. I have preached but three times and rode 170 [miles].

... November 6th [1846]—Had a good meeting at brother Hugh Rhodes,' persons from different parts of the county. They agreed it was best that I should remain and proceed to organize a Congregational church in Toulon the last Sabbath of the month....

... January 5th [1847]—... Arriving at home on Friday evening, found two fugitives from slavery had been along, with only "Christmas papers."[12] Messrs. Smith and Gordon of Farmington pursued, got out a search warrant for two stolen horses and two colored men who were supposed to have stolen them. Neither horses or men were described except that one man called himself "Major." They searched our premises in vain, however, for the birds had flown, having got a wink from friends at Farmington that they were pursued. Several constables and others followed them to Osceola, but before they reached there, the fugitives were safely out of the country.

In 1842, Zebina Eastman became editor of the *Western Citizen*. This newspaper, established in Chicago, became the leading abolitionist periodical in Illinois. The following excerpt is taken from an article published on February 23, 1847. This account is what Wright wrote about in his diary on January 5, 1847:

On the last day of December, two colored persons on horseback passed through Farmington, Fulton County, on their way to *"freedom's domain."* It was understood that they had *"Christmas passes"* only, which of course must soon expire. Two persons in the *form* of man—a *Mr. Gordon* and a *Mr. Smith,* of Farmington, thinking no doubt, that by arresting and detaining these fugitives they would readily secure a reward of *several hundred dollars* from their former masters, who would probably advertise them, resolved to spend their *"New Year's"* in pursuit.

Accordingly, in the afternoon of *"New Year's,"* they presented themselves before a justice of the peace for Stark County, and made an oath that they believed a larceny had been committed by two colored persons from Missouri, and desired a warrant to be issued for searching the premises of S.G. Wright, W.W. Webster, and N. Wyckoff, for two horses, and two colored persons, one of them calling his name "Morgan." Our well-meaning justice was not willing to issue a warrant where no *description* of property or persons could be given, and where evidently there was nothing but suspicion; and instead of wanting horses they only wanted to send two men back into slavery—or rather make a few hundred dollars by doing so.

However, they resorted to the house of a *Mr. Arnold,* who is much distinguished for his zeal in prosecuting abolitionists, and the over-persuaded Justice issued an *"illegal search warrant,"* as requested.

A constable by the name of White, was so seized with *colorphobia* as to dare violate the *express statute* of our State, and serve the warrant in the night.

About 9 o'clock in the evening, as the family of Rev. S.G. Wright were engaged in devotional exercises, they were disturbed by the intrusion of the constable and his posse, who has thus laid himself open to an action for trespass before our next Circuit Court. At this time, however, the persons sought were some twelve miles on their way toward "Freedom."[13]

Continuing with Wright's diary:

> ... July 26th [1847] — Sat. a black man from slavery came here & I carried him on the public highway by daylight, & in the middle of the day to the next station.
> ... April 3rd [1848] — ... Wed. eve. James E. Burr[14] of Mission Penitentiary notoriety, was here & gave his history to a pretty full house. Attention good. Sent Edward with Burr to Canton to work this summer with his Uncle George....
> ... June 6th [1848] — Friday carried a fugitive to Osceola and preached at half past four....
> ... June 11th [1848] — Tues. I brought a colored man fr. H. Rhodes to town, & he went on by day with a company from Osceola, & next day on in the stage to Princeton. All which shows that the railroad has risen nearly to the surface here....
> ... July 24th [1854] — Last week I assisted some in the harvest field and prepared one sermon. On Friday 5 fugitives came here who had escaped from their master in labor in Fremont County,[15] Iowa as he was taking them through from Mississippi to Salt Lake. I carried them up to Esq. Autin's in the daytime. They were intelligent for men who could not read. One of them said he would not be taken back alive, for he had determined on liberty, or death with him....

In 1906, the Reverend John Todd published a book entitled *Early Settlement and Growth of Western Iowa and Reminiscences*. In the eighth chapter, Todd tells a story of helping the very same fugitives in western Iowa that Samuel Wright wrote about aiding in western Illinois. Todd's account starts on Independence Day; Wright's assistance to these runaways took place a few weeks later. The Reverend Todd's account reads, in part, as follows:

> On the evening of the 4th of July, 1854, there came into our quiet village a traveler with his family and several colored people, three covered wagons and a carriage. The father, mother and daughter rode in the carriage. They were on their way from Mississippi to Salt Lake and would have crossed the river at Nebraska City, as their most direct route, but, on account of the rush of emigration, and the freighting across the plains, the ferry at that point was crowded, and to avoid the crowd this company had passed on, intending to cross higher up. They camped for the night on the west side of Main Street, and about mid way between Elm and Orange Streets. There were six slaves and two of them got water from Jesse West's well, near which the first hotel in Tabor was then in process of building. Whether stimulated excessively on America's natal day by large draughts of freedom and independence, or whether the circumstances conspired to such a result, or both prompted the deed, certain it is that the builders found an interview with the darkies and learned that they were slaves; that five of the six, a father, mother and two children, with another man, were anxious to escape from slavery, but that the other slave woman didn't want to leave her master and couldn't safely be trusted with their plans. Arrangements were then made, the five desirous to go were met at the corner by the hotel in the night and conducted to and across the Nishnabotna and concealed in the bushes.... They made their way to a settlement of Quakers in the vicinity of the Des Moines River, and there leaving them in safe hands....
> The fugitives reached the Queen's Dominions in safety, but their master, who we were credibly informed was a Mormon elder, on his way from Mississippi to Salt Lake, was not willing to let his slave property escape, without at least an effort to

Homes of
Rev. Samuel G. Wright

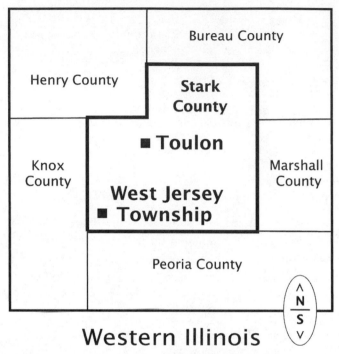

Western Illinois

Brenda Patterson, BG Patterson Graphics.

recover it. On rising in the morning after the exodus, there was an unusual stillness about the camp. No one was astir. Fires were not lighted. The teams were uncared for, nor was breakfast being prepared. All seemed at a stand still. He stepped out, and looked in all directions, but saw no trace of the missing slaves. The reputation of the people of Tabor, as being in sympathy with fleeing fugitives, was too well known to admit of his taking counsel with them in this emergency. But in a neighborhood a few miles south of Tabor sympathizing friends were found. The news was soon heralded abroad. The dastardly deed was denounced.... A good number of pro-slavery sympathizers came together. A general slave hunt was planned and the groves, and thickets, and tall grass, and timber bordering both sides of the Nishnabotna River — every place where they might be concealed was carefully searched. But one of those, who aided in the search, was at heart a friend of the fugitives, and was careful to do the searching around where he knew they were hid, and just as careful *not* to find them.... New conductors, both of whom passed to their reward many years ago, took charge of the train. When they [the slaves] had proceeded some distance on their way they met a man on horse back of whom they inquired the way to Quincy.... They ran the gauntlet of pro-slavery servility through Iowa, Illinois, Indiana and Michigan, and found freedom in Queen Victoria's land.[16]

John Todd was very familiar with Knox College, its trustees, faculty, and many of its students. Todd was instrumental in establishing Tabor College in Iowa, an anti-slavery institution modeled, in part, after Oberlin and Knox colleges. The July 1854 accounts of John Todd and Samuel Wright definitely confirm the interrelationships of UGRR operators that sometimes, as in this case, extended for very long distances across Illinois and Iowa. During the mid–1850s, the Tabor settlement started sending fugitive slaves to Galesburg.[17]

Continuing with Wright's diary:

> September 18th [1854]—Sabbath—preached three times and after I got to sleep, was awakened by the arrival of a fugitive on UGRR—I went and carried him to Mr. Winslow.
>
> ... October 11th [1858]—I went to Geneseo to endeavor to get Hattie Wells to come & teach in our school. I failed & it rained next day, so I had a hard time reached home last Thurs. & went to Galesburg to hear Lincoln & Douglas.[18] A crowd supposed to number 20,000 were there. Douglas' personal appearance I like much better than I expected to, but his style of speaking was very hard to listen to. It was disjointed as if he could not be heard if he spoke two words without a pause between. Probably from a great effort to be heard by all. Lincoln made no such effort, but was I think heard quite as far as Douglas, & yet spoke right along....
>
> ... December 12th [1859]—Last week I prepared a sermon on slavery, suggested by Harpers Ferry raid, and execution of Brown ... the notice that the subject would be presented was given out the Sabbath before, and roused much feeling among all the Democrats of the place, as if it was to be a political attack. The house was crowded beyond what it ever was before on the Sabbath—people came in from miles, and it was said every Democrat was there. I tried to improve the occasion to make a deep impression of the wickedness of the system of slavery. Not only because of the oppression of the slave, but of the evils it brings upon the white population, to rouse them to perpetuate opposition to it, I hope it was not in vain. I have seldom seen a more attentive audience.[19]

Accounts of one of the most bizarre Underground Railroad incidents anywhere in Illinois can be found in the *Historical Encyclopedia of Illinois and Knox County* edited by Newton Bateman, Paul Selby, W. Selden Gale and George Candee Gale published in 1899. It details a most unusual attempt on the part of a Mississippi slave owner to establish his right to own and keep a slave in northern Illinois:

> Among the incidents of "Underground Railroad" in Illinois is one which had some importance politically, having for its climax a dramatic scene in Congress, but of which, so far as known, no full account has ever been written. About 1855, Ephraim Lombard, a Mississippi planter, but a New Englander by birth, purchased a large body of prairie land in the northeastern part of Stark County, and, taking up his residence temporarily in the village of Bradford, began its improvement. He had brought with him from Mississippi a negro, gray-haired and bent with age, a slave of probably no great value. "Old Mose," as he was called, soon came to be well known and a favorite in the neighborhood. Lombard boldly stated that he had

brought him there as a slave; that, by virtue of the Dred Scott decision (then of recent date), had had a constitutional right to take his slaves wherever he pleased, and that "Old Mose" was just as much his property in Illinois as in Mississippi. It soon became evident to some, that his bringing of the negro to Illinois was an experiment to test the law and the feelings of the Northern people. This being the case, a shrewd play would have been to let him have his way till other slaves should have been brought to stock the new plantation. But this was too slow a process for the abolitionists, to whom the holding of a slave in the free State of Illinois appeared an unbearable outrage. It was feared that he might take the old negro back to Mississippi and fail to bring any others. It was reported, also, that "Old Mose" was ill-treated; that he was given only the coarsest food in a back shed, as if he were a horse or a dog, instead of being permitted to eat at table with the family. The prairie citizen of that time was very particular upon this point of etiquette. The hired man or woman, debarred from the table of his or her employer, would not have remained a day. A quiet consultation with "Old Mose" revealed the fact that he would hail the gift of freedom joyously. Accordingly, one Peter Risedorf, and another equally daring, met him by the light of the stars and, before morning, he was placed in the care of Owen Lovejoy, at Princeton, twenty miles away. From there he was speedily "franked"[20] by the member of Congress to friends in Canada.

There was a great commotion in Bradford over the "stealing" of "Old Mose." Lombard and his friends denounced the act in terms bitter and profane, and threatened vengeance upon the perpetrators. The conductors were known only to a few, and they kept their secret well.[21]

The final Stark County selection comes from a letter sent to Wilbur Siebert on January 28, 1896, by Harriet Hall Blair. Her father, Dr. Thomas Hall, was one of the most prominent "agents" involved in Stark County's Underground Railroad activity. Dr. Hall, an Englishman who had graduated from the Royal Society of Surgeons in London, arrived in Stark County in 1840. Ten years later an honorary degree was conferred on him by the Rush Medical College of Chicago. Dr. Hall, along with other Stark County operators had established various options for runaway slaves as escape valves:

...W.H. Siebert, Cambridge, Mass.,

Your letter addressed to the County Auditor of Stark[e] Co. has been referred [sic] to me—I shall be glad to give you any information in regard to the "Underground Railroad" that you desire. Toulon is situated midway between Galesburg and Princeton, thirty miles from either place, so became an important station—too important to be overlooked by the slave hunters—hence the fugitives were often sidetracked until those in pursuit gave up the chase or were lured in some other direction— "Niggers Point[,]" twelve miles south of here [,] was one of these by stations—here lived W.W. Webster[,] S.G. Wright & Jonathan Pratts, all active conductors on this underground railroad—"Niggers Point" was made up of a farming community and[,] being as much as twelve miles from any town[,] it furnished a safe hiding place for the fugitives. Midway between "Niggers Point" and Toulon lived Augustus Dunn,[22] who was a fearless abolitionist, also a family of Wycuffs who aided in the work, bringing the human freight within a mile of Toulon, where Hugh Rhodes took the cargo in charge and reported to Dr. Hall who at once devised means for the safe escort of all concerned to the home of Liberty Stone,[23] who lived in Osceola[,] twelve miles farther on the route to Princeton — William Hall of Osceola was another fearless champion of the rights of the slave — the last named lived on a dairy farm a mile or more off [of] the direct route — here the darkies were regaled with fresh milk and cheese, and were followed by the prayers of these God [fearing] people. The next station after leaving Osceola was Providence in Bureau County. James Pilkerton was an active conductor at this point[,] and Daniel Clark filled the same office at Boyds' Grove a few miles distant — Owen Lovejoy was the center of the anti-slavery movement in Bureau Co., so Princeton became one of the most important Stations in the State. Rev. [Mr.] Cross of Princeton often laid aside his ministerial robes and[,] dressed as a farmer[,] he would drive to one of the stations on the underground railroad and[,] after storing his freight[,] would hasten to his home where he donned his suite of black and in an hour's time stood in his pulpit wearing a look of conscious innocence. [The] Rev. S. G. Wright and W. W. Webster of "Niggers Point[,]" [and] Owen Lovejoy of Princeton were indicted May 20[,] 1843[,] for "harboring runaway slaves." [The] Rev. [Mr.] Cross was indicted a year later for the same offence. You now have an imperfect history of sixty miles of the Underground [R]ailroad running from Galesburg to Princeton via "Niggers Point" and Toulon. Right here I will say a fugitive was never captured on this line — and when word reached the stations that those whom we had fed and sheltered at the peril of life and property had reached Canada[,] peans[24] of praise went up that made the Welkin ring.[25]

The most active period of this movement in Illinois was from 1840 to 1848 — a few fugitives passed through our count[y] (?) as early as 1838 — The murder of [the] Rev. Elijah P. Lovejoy in the fall of 1837 was really the beginning of the agitation here. You ask for "a history of my own connection with the Underground Cause." I have the honor to be the daughter of Dr. Thomas Hall of Toulon — who with all the noble men of whom I have written has finished his work — yet he still lives in the hearts of those who knew his worth.

One very savory memory of the year 1844 still abides with me, it is the recollection of washing the windows in my father's house after a mob had plastered them with eggs too ancient to be relished. Strange to relate few of the participants in the egging still live here, and they are bright and shinning [sic] lights in the Republican party. Anything to be popular! If you desire to ask other questions, do so at a later date and I will answer them if possible. You will see by these dates that I am not "a new woman[.]"

> Very respectfully[,]
> Harriet Hall Blair[26]

The headwaters of the Spoon River form in northeastern Stark County, but its two forks twist toward the Bureau County line. The eastern fork begins in Osceola township, where UGRR operators Calvin Winslow and James Buswell lived. In 1833, Buswell moved to west central Illinois and in 1836 he took up residence in Stark County. Buswell's son, James Jr., wrote after the Civil War that in the course of his father's Underground Railroad involvement he came into contact with the "notorious negro Charlie," who, after escaping from slavery in Missouri, later returned in an unsuccessful attempt to rescue his wife. Unfortunately, "Charlie" learned that she had been sold to a new owner in the south. But "Charlie," according to Buswell Jr. continued to aid "others and was an active abductor for several years."[27] The west fork of the Spoon River passed through Elmira Township, where another small "station" for fugitives was run by Joseph Blanchard and his wife.

There was now light at the end of the tunnel for fugitive slaves as they moved from Stark County into Bureau and Putnam counties. The long passage through western Illinois was nearly over.

IX

Bureau County— The Martyr's Brother

The year 1837 is remembered for the crippling economic depression throughout the country known as the Panic of '37. Land values fell, trade rapidly declined, and business in general suffered. The Panic of '37 followed a period of remarkable prosperity in the United States, but the subsequent economic collapse was so pervasive it lasted well into the next decade. Like other states, Illinois contributed to its own fiscal problems by funding overly ambitious internal improvement projects. Large state debt meant that the Panic of '37 hit the Prairie State very hard.

On the Fourth of July, 1837, the cornerstone of the new state capital was laid in Springfield. That same week Elijah P. Lovejoy wrote an editorial in the *Alton Observer* pointing out to its readers that most Americans on Independence Day could rightfully commemorate their liberty and freedom but millions of others, as slaves, were unable to join that celebration. Those who advocated slavery, of whom there were many in that part of southwestern Illinois and eastern Missouri, seethed with anger toward this extremist antislavery publisher.

By early November of that year Lovejoy had witnessed the destruction of his printing presses on three different occasions by proslavery forces. When a fourth press arrived November 6th, he and his loyal supporters stood guard to protect it from those who might again try to take it from him. The next night a drunken mob formed and the scene soon turned ugly. The abolitionist-hating rioters charged the building where Lovejoy and his friends were waiting, shots rang out, and one man in the crowd outside was killed. The mob retreated, reorganized, and the town went into a frenzy. The antiabolitionist horde then charged the building for a second time and set it on fire. When Lovejoy emerged to examine the extent of the flames, he was felled by bullets and died.

This incident was a watershed for the antislavery movement throughout the entire county. The proslavery mob, by murdering Lovejoy, had given the abolitionist crusade a martyr. Throughout the North, from Illinois to Massachusetts, the tide against slavery shifted significantly. Wendell Phillips delivered a famous and impassioned speech at Boston's Faneuil Hall about the murder of Lovejoy. This protest lecture by Phillips helped launch his career as a highly regarded and brilliant spokesman for the abolitionist cause. "After Lovejoy's death the call to martyrdom rang loud in the ear of every spokesman for negro freedom. Their endurance of maltreatment rapidly became the very fiber of the antislavery lore."[1]

Immediately following Elijah Lovejoy's murder, his brother, Owen, stepped forward and vowed to take up his brother's abolitionist crusade. He kept his word to that pledge for the next 27 years. In 1838, Owen Lovejoy moved to Princeton, Illinois in Bureau County[2] and became minister of the Congregational Church. His impact on this town was immediate and long lasting. By settling in Princeton, he managed to put himself at a strategic point on the UGRR Quincy Line (Quincy to Galesburg to Princeton) while also positioning himself to help fugitives coming directly east from the Mississippi and Rock rivers. In time, he became known as one of the nation's most outspoken abolitionists and notorious Underground Railroad operators.[3] Just as Samuel G. Wright experienced a negative reaction from the majority of people he encountered upon his arrival in Stark County, Owen Lovejoy met similar animosity when he came to live in Princeton:

Courtesy of Owen Lovejoy Homestead, Princeton, Illinois.

Owen Lovejoy moved to Princeton in 1838 and became the most famous Underground Railroad agent in the state. He was the brother of martyred newspaperman Elijah P. Lovejoy, who was killed by a proslavery mob in Alton in 1837.

> It is somewhat difficult now to estimate the discouragements, the opposition, the taunts, and the secret and open resistance Mr. Lovejoy encountered upon his first coming to Bureau County. At the time but few people in Illinois had thought or

concerned themselves about either slaves or slave owners. They opposed it coming among them, and this was all. They cared but little what other States might do. They knew that the leading best men in the South, from Washington to Clay, were bemoaning in the infliction of slavery upon their portion of the country; the Southern men they knew had advocated and taken steps looking to eventual emancipation and colonization of the slaves and thus, in the slow process of time, ridding the country, not only of slavery, but of the presence of the negro. If they thought about it at all, they respected the laws of their country, without stopping to think whether the law itself was humane or cruel. Hence, it was a rude awakening to many when the new preacher, in Princeton, began to preach that slavery was the crime of crimes, and that a slave-catcher was the vilest of criminals. In conversation the other day with a citizen of Princeton, a man growing gray and who gave the information that he had always voted for Lovejoy, and for years of all men he had ever met he was the ideal, the great and good man, yet he introduced the conversation by telling

COURTESY OF OWEN LOVEJOY HOMESTEAD, PRINCETON, ILLINOIS.

Owen Lovejoy's house in Princeton, which is now a National Landmark, was used as a safe-house for a number of runaway slaves.

us, that when very young he had, with other bad boys, many and many a time from their covert thrown — at generally very safe range — clods at the "Abolitionist Preacher." The boys were acting out what they had caught around the fire-side and from older persons. They thought an Abolitionist a bad man through and through.[4]

In southern Bureau County a hideout existed in Providence, where keepers Caleb Cushing and William Pilkenton harbored fugitives. Other hiding places existed at Boyd's Grove and in Indiantown, now known as Tiskilwa. There was also a key covverture along the Stark County/Bureau County line that was managed by Liberty Stone. These were stations used prior to wayfarers being delivered to Princeton.

The cadre of Bureau County underground agents who supported Lovejoy in Princeton included the three Bryant brothers, Arthur, Cyrus and John Howard.[5] Their other brother, William Cullen Bryant, was a famous American poet and writer[6] and vocal antislavery advocate in the East. H. C. Bradsby wrote of John Howard Bryant in his *History of Bureau County, Illinois*, "Many times has he entertained fugitive slaves, both before and after the famous law of 1850, and the cruel 'black laws' of Illinois.... The unreasoning severity of these laws was an attempt to scourge men for acts of the highest Christian virtue. Their injustice and cruelty made them repulsive to a large majority of our people, and like all excessive laws, they were treated generally with contempt by good men and spit upon. Among the latter were Mr. Bryant."[7] John T. Holbrook, who lived in LaMoille, only a dozen miles northeast of Princeton, was indicted and brought to trial for aiding a fugitive slave in 1840. Holbrook was eventually acquitted, but this was the first case of its kind tried in Bureau County. Other important "agents" associated with this county's UGRR activities were Caleb Cook,[8] Roderick Frary,[9] and John Weldon.[10]

The first extended selection in this chapter is taken from N. Matson's *Reminiscences of Bureau County* published in 1872. Matson was a land surveyor with a passion for exactness and he was especially knowledgeable about the geography, people, and institutions of Bureau County. He devoted several pages of his book to that county's UGRR operation, giving particular attention to the county's most famous abolitionist and Underground Railroad agent, Owen Lovejoy. This excerpt also alludes to the underground efforts of the previously mentioned John Cross:

> In the fall of 1838, a young man, with black hair, broad shoulders, and peculiar expressive blue eyes, was seen coming into Princeton on horseback. He was alone, and a stranger, without means, being in search of a place to make his future home, and came here by mere chance. This man was Owen Lovejoy, subsequently of political celebrity. Soon after arriving here, Mr. Lovejoy was installed pastor of the Congregational Church, and occupied that position for sixteen years. From that time Princeton became a place of note; although containing but few inhabitants, and having but little commercial relation with other parts of the world, it was, nevertheless, the head center of abolitionism for the west. Newspapers of that day reported

state conventions held here, and great speeches made in favor of immediate emancipation, so that Princeton was known in abolition circles throughout the Union. Even slaves at the south heard of it, and many of them came to see it, which caused Col. Barksdale in a speech in Congress, to denounce Princeton as one of the negro stealing places in the west.

According to abolition papers of that day, an underground railroad was established, which extended from the slave states to Canada, passing through Princeton, and making it a place of changing cars. John Cross, a Wesleyan Methodist minister, who lived near La Moille, was announced general superintendent, and he was succeeded in office by Owen Lovejoy. Mr. Cross had hand bills and large posters circulated through the country advertising his business, and calling on abolitionists everywhere for assistance in carrying out his plans. His bills were not headed with a picture of a locomotive and a train of cars, but with a bobtail horse in a Dearborn wagon — the driver leaning forward and applying the whip, while the heads of two darkies were seen peering out from under the seat. Stations were established at proper distances, and agents in readiness to convey fugitives forward as soon as they arrived.[11]

A second selection from Matson's book is a particularly stirring story about an incident involving a slave tracker duped by antislavery settlers. Elijah Smith was one of the earliest settlers in Bureau County:

In the summer of 1835, two black girls, belonging to Maj. Dougherty, of St. Louis, escaped from bondage and found refuge at Mineral Point, Wisconsin. Some months after they arrived there, a professional slave catcher, named Harris, learning of their whereabouts, captured them, and was on his way to St. Louis, where he expected to receive the large reward that was offered for their return to slavery. Harris was traveling on horseback, and leading by his side another horse, on which the two girls were mounted. On a cold December night, Harris, with his two captives, whose feet were badly frozen, arrived at Elijah Smith's house of entertainment, where he procured quarters for the night. It so happened that same night that James G. Ross, of Ox Bow prairie, being on his way to Galena, was staying over night at Smith's house. Mr. Ross, being an abolitionist, was soon engaged in a warm controversy with the slave catcher, each of whom accused the other of rascality. Smith's house of entertainment consisted of a double log cabin, of two apartments, the men occupying one, and the women, with the two black girls, the other. Eli Smith and wife, with another neighbor, were there spending the evening, and on hearing the girls tell their sad story, they became interested in their behalf, and a plan was adopted for their rescue. Mr. Ross being a party to this project, proposed to take the girls to his friends, east of the river, where they would be assisted on their way to Canada.

To avoid being suspicioned by Harris, Ross complained of sudden illness, and the women gave him warm teas, but getting worse, he went upstairs to bed. Each of the cabins of which Smith's residence was composed, had a flight of stairs that met at the top. Ross, instead of going to bed, walked down the other flight of stairs, brought out his horse, hitched it on to Eli Smith's sled, and with the girls started for Hennepin. On reaching the timber, near Joel Doolittle's residence, he found the snow so near gone that his horse could not draw his load, so he left the old sled by the wayside, placed the girls on his horse, and going on foot himself, he continued the journey.

141

Harris, believing that Ross was sick in bed, gave himself no further trouble about his chattels, but went on to tell what he would do if any one should attempt to steal his negroes. Before retiring for the night, Harris went into the other apartment to see if everything was right, and he was much surprised to find the girls gone. Assisted by Elijah Smith, carrying a lantern, the barn and haystacks were searched, but without effect. Harris was in a terrible rage, accused the family of being accessory to the escape of the girls, and taking out his revolver, he swore he would shoot all about the house if they were not forthcoming.[12]

The following letter sent to Owen Lovejoy's daughter, Sarah, by Justice Olds on May 17, 1874, recounted a dramatic story about her father's involvement in aiding the escape of a slave named John:

Miss Sarah Lovejoy
Dear Madam,

I have yours of thirteenth instant requesting me to give some recollections of your father to be used by Mister Cook in speaking of him at the anticipated anti-slavery reunion. I should be most happy to comply with your request, but my recollections of those times have faded from my memory to such an extent that it is impossible to give a very clear and certain statement of anything that would be interesting. The affair in regard to John to which you refer I think I recollect as well as anything.

When your father first came to Princeton and commenced preaching *abolition*, the old church was almost unanimous in its opposition to it, but he told them he should preach it until the members were as much abolition as he was and then they would like to hear it. And this he soon accomplished. Old Doct Chamberlain, then one of the deacons, once left the meeting rather then to hear an abolition sermon, but he soon became a strong abolitionist.

The first event that brought your father into notice outside the church was his being prosecuted for entertaining a colored woman escaping from slavery. I think Mr. Cook was attending court at the time of the trail and probably recollects the history of that affair. Mr. Collins of Chicago was counsel for your father, and I think Judge Certon and Dickey were employed in the case.

The affair of John's capture and escape is perhaps as well remembered by me as anything I could relate. He came to Princeton poor and ragged, just escaped from Missouri. He was stout and robust and a good looking mulatto. He worked industriously and soon appeared well dressed, and by his steady habit and good behavior, won the respect of all who knew him. One day while mowing in the field for Enos Matson, his old master and some person with him came up behind him unperceived until close upon him and presented a pistol and ordered him to surrender. John, seeing no way of escape, gave himself up, and his master tied his hands together with a rope and led him into town as he would a stray horse. That roused all the anti-slavery spirit that then existed, and the friends of the slave soon rallied with Lovejoy at their head for the rescue. A general understanding was had among the anti-slavery men that John should not be taken away. A warrant was obtained from a justice of the peace against the slaveholder for kidnapping upon which he was arrested and taken before the magistrate for examination, he retaining his hold upon the halter that held his victim in his custody. A motion was made for the release of

John from the custody of the kidnapper, and while that was being argued, the kidnapper's friend procured a justice of the peace before whom they proposed to take John and procure papers authorizing his removal from the state. A messenger was sent to the kidnappers informing him of the proceeding and to take charge of John to conduct him to one of the offices in the court house where the justice of the peace was in waiting. As soon as John was given into the hands of the messenger the rope was cut by some one in the crowd, and being at liberty, he rushed out of the door followed by Lovejoy and a number of friends. The door was then closed by the sheriff for fear the kidnapper, who was in his custody, should escape with the crowd, and several minutes elapsed before the kidnapper's friend could get out of the court house. John ran out of the court house yard and up the sidewalk at the top of his speed followed by Lovejoy and other friends. When passing up the walk as fast he could run, he was tripped up by a man standing on the sidewalk, but he recovered himself and ran as far as Peru Street where he was put on horseback and made his way to Lovejoy's house ahead of all pursuers. The kidnapper's friends pursued their victim to Lovejoy's where they found Lovejoy himself in the front yard who forbid all persons from trespassing on his premises and held the entire crowd at bay, no one presuming to enter the yard and where he commenced an anti-slavery speech.— Soon a man was seen riding from Lovejoy's barn as fast as the horse could go in the direction of Dover with a handkerchief tied around his head, and the cry went out, there goes John! There goes John! And the crowd was soon in pursuit. But the man did not prove to be John who was in the meantime arrayed in woman's clothes with a bonnet hiding his face and put into a wagon and conveyed to a neighbor's a mile or two distant and kept till night and sent off upon the underground railroad.

I do not think of anything more at present that would be interesting, but I wish to say that Mr. Lovejoy was always true to his principles and never compromised them for expediency. He was always bold and fearless, and the objects he wished to accomplish were never concealed.

Hoping I may be able to attend the reunion, I remain as ever,

Yours truly,
Justice H. Olds[13]

Another daughter of Owen Lovejoy's, Ida, who was born in 1848, clearly indicated that her father had no problem at all with runaways arming themselves in order to fight off slave trackers. Ida recalled firsthand that when, in the late 1850s, a group of ex-slaves pulled up to the Lovejoy homestead in a wagon, her father immediately asked them if they had any weapons. When informed that they only had clubs, he told them not to hesitate to use them. Ida's grandmother was there that morning and when she asked Owen if he was sure that was the right advice, he answered "Yes, I am sure."[14]

Owen Lovejoy was elected to the United States House of Representatives in 1857, where he served until his death in 1864. [15] By 1859, Lovejoy's reputation as a leading antislavery crusader was well-known throughout the North and South. A sample of his writing below helps to explain his reputation as a captivating orator. Owen Lovejoy is a perfect example of what James and Lois Horton mean in their book, *Hard Road to Freedom*, "the American Anti-Slavery Society and its supporters published flurries of pamphlets, sermons, and newspapers but their most effective agents were anti-slavery speakers."[16] The following selection includes excerpts taken from a speech made on the floor of the U.S. House by Lovejoy on February 21, 1859:

Within the last five lustrums,[17] a strange fanaticism has made its appearance in this country — a fanaticism at once monstrous and malign. Twenty-five years ago, by the universal sentiment of the country, Slavery was deemed a moral, social, and political evil; a wrong to the slave, an injury to the owner, a blight on the soil, a detriment to all the best interests of the communities or States where it was found, and, in its reflex influence, a reproach and damage to the whole country. By many, it may be, this evil was considered incurable, but still an evil. But within the period indicated, a different sentiment has sprung up. This fanaticism deems Slavery not an evil, but a blessing.

Formerly by all, and still by all right thinking men, Slavery was regarded as a hag, ugly, deformed, wrinkled, and covered with the daub and paint of harlotry; but now we are told it is an angel of beauty, a virgin decked in bridal attire, to be gazed on with complacency and love! Candidates who aspire to gubernatorial honors are made to renounce opinions held a quarter of a century ago, and give in their adhesion to this new dogma, to wit: that Slavery is a blessing. It is not any longer the question how a cancer can be cured — whether by knife or caustic, or other remedial agencies — but to have a cancer is now proclaimed to be a sound and normal condition of the human system, the highest type of health, and, if on the face, an ornament and beauty spot. Every one, to enjoy perfect health must have this form of disease gnawing at his vitals. The spirit of this fanaticism has taken possession of the Democratic party, and worked therein a wonderful and almost incredible transformation; for since the Ages drew up the reins and started on their journey, I do not suppose they have witnessed such a stupendous Lie as the Democratic party now is. I speak of the organization, without any reference to the individuals who compose the party. "From the sole of the foot even unto the head, there is no soundness in it; but wounds, and bruises, and putrefying sores: they have not been closed, neither bound up, neither mollified with ointment" — unmedicated and unbandaged, it drips with its fetid putrescence....

... Now, I am reckoned as ultra and extreme as most on this subject, and yet, no one has ever heard me say anything against the South. It is only against Slavery that I have spoken, and I propose to assail that only in those modes justified by the Constitution; yet I am sectional, and Republicans are sectional. When they only seek to prevent the extension of a system which is under the ban of the civilized world, they are charged with being sectional. In Illinois, we have supped full of this horror. And what is the proof? Oh, we have no delegates from slave States to attend our National Nominating Conventions. Why have we none? Mark; because if delegates attend these Conventions they are mobbed and driven into exile....

And this reminds me to say that the Democratic party, led on by this insane fanaticism, which holds slavery to be morally right, under the guidance of a political harlequin and trickster, has proclaimed the constitutional right of Slavery to go into the Territories without let or hindrance. Plighted national faith is broken and dishonored! Principles once declared sacred by this very leader, and said to be canonized in the hearts of the American people, are ruthlessly and recklessly trampled under foot. We had an angel of Liberty stationed at the portals of our Territories. For thirty years, this sentinel had kept watch and ward, and guarded that magnificent domain as the heritage of Freedom, and, with the flaming sword of the ordinance of the patriots of the olden time, kept out Slavery from this Eden. Who chased away this angel, and broke down the walls that enclosed that empire, consecrated to the sons and daughters of Freedom as a dwelling place and some, as long as the sun and moon should endure? Who did this ruthless, reckless, damnable work? The Democratic party, under the leadership of the individual I have indicated. Under what plea was Slavery thus allowed to enter in and ravage the heritage of Freedom? On the same ground that the madman opens the pest house to let leprosy, plague, and cholera, rush forth, as did the winds from the fabulous cave, to walk at midnight and waste at noonday. A man with a contagious disease must not stay in his own house, nor be confined in the hospital, but must be allowed to roam abroad, to spread disease and death among his fellow men! What is this, but the veriest madness that ever raved in Bedlam! I know it is said that there are two wings to the Democratic party. I am aware of that, and I know, also, that both wings belong to the same vulture, and, although one has been slightly out of joint, it has now got back to its place, and both will flap in unison, to bear the carrion bird back to gorge and fatten on the carcass where it has gorged and fattened so long....

... Honor thy father and thy mother, is the requirement of the Bible. Slavery utterly annuls this command. The owner claims honor and obedience, to the utter disregard of parental authority and parental claims. Whoever thinks of a slave child obeying his parent in preference to his master? The very suggestion is preposterous. Does the Bible sanction a system that abrogates its own injunctions...?

... Suppose, now, this system, all reeking with lust, incest, crime, and cruelty, is brought out and placed under the blaze of Christianity. Whatsoever ye would that men should do unto you, do ye even so unto them; for this is the law and the prophets. This is the condensed summary of the whole Bible. Who has the hardihood to say that the practice of slaveholding is consistent with this injunction? What, in the New Testament, is the classification of slaveholders? It places them with murderers of fathers and murderers of mothers....

... The Slavery Democracy prates and chatters about "negro equality" "Black Republicans" and "nigger stealing," to use its classic phrase and improved orthography. It has or affects to have, a great horror of "niggers." And any one who advocates the principles of human Freedom, as they were enunciated and laid down in enduring forms by the Fathers of the Republic, is a "woolly head," and these same Democrats have learned to speak of them with a peculiar nasal twist. *Naso contemnere adunco.* You would suppose that these gentlemen, whose olfactories are so sensitive and acute, never saw a nigger, unless in a menagerie. And yet, would you believe it! the very first service rendered him on earth is performed by a nigger; as an infant, he draws the milk which makes his flesh and blood and bones from the breast of a nigger; looks up in her face and smiles, and calls her by the endearing name of "mammy," (*Incipe parve puer. Cognoscere risu mairem.*) and begs, perhaps, in piteous tones, for the privilege of carrying "mammy" to the Territories; he is undressed and put to bed by a nigger, to eat food prepared by a nigger; every service that childhood demands is performed by a nigger, except that of chastisement which from the absence of good manners in many cases, it is to be feared is not performed at all. When he reaches manhood, he invades the nigger quarters, to place himself in the endearing relation of paternity to half nigger....

... And now, what about this negro equality of which we hear so much, in and out of Congress? It is claimed by the Democrats of to-day, that Jefferson has uttered an untruth in the declaration of principles which underlie our Government. I still abide by the Democracy of Jefferson, and avow my belief that all men are created equal. Equal how? Not in physical strength; not in symmetry of form and proportion; not in gracefulness of motion, or loveliness of feature; not in mental endowment, moral susceptibility, and emotional power; not socially equal; not of necessity politically equal — not this, but every human being equally entitled to his life, his liberty, and the fruit of his toil. The Democratic party deny this fundamental doctrine of our Government, and say that there is a certain class of human beings who have no rights. If you maliciously kill them, it is no murder; if you take away their liberty, it is no crime; if you deprive them of their earnings, it is no theft. No rights which another is bound to regard...!

Sir, I never will do this. I never will degrade my manhood, and stifle the sympathies of human nature. It is an insult to claim it. I wish I had nothing worse to meet at the judgment day than that. I would not have the guilt of causing that wail of man's despair, or that wild shriek of woman's agony, as the one or the other is captured, for all diadems of all the stars in heaven.

It is desired to call attention to this fact? Proclaim it then upon the house tops. Write it on every leaf that trembles in the forest, make it blaze from the sun at high noon, and shine forth in the milder radiance of every start that bedecks the firmament of God. Let it echo through all the arches of heaven, and reverberate and bellow along all the deep gorges of hell, where slave catchers will be very likely to hear it. Owen Lovejoy lives at Princeton, Illinois, three quarters of a mile east of the village, and he aids every fugitive that comes to his door and asks it. Thou invisible demon of Slavery, dost thou think to cross my humble threshold, and forbid me to give bread to the hungry and shelter to the houseless! I BID YOU DEFIANCE IN THE NAME OF MY GOD![18]

Lovejoy was not done with firey speeches to Congress. The following spring he became embroiled in a very lively affair on the House floor that H. C. Bradsby wrote of in his *History of Bureau County, Illinois*:

April 5, 1860, Mr. Lovejoy had the floor in the House of Congress, and commenced a speech on the subject of the state of the Union. It was the moment of the commencement of those turbulent times that climaxed in blood and war.... The scene in the halls of Congress on this occasion is probably without a parallel in history. He had talked but a few minutes, when Roger A. Pryor, of Virginia, rose up from the Democratic side of the House and menacingly approached Mr. Lovejoy, said, "You *shall not* come over to this side of the House and shake your fist in our faces — *you shall not.*" Many members were at once on their feet, one side demanding Lovejoy to speak from his seat; the other side vociferating he should speak — should not be intimidated. The Speaker was rapping for order, members much excited, many talking at the same time. Barksdale, of Mississippi, approached Lovejoy, called him a "black-hearted nigger thief and scoundrel," and from several were hurled all manner of epithets, as "perjurer," "nigger-thief," etc., etc. Confusion reigned supreme. The temporary Speaker called the Speaker to the chair and finally quiet was secured by Mr. Lovejoy leaving the area and delivering his speech from the clerk's desk. It seems there was a rule requiring each speaker to speak from his seat or the clerk's desk. Amid all this hubbub the only remark that escaped Mr. Lovejoy's lips was, "I cannot be intimidated." When quiet was restored he resumed from the clerk's desk. He hated slavery with the consuming, relentless hatred of an intense combative nature, and he was the supreme master of bitter, cutting taunts, which he flung into the faces of the Southern members with a serene and galling calmness. He told of a Presbyterian elder of Tennessee, taking his slave, "laying him down on his face on the ground, his hands and feet extended to their utmost tension and tied to pickets, and the Gospel whipped into him with the broad side of a handsaw, discolored whelks of sanctification being raised between the teeth every time this Gospel agency fell upon the naked and quivering flesh of the tortured convert." [Laughter]. Lovejoy resuming: "I swore to support the Constitution, because I believe it." Barksdale interrupting: "You stand there an infamous, perjured villain." [Calls to order.] Ashore, "Yes, he is a perjured villain; and he perjures himself every hour he occupies a seat on this floor." [Renewed calls to order.] Mr. Singleton: "And a negro-thief into the bargain." Lovejoy: "I do not believe in their construction of the Constitution." The speaker then proceeded at some length unmolested, in which he argued that the Constitution did not countenance slave-holding. Soon after he had finished this part of the address and was again pouring the vials of his wrath upon slave-holders on the confusion and interruptions were again on foot. He, when asked questions, only once so far noticed his questioners as to say: "I decline to yield to the floor." Toward the conclusion of his speech, however, he fired a parting salute at the fire-eating fellows who had so heaped upon him coarse epithets. "I did intend to taunt you about Harper's Ferry, but I believe I will not. I am willing to concede that you are as brave as other men, although I do not think you show it by this abusive language, *because brave men are always calm and self-possessed*. God feels no anger, for he knows no fear."

"Refuse or neglect this," [to abolish slavery]; "refuse to proclaim liberty through all the land, to all the inhabitants thereof, and the exodus of the slave will be through the *Red Sea*."[19]

In the summer of 1860, Owen Lovejoy gave the following firsthand account of having once helped a fugitive slave woman escape. The story was given during a speech he delivered in Greenup, Illinois, in Cumberland County. This part of Illinois, for the most part, was unsympathetic to abolitionists and when the account by Lovejoy was over, it left some in the audience angry; others were in tears:

On a plantation, in the distant Southland, in the low miasmatic swamps, there was a woman. She was young, handsome, and under God's law had as much right to live and control her own actions as any of us. She was of one-eighth African blood, just like your blood and mine. The overseer of the plantation where she was held in bondage sought to persecute her because she would not assent to his advances. She escaped into the swamps. Bloodhounds were set on her trail. She boarded a little steamboat which plied on a small river which emptied into the great Father of waters. In the fullness of time she landed at the first station in Illinois, name not given, and proceeded from station to station. Finally she arrived in Princeton. I myself was the keeper of that station at Princeton. She came to my house hungry and told me her story. She was fairer than my own daughter, proud, tall and beautiful. She was naked and I clothed her; she was hungry and I gave her bread; she was penniless and I gave her money. She was unable to reach the next station and I sent her to it. So from station to station she crossed the Northland far from baying dogs on her trail, and out from under the shadow of the flag we love and venerate, into Canada. Today she lives there a free and happy woman.[20]

Owen Lovejoy died on March 25, 1864. The invocation at his funeral was delivered by Henry Ward Beecher.[21] When Abraham Lincoln was informed of his death, the president remarked, "Lovejoy was the best friend I had in Congress."[22]

X

The Underground Railroad Moves on Steel

It is ironic that the single event that altered the way the Underground Railroad operated in western Illinois was the arrival of the real railroad. The development of railroads in Illinois was stymied for a variety of reasons but suffice it to say that by 1850 only 111 miles of track existed in the entire state.[1] In many other states the UGRR and real railroads functioned and grew simultaneously.[2] It is noteworthy that most of the language used by the Underground Railroad organizers in Illinois (stations, agents, conductors, superintendents, passengers, cargo, etc.) was being used by the region's legion of "operators" well before real trains were moving across the state. It is not difficult to imagine why escaped slaves were eager to hitch a ride on the steel if they had the opportunity. Runaways could reach safety much sooner this way instead of working their way to freedom county by county and hideout to hideout. Just as a trip by boat had always been more desirable than traveling on foot or by wagon, now fugitives hiding as stowaways on freight train cars were able to make even quicker and safer journeys to freedom. By 1860, over 2,800 miles of track had been put down across Illinois.[3]

With slavery legal in states both to the south and west of "its waterways, state roads and later its railroads, [Illinois] gave direct and well defined outlet to the Great Lakes and the borderlands of freedom beyond."[4] But S. J. Clarke's *History of McDonough County, Illinois* recounts a story of two runaways who, despite traveling by rail, nearly didn't make it out of Macomb, Illinois:

> On the morning of the thirty-first of December, 1862, two negro men were taken from the Eastern bound train of the C. B. & Q. R. R., at the depot in Macomb, by a citizen of this county, who claimed they were runaway slaves, and who felt it his duty or privilege to take them back and deliver them over to the gentle and fatherly care of their "master." Whether this man had ever heard of the emancipation procla-

149

'REINDEER' - 1853

The first steam engine to pull railroad cars through western Illinois was called the Reindeer. Runaways began escaping on trains in the mid–1850s following the construction of the CB&Q Railroad.

mation of President Lincoln or not we cannot say, but presume not, or if he had he regarded it as "unconstitutional," and therefore invalid. By returning them to their owner or owners he thought he would receive enough money to keep him in whisky and tobacco for some time. At this time the Eastern and Western bound trains connected at this point, and it was the design of this zealous fugitive slave law man to hurry the negroes on board the Western bound train and take them back. Luckily this train was a few minutes late. John Q. Lane was at that time the City Marshal, and happened to be at the depot, and the negroes made known to him their condition, stating they were traveling on a pass from their master, and that it had been taken from them by this advocate of the laws. Mr. Lane told them to get in the omnibus, and he would take care of them. By oaths and threats this was sought to be prevented, but the Marshal "didn't scare worth a cent." He took the negroes to the Randolph Hotel, where they were kept under guard that day and night. The party capturing them, inflamed by liquor, went to the hotel and demanded them of the landlord, the Hon. William H. Randolph, who then occupied that position. Mr. R., not liking the style of the gentleman, ordered him from the house, and accelerated his speed by a not very gentle kick. The man left, swearing vengeance. The negroes were held by friends until 12 o'clock at night, when they were informed that, agreeable to the proclamation of the President of the United States, they were free men, and could come and go as they pleased, being beholden to no man.[5]

In some cases abolitionists provided tickets and forged "free papers" to escapees which allowed them to travel in passenger cars. This was risky business, however, because one could never be sure when detectives and slave catchers might pass along the aisles looking for suspicious travelers. The need to travel by traditional secretive means in attempts to escape continued, of course, because locomotive travel was not available to all runaways.

In the midst of the Prairie State's railroad development, the Kansas-Nebraska Act was passed in 1854. Illinois senator Stephen A. Douglas[6] guided the legislation through Congress and it changed the nation abruptly. In effect, it cancelled that part of the Missouri Compromise that had prohibited slavery north of parallel 36°30', thereby opening up the possibility that slavery could be extended into the territories. Douglas, the northern Democrat, was courting southern Democrats in hopes of someday gaining the presidency; he designed a law that clearly served the interests of slaveholders. The law enraged abolitionists as well as many in the North who were less radical on the slavery issue. The chief political casualty was the Whig Party because out of the resulting turmoil northern Whigs, antislavery Democrats and Free-Soil Party loyalists, formed the Republican Party. The reaction against the Kansas-Nebraska Act in western Illinois's Knox County was strong and vocal. Anti-Nebraska meetings were held in Galesburg, Knoxville, and Victoria. In October 1854, Knox College president Jonathan Blanchard and Senator Douglas conducted a lively and spirited debate on the subject before a large crowd in Knoxville. Following President Blanchard's lead, scores of Galesburg antislavery advocates became Republicans and in 1856 John C. Fremont, the new party's first presidential candidate, won Knox County thanks to the Galesburg vote.[7] Clark E. Carr,[8] who spent most of his adult life as a key figure in Republican Party politics on both the state and national level, recalled the following in his book, *My Day and Generation*:

> Galesburg was the most enthusiastic Republican town in all that region. Most of the people were really abolitionists. One of the fundamental tenets of the founders of the town was earnest and eternal antagonism to human slavery. The town was known and recognized throughout the West, especially in the adjoining slave State of Missouri, as an "abolition hole." Even the slaves knew that if they could in a dash for liberty reach Galesburg, they would find a safe hiding-place where they would be cared for and concealed and protected and helped on in their flight to Canada, to the next "underground railway" station.[9]

The most immediate and startling effect of the Kansas-Nebraska Act was the violence that erupted shortly thereafter between antislavery and proslavery forces, in

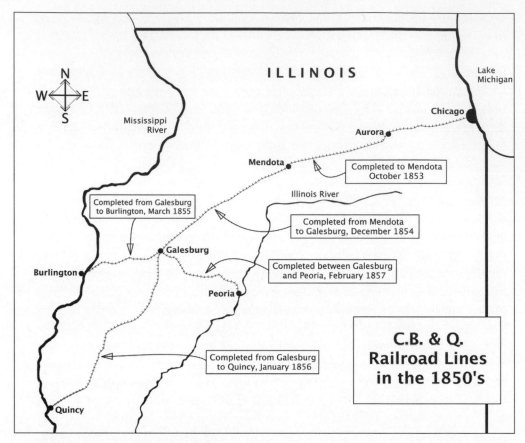

BRENDA PATTERSON, BG PATTERSON GRAPHICS.

what came to be known as "bleeding Kansas." On both sides, numerous people were injured and some 200 were killed.

The Chicago, Burlington and Quincy Railroad (CB&Q) profoundly changed western Illinois. It opened up the region to thousands of immigrants, radically increased its population and dramatically quickened its economic development. *The Monmouth Atlas* (Warren County) reported on March 9, 1855, that "the railroad is putting new life and activity into everyone. Business is going ahead rapidly ... all kinds of produce can now be turned into cash at high prices and if farmers do not get rich it will certainly be their own fault."[10] The railroads also brought industry into western Illinois and the character of the region was substantially altered. When Abraham Lincoln was elected president in 1860, Illinois ranked fourth among states in population and wealth.[11]

The CB&Q reached Mendota, in north central Illinois, by October 1853. It arrived in Galesburg in December 1854; was connected to Burlington, Iowa, in March of 1855; and extended to Quincy in January 1856. When tracks were completed west from Burlington to Ottumwa, Iowa, on the Des Moines River, September 1, 1859, a passenger could travel the 280 miles from there to Chicago in approximately 15 hours. In a letter to Wilbur Siebert, Emma Chapin,[12] who was well-informed about the UGRR in western Illinois, recalled that "after the railroad was built in 1855 he [a runaway] was smuggled on the train when it stopped at the water tank." In another correspondence to Siebert, W. C. Collins identified "Solomon Kimbell of Galesburg," as a train conductor employed by the railroad as having "extensive personal experience in hiding negros."[13] Chapman's *History of Knox County, Illinois* reports that "after the railroad was built from Chicago to Quincy in 1854–56 the refugees would get aboard freight trains at Quincy and go right through without much local help along the route."[14] The "Q" line, according to E. E. Calkins, "offered a new means of transportation, and companies of Negroes were sent through in freight cars, which eased the burden of the agents, and made pursuit even more difficult."[15] One method used to help smuggle runaways on board a freight train coming into Galesburg from the south was to place a lighted lamp in a designated window close to the tracks on the outskirts of town. When certain engineers saw this signal, they would slow the train to a snail's pace, allowing the fugitives to jump onboard before the locomotive resumed speed for the trip to Chicago.[16] John Conger wrote in the *History of the Illinois River Valley*, that "the Underground Railroad had a widespread following in the upper valley largely free from the southern influence. Its effectiveness was greatly increased when the Chicago, Burlington and Quincy, the Rock Island, and the Illinois Central Lines gave access to Canada by way of the Great Lakes."[17]

One of the first Galesburg men hired to work on the CB&Q Railroad was resident William Patch. A passenger train conductor, Patch was a member of the Congregational Church and a good friend of the Reverend Edward Beecher. On one occasion Patch helped put two fugitives, who had been hiding at Beecher's house, aboard a train heading north.[18]

According to H. C. Bradsby in his *History of Bureau County, Illinois*, Princeton "agent" John Bryant used the "Q" tracks to send fugitives toward Lake Michigan. "In 1854 he [John Bryant][19] had as many as fifteen runaway slaves on his place at one time. He aided all he could to reach Chicago, sending them in broad daylight over the Chicago, Burlington & Quincy Railroad to Dr. Dyer, of Chicago."[20] Dr. C. V. Dyer, a well-known Chicago UGRR agent, had been receiving fugitives at his home since the mid–1840s. "In 1846, for example, Dr. Dyer, a prominent physician, employed a fugitive slave from Kentucky in his house. When his master seized him, Dyer rescued the fugitive and beat off the Kentuckian with his cane."[21] Dyer later became president of the CB&Q Railroad, which helps to explain why many fugitive slaves were transported on that company's lines through Illinois.

An article that appeared in a 1934 supplement to the *Galesburg Post* discussed the importance of the CB&Q's extension south to Quincy to the operation of the UGRR in the Galesburg area. The author of the article identified as a "contributor" seems to have been remarkably familiar with the history of the black community in Galesburg. The writer referred to many early black settlers in the town, such as Joe Barquette [Joseph Barquet], Frank Gash, and Levi Henderson. The story confirmed that once steam-powered engines started passing through Galesburg the operation of the local Underground Railroad was substantially changed:

> This article is not intended as constituting at all a complete history, but in many of the essential parts it may recall some of the earlier colored people who lived in Galesburg, their position and some of their descendents.
>
> Galesburg was settled by pioneers from Oneida County, New York, who came here almost to a man and family thoroughly permeated with the anti-slavery sentiment. I have no authority for saying that any colored residents came earlier than 1850, though the college was then thoroughly established here and was about to graduate its first class, but the underground railroad was then beginning its more active operations and Galesburg was one of the well-known stations along that travel.
>
> In all probability even prior to the underground railroad, colored people undoubtedly drifted here finding a welcome amongst the earlier settlers. But the main source of operation, as I think it is generally understood, was by means of the railroad when the extension was made of what is now the Burlington, as far south as Quincy, Illinois. Its then Superintendent was generally believed to have been the moving cause of a great many colored refugees from Missouri, especially in the neighborhood of Palmyra and Hannibal.
>
> The Negro was to very many of the early settlers entirely unknown, many of them never even having seen one.[22]

Even if an absconder could not get on board a train, he or she could follow the silver ribbon of track line on foot. Either the CB&Q or the Illinois Central (ICRR), incorporated in 1851 through central Illinois, would have provided a route all the way to Chicago. The ICRR was completed from Cairo at the southern tip of Illinois, to Chicago and from Centralia to east Dubuque, Illinois, by 1856. According to Siebert, the Illinois Central was an important escape route for fugitive slaves. Glennette Turner in *The Underground Railroad in Illinois* identifies George L. Burroughs as a free black who worked as a porter on the ICRR. This was an ideal job for someone helping to keep runaways out of sight between the Ohio River and Chicago. She also discussed other underground activists in southern Illinois who sent slaves north on the real railroad:

> James Wilson continued his UGRR work when he moved from Sparta to Centralia. After the I.C. was built in 1854, he and George McGee and several I.C. employees used the railroad to "do the work of the UGRR." An I.C. freight conductor, Larry Wiggins, would unlock the boxcars at night and hide UGRR passengers with

enough food to last until the train reached Chicago. One or two coach conductors also cooperated by "forgetting" to collect tickets from any UGRR passengers.[23]

In 1855, slave owner Thomas Rodney, of Mississippi County, Missouri, determined that an employee of the ICRR had given a train ticket to one of his slaves. After Rodney tracked the fugitive to Chicago, he discovered that abolitionists there had the former slave sequestered beyond his reach. Two years later, a Missouri slave who had enjoyed passage on the Illinois Central, was the key figure in a suit brought before the Illinois Supreme Court by his punitive owner against the railroad. The Illinois high court ruled in favor of the ICRR.[24]

On April 5, 1861, an announcement appeared in the Chicago *Journal*, an antislavery newspaper, advising blacks in the city who did not have certificates of freedom to "make tracks for Canada." Information had reached the Chicago black community suggesting that waves of federal marshals were about to sweep through Chicago and other northern cities, looking for escaped slaves. Four railroad freight cars were chartered to carry fugitives to an embankment point on Lake Michigan. The *Journal* gave this account of the departure scene:[25]

> All day, yesterday, the vicinity of the Michigan Southern depot was a scene of excitement and confusion. After the religious services at the Zoar Baptist Church in the morning, which was densely attended, the leave-taking commenced ... the fugitives and their friends, going from door to door, bidding each other good-bye and mingling their congratulations and tears....
>
> ... As the hour of departure ... drew night, the streets adjacent to the depot and the immediate vicinity of the four cars ... were thronged with an excited multitude of colored people of both sexes and all ages. Large numbers of white people also gathered from motives of curiosity, and stood silent spectators of this rather unusual spectacle. The four cars were rapidly filled with the fugitives, numbering one hundred and six in all, and embracing men, women, youth and infants....
>
> ... After all were aboard, ... the immense crowd pressed up to the cars and commenced the last farewell.... Here and there was one in tears and wringing the hands, but the majority were in the best of humor, and were congratulated by their friends lingering behind, that tomorrow they would be free....
>
> ... The larger proportion of the fugitives were stout, able bodied young men, many of them well dressed and some of them almost white.... The elder ones evinced no levity but acted like those who had been hardened by troubles, and were now suffering a lot foreseen and prepared for....
>
> ... But all were finally stowed away, the bell of the engine sounded and the train started and amid lusty cheers, many-voiced good-byes and the waving of hats and handkerchiefs as far as the eye could see. The fugitives heartily responded and the train vanished in the distance....
>
> About one thousand fugitives have arrived in this city since last fall, a large number of whom have left within the past few days.[26]

The number of fugitive slaves who actually passed along the western Illinois Underground chain or throughout the entire state, no matter what means of escape was used, will never be known. There is little doubt that following the passage of the Compromise of 1850 the traffic increased significantly.[27] In her previously mentioned 1917 article on the Illinois UGRR, Verna Cooley addressed the question of how many runaway slaves actually passed through the Prairie State:

> From 1850 to 1860 was the period of the road's greatest activity, accelerated by the Fugitive Slave Law of 1850.[28] The reaction of the conductors toward this law was that of defiance, hence they displayed added zeal in aiding fugitives. After the signing of the bill, a storm broke over the North with violence, political conventions, abolition meetings, and religious organizations poured forth a deluge of resolutions and petitions against the law. The *Western Citizen* printed a petition for the repeal of the bill to be cut from the paper and circulated throughout the State. It was asserted that scarcely a man could be found who would not sign it. The colored people of Chicago saw that if this law were enforced no colored person in the United States would be free from liability to slavery, hence they considered it expedient to appoint a vigilance committee to watch for attempts at kidnapping....
>
> ... The problem became so grave for Missourians that in 1857, the General Assembly, by joint resolutions, instructed the Missourian representative in Congress to demand of the Federal Government the securing of their property as guaranteed by the Constitution, and in particular against the action of certain citizens of Chicago who had aided fugitives to escape and had hindered and mistreated Missouri citizens in search of their slaves. In 1859 the *Western Citizen* made the following estimate of the activity of the Underground Railroad, rather extravagantly phrased, but nevertheless indicating the degree of boldness with which they advertised it. "The road is doing better business this fall than usual. The Fugitive Slave Law has given it more vitality, more activity, more passengers, and more opposition, which invariably accelerates business. We can run a lot of slaves through from almost any part of the bordering states in Canada within forth-eight hours and we defy the slave holder to beat that if they can."
>
> These reports of the activity of the Underground Railroad mean nothing if one does not know how many fugitives were actually aided. It was no doubt a tendency of these people who harbored and secreted the slave, under the spell of danger and adventure, to exaggerate the extent of their secret undertaking. However, when numbers are given, with due allowance for over estimation, one can see concretely the degree of the road's activity. The entire number of fugitives who escaped annually from the South has been roughly estimated at two thousand. Reports of numbers transported on the Underground Railroad through Illinois tends to substantiate this estimate. When one considers the number of termini from the East to Iowa and that each aided fully as many as Chicago, it is not difficult to account for the two thousand. Take, for example, some numbers given in 1854 by the *Western Citizen*. Fifteen fugitives in the fore part of one week arrived in Chicago by the Underground Railroad. December 16, 1854, it was reported that since May 6, 1854, four hundred eight-two were taken by the Underground Railroad across to Canada from Detroit. As many as twenty at a time were said to have left Chicago for Canada and freedom. The largest number found in this year was given for the three months ending September 1, 1854, one hundred "Seventy"-six passengers, and for the three months ending December 1, one hundred twenty-four, which made a total of three hundred for six months.[29]

X. The Underground Railroad Moves on Steel

The flight to freedom above ground or under ground did not end with the beginning of the Civil War. The Emancipation Proclamation, announced by President Lincoln after the North had finally achieved a major victory in the eastern theater of the war at Antietam (Sharpsburg) officially took effect on January 1, 1863. Lincoln's proclamation freed only "persons held as slaves within any state or designated part of a state, the people whereof shall then be in rebellion against the United States." Therefore slaves in most of Missouri and Kentucky were not free and consequently many of them continued to flee. Ira Berlin and Leslie S. Rowland write in *Families and Freedom*:

> The Emancipation Proclamation had no bearing on the slave states that had remained in the Union — Delaware, Maryland, Kentucky, and Missouri. Slavery retained full standing within their bounds. Although military activity at times created opportunities for slaves to escape their bondage, official policy dictated support for the slaveholders' authority.[30]

Even blacks that had been freed by the Emancipation Proclamation found themselves vulnerable if they chose to travel across a border state like Kentucky where slavery remained, for the most part, legal:

> Hundreds of former slaves from the seceded states forfeited their newly won freedom when they tried to travel northward through Kentucky, where slavery remained intact. Even freed people with protection papers from high-ranking military officers were halted at the Ohio River under state laws forbidding public conveyances to transport slaves without their owners' consent. State and local officials arrested the freed people as fugitive slaves, advertised for their masters, and sold them to new owners when no one registered a claim. They had escaped slavery in the Confederacy only to be re-enslaved in the Union.[31]

Black population in safe towns within the three rivers, like Galesburg, continued to grow rapidly after 1863.[32] But animosities toward blacks, fugitives or not, was so strong outside Galesburg in the spring of 1863 that the mayor of the city wrote a letter expressing his concerns to General Jacob Ammen, who was based in the state capitol. The correspondence confirms the wide gulf in attitudes between the residents of Galesburg and citizens living in the outlying rural communities. It was nearly as vast as it had been over 25 years earlier, when George Washington Gale established his college town:

> I understand from the papers that you have charge of military matters in this State. Such being the fact, I wish to hear from you how to proceed to exterminate the rebels in this part of Illinois. In parts of this County, Negroes are not allowed to work for respectable farmers: Meetings are openly held denouncing the War and proposing opposition to any draft. Cheers open and loud for Jeff Davis. Is there any remedy? Please let me hear from you in regard to this matter.
>
> J.F. Dunn, Mayor
April 25, 1863
Galesburg, Illinois[33]

A short newspaper article appearing in the *Quincy Whig Republican* that same spring illustrated the extent to which blacks could count on the city's judicial authorities to protect them from abuse and attack. The newspaper headline reads "Mob Spirit at Galesburg":

> A drunken white Copperhead named Waddell assaulted a sober darkey at Galesburg the other day, whose name (unfortunately for the nigger) was Dick Richardson, an ostler in a livery stable. After receiving one blow and a great many choice Democratic epithets, and a second blow being on the way, Dick rallied and knocked Waddell down. The latter then entered a complaint in Court, and on hearing the case, the justice decided, "Served him right."[34]

The black population of Galesburg had grown to well over 600 by 1870 from just under 100 in 1860. The account of James O. Washington, an 87-year-old former slave, provides firsthand evidence of this startling influx. Washington, whose mother was a slave on a small farm and whose father lived on a nearby plantation, was born in Mason County, Kentucky, in 1853. He gave this account of why he and his family came to Galesburg and his story confirms connections that had existed for many years between the city's free blacks and slaves in border states:

> After Mr. Lincoln freed us slaves and our masters let us go, my mother, father, and nine brothers and sisters and I started on the road to Galesburg, in an old covered wagon. There were two particular families of colored folks living here [in] Galesburg then — that had been writin us for several years to get us to come here to Galesburg. They'd run away several years before.[35]

E. E. Calkins, commenting on this increased passage of blacks into Galesburg and other western Illinois towns, wrote:

> One result to Galesburg and other cities similarly involved was to give them a colored population above the average in quality. As has been seen, some of the runaways remained, and others came back, and with the beginning of the Civil War the accession increased ... there were many references to the "contrabands" in old letters from Galesburg to Friends in the East.[36]

Along with Joseph Barquet and his Galesburg recruits in the 54th Massachusetts, thousands of other men and women left western Illinois to help the Union during the Civil War. Fountain Watkins, who was from Peoria County and known as the laughing abolitionist, had two sons die in the Union army while fighting in the western theater of the war. William J. Phelps, owner of the Phelps Barn signal station, saw his son, William E., appointed minister to Russia in 1862. John Buford, from Rock Island County, studied briefly at Knox College, later graduated from West Point and he went on to become one of the heroes at the Battle of Gettysburg. Henry Clay Work, the son of Quincy's Alanson Work, who spent over three years in the Missouri state penitentiary for trying to help slaves escape, grew up to become a composer. He wrote, among other songs, "Marching Thro' Georgia." Mary Ann "Mother" Bickerdyke was a renowned Civil War nurse from Galesburg of whom General William T. Sherman supposedly said, "She outranks me." Julian Bryant, the son of Arthur Bryant and nephew of John and Cyrus, all three of whom had worked in the Bureau County Underground Railroad network, accepted an appointment in 1863 as major of the newly organized First Mississippi Infantry, a black unit. In the graveyards of western Illinois one can find numerous stone markers with the names of Union soldiers who did not return to the Prairie State alive.

The Civil War finally ended with the collapse of Confederate armies across the south in the spring of 1865. The passage of the Thirteenth Amendment, which abolished slavery, and was ratified on December 18, 1865,[37] finally ended forever the great exodus of fugitive slaves to freedom, however tenuous, in the north including the prairie lands of Illinois. The United States of America had struggled with the slavery question from its inception. Abigail Adams described the crux of the dilemma that would face the nation for decades when she wrote to her husband John during the early days of the republic: "It always seemed a most iniquitous scheme to me—[to] fight ourselves for what we are daily robbing and plundering from those who have as good a right to freedom as we have."[38] From the passage of the Fugitive Slave Law in 1793, to the Missouri Compromise,[39] the Mexican War,[40] the Compromise of 1850 and finally the Dred Scott[41] decision, the nation tried to deal with this issue in various ways; all were in vain. In the meantime the United States had become the "Mecca of slavery."[42] These political strategies only bought time until the deep differences separating Americans on this issue were finally resolved by the ravages of war. For slightly more than fourscore years a very distinct way of life had evolved in the South, a region that particularly prized the status quo. The very existence of the southern master/slave society was at stake. During the 30 or 40 years prior to the Civil War, the Southern strategy was to maintain legislative strength against abolitionists and the more aggressive activities of the Underground Railroad. As a result, the existence of slavery did not allow the nation to ever truly embrace the principles of liberty and justice for all until the institution was finally abolished. The wedge that slavery drove between Americans was so fundamental, and the damage done to blacks so profound and pervasive that the "race question" remains one of the most significant domestic issues in the nation.

If the Civil War was America's great epic adventure, then surely its companion saga was the story of runaway slaves and the committed black and white antislavery activists, who helped them. The Civil War is rich in documentation, as is the political ferment surrounding slavery from which the war arose. Less well documented is the dramatic and inspiring era in our history which was the operation of the Underground Railroad. When the war was over, one of our nation's most clandestine and secretive dramatic chapters closed and its true story was only really known by a handful of its participants.

Notes

Chapter I

1. The Big Dipper's pointer stars Merak and Dubhe show the way to Polaris, located at the tip of the Little Dipper's handle.

2. Turner, *The Underground Railroad in Illinois*, 50, 56.

3. "I knew how to kill the scent of dogs when they came after me: I could do it with red pepper. Another way which I have practiced is, to dig into a grave where a man had been buried a long time, get the dust of the man, make it into a paste with water, and put it on the feet, knees, and elbows, or whatever I touched the bushes. The dog won't follow that." Account of ex-slave John Warren (Drew, *The North-Side View of Slavery*, 186).

4. Turner, *The Underground Railroad in Illinois*, 54.

5. Although there is not definitive proof that the "Phelps Barn" was used as a UGRR signal station there is strong evidence: (1) oral history about the barn passed down over generations of Elmwood residents; (2) William J. Phelps was a known antislavery advocate; (3) the barn's close proximity to other Underground Railroad operators familiar with Phelps; (4) the fact that Phelps was made a trustee of Knox College by President Jonathan Blanchard, an outspoken abolitionist and UGRR operator, who only appointed men to the board who shared his antislavery attitudes; (5) a speech delivered after the Civil War by William J. Phelps's youngest

son describing how he had once, as a boy, while alone one day on the family farm, helped a fugitive escape; and (6) the existence of the carved cross shape.

6. The Underground Railroad headed in every direction out of southern states — across the Caribbean Sea and along the Atlantic sea coast. It extended as far west as California, traveled into Mexico, passed over the ocean to Europe and Africa and moved through every northern state toward Canada. Some slaves, who were taken on trips abroad by their owners, chose to escape after they arrived in foreign lands.

7. In southeastern Iowa, UGRR operator Dr. Edwin Janes, who feared that bounty hunters might be waiting at the bridge over the Skunk River between Denmark and Augusta, reputedly used cider barrels to float fugitives across the river at an isolated location.

8. The Underground Railroad borrowed the language of real railroad terminology. "Operators" and "agents" maintained hiding places called "stations," for runaways. "Conductors," "carriers" and "brakemen" actually moved fugitive "passengers" or "cargo" but in numerous cases these roles were interchangeable.

9. Gara, "The Underground Railroad in Illinois," 519.

10. Letter from Emma M. Chapin to Wilbur Siebert, January 11, 1896.

11. In the Hannibal, Missouri, area, across

the Mississippi River from Illinois, free blacks were the only ones helping to make arrangements for runaways to escape. Delphia Quarles, a free black woman in Hannibal, was an operator and, in addition, was a mail courier for the UGRR. Quarles was identified and warned in the Hannibal press in 1857 as a "certain free woman in that city ... who has received several letters from fugitive slaves in Chicago and has slyly distributed them among the slaves of Miller Township" (Dempsey, "Heroes, Previously Unnamed, Played an Important Role in our History"). Quarles left the area shortly thereafter.

12. Berlin, *Generations of Captivity*, 244.

13. *Galesburg Evening Mail*, June 19, 1909.

14. Franklin and Schweninger, *Runaway Slaves*, 224.

15. Ibid., 225.

16. Ibid.

17. This water giant of the Prairie State starts where the Des Plaines River and Kankakee River meet and is fed by such prominent rivers along its course as the DuPage, Fox, Vermillion, Spoon, and Sangamon. The Illinois River and its tributaries drain over 40 percent of all the water that falls upon the state.

18. A steady stream of escaped slaves passed through the southeastern most part of Iowa from northeast and northern Missouri. Another significant route moved fugitives over a bow-shaped line starting in the southwest corner of Iowa, arching through the state's central counties and finally peeling off in several directions toward stops on the Mississippi River or north to Wisconsin and Minnesota.

19. To a limited degree, tall grass prairies existed in Ohio, Indiana, and Wisconsin; tall grasses also thrived in western and northern Minnesota.

20. "In the prairie country occasional stands of trees rose like islands from the grassland. Here the word 'grove' came into use ... each season the appearance of the grassland changed for over its long swales and swells the prairie wore a coat of many colors" (Havighurst, *Land of Promise*, 5).

21. The primary species found there were deer, wolves, foxes, prairie chickens, wild turkeys, squirrels, rabbits, quail, grouse, rac-

coons, opossums, and various large snakes including rattlesnakes.

22. Turner, *The Underground Railroad in Illinois*, 57.

23. Nelson, *Illinois*, 87.

24. A precise definition of the term "Underground Railroad" is difficult to state, but for the purpose of understanding it in west central Illinois it should include those individuals who only occasionally gave aid and comfort to fugitive slaves in addition to those whose help was more frequent.

25. Blockson, *The Underground Railroad*, 201.

26. In a speech celebrating and recalling the establishment of the United Presbyterian Church of Somonauk, Illinois (DeKalb County), in the previous century, Dr. O. L. Schmidt, president of the Chicago Historical Society described Illinois UGRR "routes" as follows: "To ask for a map of the Underground Railroad is to ask for a map of the routes by which the wily fox evades the hounds. Circumstances and close local knowledge determined them" (Schmidt, "Somonauk United Presbyterian Church," 708).

27. This is *not* to suggest there was not Underground Railroad activity in St. Louis. In fact, the city had a well-organized UGRR network. Among the leading Underground figures in Missouri's largest river city were John Berry Meachum, a former slave who became a successful businessman and educator; Mary Meachum, who jeopardized her own life helping runaways escape; the Reverend Artemus Bullard, who built and operated "Rock House"; and Moses Dixon, a free black who led a group of UGRR sympathizers called the Knights of Liberty. By 1860, there were 3,572 free blacks living in Missouri and approximately one-half of them lived in St. Louis. The city of St. Louis experienced a population explosion after the War of 1812 and grew into one of the largest river ports in the United States. The Missouri River empties into the Mississippi just above St. Louis and the city became a commercial giant with river traffic running north and south while railroad lines spread from the transportation center in every direction.

28. Calhoun County is stretched narrowly

between the Illinois River and the Mississippi River at the southern tip of the three rivers triangle. Hamilton (*History of Jersey County, Illinois*, 188–89) offers this account of a free black who came into the county looking for a stolen horse: "Under this arrangement George [Washington] was sent to Calhoun County, where the public sentiment was very strong against the colored from the slave state of Missouri. Many slaves from that state, from time to time crossed the river, and thence found their way to the 'underground railroad,' and through that means reached Canada. But woe to the colored man or woman, whether fugitive slave or not, that fell into the hands of the people of that county. If they could be kidnapped or smuggled across the river, regardless of law or justice, they were sure of a trip to the cotton fields of the south, where a man like George [Washington] was worth at least $2,000.00. George [Washington] was arrested by these people as a runaway 'nigger,' and put in the jail at Gilead, then the county seat of that county. This jail was constructed of large logs, hewed square and laid on top of each other, dowelled together with wooden pins. The sides, bottom and top were made of the same kind of timbers, the only means of entry was a hole in the top of a ladder. George [Washington] had been in this jail for a day or two, when Clarence M. Hamilton, being then in business in Gilead, hearing there was a runaway 'nigger' in jail, went up to take a look at him, and then made the discovery that it was George [Washington], with whom he was well acquainted, and he thereupon took the necessary steps to secure his release. This was a very narrow escape for George [Washington], and he never ventured into that county again."

29. Horton and Horton, *Hard Road to Freedom*, 142.

30. The Alton Underground Railroad was dominated by blacks with Priscilla Baltimore, a particularly well-remembered operator. The contributions of Charles Hunter, a white abolitionist, were also very significant.

31. John Hossack, a Scottish immigrant who lived in a magnificent Greek Revival house, was the most actively involved UGRR agent in Ottawa.

32. Some of the key figures associated with the Chicago Underground Railroad were Emma Jane Atkinson, Henry Bradford, Philo Carpenter, Calvin DeWolf, Dr. C. V. Dyer, Mary Dyer, Zebina Eastman, Barney Ford, Louis Isbell, John and Mary Jones, Sylvester Lind, J. E. Roy, and Henry Wagoner. Chicago was far and away the leading Underground Railroad center in Illinois. It was the city where most UGRR activists lived, where the largest number of stations existed, and it was the safest place, other than Canada, for fugitives to stay.

33. In this region the Covenanter Church harbored fugitives and in 1851 a gang of slave trackers from New Madrid County, Missouri, headed toward Sparta for an escaped slave, but they encountered armed abolitionists and fell back across the Mississippi River without the runaway.

34. Macy, *The Anti-Slavery Crusade*, 126.

35. Franklin and Schweninger, *Runaway Slaves*, 23.

36. "Added to the slave's fear of the lash was the dread of being separated from loved ones. To be sold away from his relatives or stand by and see a mother, a sister, a brother, a wife, or a child torn away from him was easily the most traumatic event of his life" (Blassingame, *The Slave Community*, 297).

37. Bartlett, "How Did Uncle Joe Get Home?"

38. In Missouri a slave found guilty of bartering, selling or delivering liquor to another slave was commonly punished with 25 lashes and occasionally put in jail.

39. "Lying out" or "laying over" referred to slaves who only temporarily left their owners for a variety of reasons before returning to their masters. But for some slaves a lay over was good experience for it allowed them the opportunity to practice before running away for good.

40. Franklin and Schweninger, *Runaway Slaves*, 23.

41. "Throughout the entire antebellum period [1830–1860], the number of blacks in the area [counties Adams, Calhoun, Fulton, Hancock, Knox, Peoria, Pike, Schuyler, Warren, Brown, Henderson, McDonough, Marshall, and Stark] never quite reached four-tenths of one percent of the total population"

(Bridges, "Dark Faces on the Antebellum West Central Illinois Landscape," 67).

42. "For a master the return of a fugitive slave was a matter of dollars — lots of them. Slaves, worth between $500 and $1,200, were extremely valuable possessions; but also at stake was an issue of constitutional right. Masters often spent more than a slave was worth to assert their rights as slave owners under the Constitution" (Finkelman, "Slavery, the 'More Perfect Union,' and the Prairie State," 261).

43. Letter from Emma A. Chapin to Wilbur Siebert on January 11, 1896, found in two reels of microfilm, Illinois Historical Society, Springfield, Illinois.

44. Patten and Graham, *History of the Somonauk United Presbyterian Church*, 59–60.

45. Merkel, "The Underground Railroad and the Missouri Borders, 1840–1860," 274.

46. Source: Terry Swails, meteorologist, KWQC, Davenport, Iowa.

47. In Maryland, for instance, free blacks increased by 350 percent from 1755 to 1790. In 1782 Virginia made it legal for private citizens to free their slaves. By 1790, 4 percent of that state's black population was free.

48. The death rate of slaves in the United States was high. Therefore slave owners often required slaves to have children and this *enforced breeding* often resulted in a female slave having four or five children by the time she was 20 years old. Hannah Jones, an ex-slave born in Cape Girardeau, Missouri, left this record of slave breeding: "Ben Oil had 100 niggers. He just raised niggers on his plantation. His brother-in-law, John Cross raised niggers, too. He had 125 niggers. He had a nigger farm. His other brother-in-law we call old man English, had 100 niggers. Dey all jes' had nothin' else but niggers" (White, "Bred Slaves Like Stock").

49. McPherson, *Battle Cry of Freedom*, 89–90.

50. Macy, *The Anti-Slavery Crusade*, 46–47.

51. By the early 1840s the American Anti-Slavery Society had become so fragmented and embroiled in competitive feuds that it finally dissolved. But for a significant period of time it provided crucial leadership, important organizational structure and a networking membership that was central to the antislavery movement.

52. The city and college, started by the same people, were established in 1837. This was only five years after the region was considered "safer" for settlers because Native Americans had nearly all been driven from the state following the conclusion of the Black Hawk War of 1832. Black Hawk had, years earlier, been part of Tecumseh's failed collective resistance to Euro-American westward expansion. In 1832, Black Hawk led a small band of Native Americans which included his Sauks, with some Fox, Winnebago, and Kickapoo allies, against the state and federal governments. They were pursued from Illinois into Wisconsin and destroyed at the Battle of the Bad Axe River. Among those who chased Black Hawk down were Abraham Lincoln, Jefferson Davis, and Winfield Scott. The Kickapoo were probably the last to be forced out of Illinois, though some Sauk, Fox and Pottawatomies lingered in the area.

53. George Churchill, who is regarded as the founder of Galesburg public schools, wrote this in *Galesburg History*, published as two articles in the *Galesburg Republican-Register*, July 29 and August 5, 1876: "Her citizens [Galesburg] would be true to her Puritan blood, and their oft expressed anti-slavery sentiments and to their country one and inseparable. The first and chief constructive undertaking of the colonists was to build up a Christian college; their first and chief destructive one, the overthrow of slavery; hence arose many contests between the colonists and the people of the surrounding country, who, many of them being from the Southern States, were defenders of slavery — and of the black laws of the State forbidding all aid to fugitives from slavery. A branch of the famous 'underground railroad' ran through Galesburg and had a depot here, and it is generally believed that the road did a paying business in furnishing dark colored citizens to our Canadian neighbor, while it certainly involved some of the Galesburgers in troublesome law suits and attendant damages. Very few sympathizers did the Mexican War find in this locality — for it favored too much of the advantage to the 'divine institution'; but when the 'Kansas troubles' broke out, the Free State men of

Kansas received the hearty sympathy and aid not only of Galesburg, but of Knox County, for to Galesburg and Knox County belongs the honor of sending the first carload of provisions and supplies to the sufferers there, and not one carload only went there, but very many followed, and that as long as there was need of outside help."

54. *Galesburg Evening Mail*, February 1, 1890.

55. "Galesburg is a flourishing city of about eleven thousand inhabitants. It is situated in a beautiful and healthful section of country known as the 'Military Tract,' and is about midway from the Mississippi and Illinois rivers.... This colony was strongly anti-slavery, which character has been well sustained to the present time, thus preparing the way for their patriotic and efficient efforts in various ways for the great Rebellion caused by slavery" (*Annewalt & Lawrence's 1867 Galesburg Directory*, 13).

56. Lovejoy's *Extra* said, in part, that "The slavery question in this country, and especially in this state, is of commanding interest to us all. No question at the present time, exerting so strong an influence upon the public mind.... The whole land is agitated by it.... It is earnestly to be hoped that there will be a full attendance at the Convention. Let all who feel deeply interested in this cause, not only attend themselves, but stir up their neighbors to attend.... Take away the right to free discussion — the right under the laws, freely to utter and publish such sentiments as duty to God and fulfillment of a good conscience may require, and we have nothing left to struggle for."

57. George Avery, a deacon of the First Church, lived and farmed on the "Monmouth Road" west of Galesburg and was a local UGRR "shepherd." Shortly after Avery arrived in Knox County, he was asked by the widow of one Colonel Mills to take responsibility for a 12-year-old-black child who the Mills had brought from New York to Illinois. Avery agreed to take care of the boy but was required to pay taxes on him, like chattel. Avery contacted authorities in New York who, in turn, sent "free papers" eliminating the tax.

58. Edward Beecher came to Galesburg to become the minister of the First Congregational Church in 1855. He was formerly president of Illinois College in Jacksonville, had been closely associated with E. P. Lovejoy, and his reputation as an unflinching abolitionist preceded his arrival in Galesburg.

59. Jonathan Blanchard was educated at Middlebury College and the Lane Seminary in Cincinnati. He left Ohio in 1846 to become the second president of Knox College. Immediately prior to his arrival in Illinois he had received nation-wide attention in the "Queen City" following a four-day debate with N. L. Rice on the "sin of slavery." In 1860 Blanchard became the president of Wheaton College in northern Illinois.

60. Hirim Mars was an early resident of Galesburg who knew Samuel Hitchcock personally. Mars gave a speech to the Knox County Historical Society in 1909 where he recalled hearing Hitchcock himself detail a story describing an unusual way ex-slaves were transported out of Galesburg on a night passage: "He said one night there was a knock on the door ... and there stood four passengers for the trip. [He spread] straw over the bottom of the wagon bed, put two of his passengers with their heads to the rear in and two with their heads to the front, then piled over them a lot of sacks filled with straw and chaff to represent a load of grain that he was on the way to Chicago to market, as was frequently the custom in those days. He delivered his passengers safely to the next station, turned them over to the next conductor, and returned home before daylight, as it was the custom not to go farther than they could return within that time, thus avoiding suspicion."

61. Siebert, *The Underground Railroad from Slavery to Freedom*, 405; Muelder, *Fighters for Freedom*, chapters 7, 17; Boyes and Jelliff, *Annals of Knox County*, 173, 175; Calkins, *They Broke the Prairie*, 221–29.

62. Berry and Blassingame, *Long Memory*, 61.

63. They were mostly from upper state New York. "These folks were so susceptible to religious revivals and Pentecostal beliefs that their region was called 'The Burned Over-District'" (Morison, *The Oxford History of the American*

People, 517). The town's founder, George Washington Gale, was born in Dutchess County, New York, in 1789. He experienced a "peculiar emotional experience known as conversion" and "received a divine message ... from that time, consciously or unconsciously, his sole concern was religion, his sole preoccupation saving souls" (Calkins, *They Broke the Prairie*, 37–38). Gale was licensed to preach by the Hudson Presbytery in September 1816 and was the mentor of the famous revivalist preacher Charles Grandison Finney. In New York, Finney enjoyed remarkable success as a revivalist and his captivating fire and damnation delivery swayed thousands of converts. This spellbinding style was popular with many Americans during the Second Great Awakening. In 1837 Finney joined the faculty of the widely known Ohio abolitionist school Oberlin College and he served as the president of that institution from 1851 to 1866.

64. Harris, *The History of Negro Servitude in Illinois*, 142.

65. In 1775, the Quakers formed the first antislavery society in Philadelphia.

66. John J. Miter lived among the Hoosier residents of Knoxville for a brief time and was one of Theodore Weld's famous "Seventy."

67. Chambers, *Reminiscences of Early Days*, 6–7.

68. One remarkable 19th-century alumnus of the Galesburg college was Hiram Rhoades Revels. In the annals of the United States Senate, there have been few moments more dramatic than the day in 1870 when Revels took the oath as United States Senator from the state of Mississippi. By so doing, he filled the seat previously held by Confederate president Jefferson Davis. Revels was born in North Carolina and had been educated at the Knox College Academy in the late 1850s. In the Library of Congress a brief writing of Revels mentions his efforts to aid runaway slaves: "When in free states, I always assisted the fugitive slave to make his escape." According to James and Lois Horton in *Hard Road to Freedom*, Pennsylvania senator Simon Cameron said that he had warned Jefferson Davis that "a negro someday will come and occupy your seat." That "negro" was Hiram R. Revels who went on to become

president of two black colleges, Alcorn A&M and Mississippi State College for Negroes.

69. Muelder, *Fighters for Freedom*, 191.

70. According to Angle and Beyer (*Handbook of Illinois History*, 29), Philippe Francis Renault was responsible for bringing the first slaves to Illinois in 1720. Renault was director of mines for the Company of the West. This venture eventually failed but slavery remained in Illinois thereafter.

71. These black laws did not stop black migration into Illinois. "Between 1820 and 1860 the Prairie State's total black population increased by more than 500 percent, from 1,374 to 7,628. In 1850 half the blacks recorded by the census were born outside the state. In the decade from 1850 to 1860 the Illinois black population increased by over two thousand — a 40 percent jump" (Finkelman, "Slavery, the 'More Perfect Union,' and the Prairie State," 257–58).

72. Dr. O. L. Schmidt, president of the Chicago Historical Society, noted in his 1925 speech that "as different as day and night were the little Puritan communities of northern Illinois ... these men had a Puritan passion for remaking the world as they thought God willed it to be." But Schmidt also believed that the operators enjoyed "the thrill of outwitting and escaping pursuers" (Schmidt, "Somonauk United Presbyterian Church," 706).

73. Chambers, *Reminiscences of Early Days*, 7.

74. Bobrick, *Testament: A Soldier's Story of the Civil War*, 16.

75. Gara is absolutely right in regard to blacks *not* being given proper credit for their important Underground Railroad activism in Illinois: "While some abolitionists seemed to find work in the underground railroad merely an exciting diversion, Negroes in Illinois took a more sober view of the events relating to its operations. Free Negroes were often involved in fugitive rescues, and frequently such rescues were reported in the press as the activity of a 'Negro mob.' Both the free Negroes and fugitive slaves had a more vital and personal interest in the fugitive question than the abolitionists, who viewed it partly as an indirect method of attacking the institution of slavery.... In retro-

spect, the role of the Negro is frequently neglected in discussions of the underground railroad. Those who lived in the pre–Civil War period, however, did not overlook the Negro's contribution. The presence of free Negroes in slave states was sometimes considered to be an open invitation to slaves to escape. From time to time St. Louis newspapers called attention to this danger. In 1841 an item in the *Daily Evening Gazette* pointed out that free Negroes and hired slaves working on riverboats had an opportunity to talk with slaves of other southern states and also with the free Negroes and abolitionists of Illinois and other free states" (Gara, "The Underground Railroad in Illinois," 508–28). Gara is, however, uninformed and generalizes to an unfortunate extent about the "romantic interpretation of the Underground epic" in the Prairie State. In some cases, he is most certainly correct about these exaggerations, but in many instances he is utterly unaware of the Illinois UGRR organization, operation, interconnection and networking.

76. Gara, *The Liberty Line*, 2–4, 42–44, 47, 58–59, 62.

77. Coleman, *Slavery Times in Kentucky*, 228. This quote is from narrative of William W. Brown, a runaway slave.

78. "His two greatest enemies were the white man and hunger. The latter problem he solved by appropriating ears of corn from the fields or barns, chickens from chicken houses, or, if desperate, he begged for food in the slave quarters or ate garbage. But the white man was, by far, the runaway's most deadly enemy. If the slave was surprised by an ignorant white man, he flashed any piece of paper with writing on it in front of his face and usually succeeded in deceiving his adversary. When accosted by a white man he could not deceive, he ran. If cornered, he sometimes fought and killed his pursuers" (Blassingame, *The Slave Community*, 200–201).

79. Garretson, "Traveling on the Underground Railroad in Iowa," 427–28.

80. Ellsworth, *Records of the Olden Times*, 572.

81. Some white western Illinoisans "worked actively to improve the lot of those [blacks] living among them, or those who wished to escape

slavery's chains in the border states ... contrary to what some scholars have recently alleged, there is ample evidence in newspapers and private correspondence that the Underground Railroad was very active in western Illinois." And, "the majority of white residents remained hostile to blacks" but there is "evidence of a sizable number of [whites] in west central Illinois sympathetic to the plight of blacks in their midst, and even more so for those in bondage" (Bridges, "Dark Faces on the Antebellum West Central Illinois Landscape," 72).

82. In 1860, after living in Canada for several years, Anderson was accused of killing a white man in Missouri who tried to prevent him from escaping. There followed a lengthy period of litigation that received widespread public attention in Canada, Great Britain, and the United States, but Anderson was never forced to return to the states.

83. In Rock Island County, Dr. Thomas Baker, Robert Delany, Michael and Abram Hortzell, and F. M. Smith helped send fugitives up the Rock River or east toward Princeton. In 1846, C. B. Waite started publishing the "Liberty Banner," an antislavery newspaper, in the city of Rock Island. He traveled throughout the area soliciting subscriptions but after a short time this venture ended for want of subscribers. Waite moved to Chicago in 1853 and in 1862 was appointed chief justice of the Utah Territory by President Lincoln.

84. Blassingame, *Slave Testimony*, 353–57.

85. Coffin, *Reminiscences*, 254–55.

86. When Garrison's *Liberator* first appeared, the majority of its "initial subscribers" were blacks (Berry and Blassingame, *Long Memory*, 63).

87. Horton and Horton, *Hard Road to Freedom*, 137.

88. Morison, *The Oxford History of the American People*, 159.

89. Knox College's second president, Jonathan Blanchard, was also one of the "Seventy."

90. Wilbur Siebert provided the pioneer study on the Underground Railroad. He sent numerous circular letters throughout the north asking for information about the operation of the UGRR. Siebert asked seven basic questions

about (1) routes followed, (2) time frames of UGRR activities, (3) operational methods, (4) important or unusual incidents, (5) personal involvement of correspondents, (6) names of operators, and (7) a biographical sketch. The true worth of these letters is not their face value, but in using them as a means of confirmation from other reliable sources. Some scholars have dismissed these letters to Siebert out of hand as sentimental retrospectives but that, unfortunately, is an example of "throwing the baby out with the bath water" for some can help verify actual underground activity, though other vague, fanciful, and unsubstantiated accounts cannot.

91. Siebert, *The Underground Railroad from Slavery to Freedom*, between 113 and 114.

92. The Green River flowed just above the northern boundary of the Military Tract.

93. In 1841 Queen Victoria pronounced that fugitive slaves from the United States were free as soon as they landed on British soil.

94. A term adopted by some settlers from Native Americans that means a crossing of trails.

95. Also located in Henry County was the city of Geneseo which was a critical UGRR stop. Here the Allan brothers, James and William T., along with Roderick R. Stewart and E. M. Stewart served as important "shepherds." Fugitives were sent from that town northeast hugging the Rock River or they were sent due east to Princeton. "Hardly had the cabins been built before Geneseo became a station of the Underground Railroad for the poor runaway slaves soon learned where friends were ... and at night, or under grain or hay, even in the daytime, some of the young men of the colony would get them on, to the next station, toward a land of safety" (Taylor, "History of the First Congregational Church of Geneseo," 118–19).

96. A UGRR term meaning a number of hideouts available close to each other.

97. Northerners who sympathized with the South during the Civil War.

98. Cooley, "Illinois and the Underground Railroad to Canada," 81.

99. Brown, *The Slave Narrative of Williams Wells Brown*, 57.

100. This proslavery sentiment was so deep-seated that when the Confederacy was first forming after Lincoln's election as president, there was some discussion in southern Illinois about forming a separate state of Egypt. The new state would be part of the Confederate States of America. Stephen Douglas hurried to these southern counties to help convince those wavering on the issue to stay with the Union.

101. Pirtle, *Escape Betwixt Two Suns*, 1–4, 15–16, 50–57, 59–60, 63, 88–92, 103, 105–107, 109, 113.

102. Calkins, *They Broke the Prairie*, 121–23.

103. *Galesburg Republican Register*, June 20, 1904.

104. Muelder, *Fighters for Freedom*, 214.

105. Ibid., 85.

106. Many states, including Illinois, passed personal liberty laws aimed at prohibiting the kidnapping of blacks in order to prevent them from being taken into a slave state for sale. But these laws were not enforced in the Prairie State and it was not until 1855 that a bona fide law of this kind was enacted.

107. *The History of Peoria County*, 442.

108. Berlin, *Generations of Captivity*, 236.

Chapter II

1. Nearly every former U.S. president has seen his "star" gradually fade after leaving the White House but such was not the case with John Quincy Adams. He was later elected to the U.S. House of Representatives, where he decried slavery as "an outrage upon the goodness of God." John Quincy Adams became one of the lawyers for blacks from the mutinied slave ship *Amistad*. He led the fight in Congress against the "gag rule" that for years had forbidden the topic of slavery to even be debated by the House.

2. *Rand McNally Atlas of American History*, 40.

3. The slave population of Missouri grew steadily over the decades and the price of slaves increased as time passed. Gradually demand exceeded supply and the value of slaves rose. Prices eventually reached a peak just before the Civil War broke out. In 1860 a so-called top male slave sold for approximately $1,300 and a

top female slave for about $1,000. The Missouri census of 1820, when that state gained statehood, listed 9,797 slaves; by 1860 the number of bondsmen had swelled to 114,931.

4. "Bounties were established for Illinois abolitionists and negros suspected of being fugitives. The committees (anti-abolitionist society) further recommended that Illinois abolitionists known to have helped fugitive slaves be kidnapped and taken to Missouri" (*Western Citizen*, January 18, 1854).

5. Dempsey, "Heroes, Previously Unnamed, Played an Important Role in our History."

6. Calkins, *They Broke the Prairie*, 226.

7. Frazier, *Runaway and Freed Missouri Slaves and Those Who Helped Them, 1763–1865*, 174.

8. Richardson, "Dr. David Nelson and His Times," 434, 443, 451, 453.

9. Weld, *American Slavery as It Is: Testimony of a Thousand Witnesses*, 86.

10. The Reverend Samuel G. Wright, who lived nearly 100 miles as the crow flies northeast of Quincy, wrote in his personal journal on January 9, 1843, that his horse went lame while "conducting along Dr. Eels." Wright's entry in his journal gives credence to the fact that the UGRR was already being organized through western Illinois by the early 1840s.

11. Muelder, *Fighters for Freedom*, 197.

12. *Galesburg Evening Mail*, June 19, 1909.

13. Frazier, *Runaway and Freed Missouri Slaves and Those Who Helped Them, 1763–1865*, 135.

14. Thompson, *Prison Life and Reflections*, 1, 14–15, 17, 31–33, 47, 54, 58–60, 62–63, 79–80, 85, 112–13, 116–18, 121–22, 131, 139, 160–62, 168, 270–71, 298, 351, 362–63, 370.

15. In Kentucky, the other slave state bordering Illinois, there were 44 people imprisoned for aiding fugitive slaves seeking freedom between 1844 and 1864 (Hagedorn, *Beyond the River*, 254).

16. Merkel, "The Underground Railroad and the Missouri Borders, 1840–1860," 277–78.

17. Tillson, *History of the City of Quincy, Illinois*, 40.

18. Magoun, *Asa Turner: A Home Missionary Patriarch and His Times*, 160.

19. Ibid., 160–61.

20. Deacon Brown's daughters were both married to the Allison brothers, who were Underground Railroad agents to the northeast of Quincy in McDonough County.

21. Letter from H. D. Platt to Wilbur Siebert found in two rolls of microfilm in Siebert's notes and letters on the Illinois UGRR.

22. East of Quincy, in Liberty, a small band of UGRR operators also "carried" fugitives.

23. Letter from J. E. Platt to Wilbur Siebert, March 28, 1896, found in two rolls of microfilm in Siebert's notes and letters on the Illinois UGRR.

24. Lee, "Slavery and Emancipation in Lewis County, Missouri," 294–317 and Moore, "An Abortive Slave Uprising," 123–26.

Chapter III

1. The Mormons, courted by both of Illinois's dominant political parties, were given a city charter. Their sect's population exploded and regional "gentiles" became frightened, alarmed and finally murderous. Joseph Smith, the Mormon prophet, was killed by a mob in Carthage, Illinois, in 1844.

2. This waterway is now called the LaMoine River.

3. Lovejoy was in fact murdered in November 1837.

4. Young, *A History of Round Prairie and Plymouth*, 12–13, 15–20, 248, 250–53, 255, 270–72, 281–86, 288–302.

5. Letter from Professor Lucy Maynard Salmon to Professor Wilbur Siebert-found in two rolls of microfilm in Siebert's notes and letters on the Illinois UGRR. "(Our) uncle Mr. Louis Calvin Maynard went when a young man from Phillipton, Massachusetts, to LaHarpe, Hancock County, Illinois.... Some years later I visited him and was shown an old attic where the negroes were concealed. He told me he could recall some thirty-seven (I think) different persons he had aided in escaping."

6. Gregg, *History of Hancock County, Illinois*, 910–11.

7. This is almost certainly Deacon Luther Birge from Fulton County who will be discussed later in chapter five.

8. This reference likely alludes to the Reverend Milton Kimball, a trustee of Galesburg's abolitionist Knox College.

9. Gregg, *History of Hancock County, Illinois*, 430–32.

Chapter IV

1. According to Glennette Turner, a prominent UGRR figure in Macomb was Judge Damon G. Tunnicliff, who kept a "hiding place in his home" for fugitive slaves.

2. Uncle Billy Allison's sons, Harmon and Andrew, were key Underground Railroad agents in McDonough County. Harmon and Andrew were married to Beulah and Lucinda Brown, whose father, George Brown, was actively involved with the Quincy UGRR.

3. Hemp grows from the tough fiber in its stem and is used for making strong cord or rope. The tedium and danger of working at a hemp plant were well-known in the past. This work tore up a worker's hands and easily led to infection. In England it was work often done by convicts and the inmates of workhouses.

4. In Memphis, Tennessee, UGRR "agent" Jacob Burkle, a man of considerable wealth who owned a large stockyard close to the Mississippi River, helped send slaves north on the "River Jordan." He would bribe steamboat captains to take fugitives onboard after dark.

5. Indigo is a blue dye obtained from plants from the genus *Indigofera*. Indigo was placed in a vat where its contents would ferment, yielding acid and producing sulfur gases. Queen Elizabeth I forbid indigo dye production within five miles of her estates because of the noxious smells it created.

6. Blazer, "The History of the Underground Railroad of McDonough County, Illinois," 579–91.

7. Upper Alton is just south of where the Illinois River and Mississippi River meet at the southern tip of the three rivers triangle, in Hardin County.

8. Clarke, *History of McDonough County, Illinois*, 273–74.

9. Conger, *History of the Illinois River Valley*, 131.

10. Frazier, *Runaway and Freed Missouri Slaves and Those Who Helped Them, 1763–1865*, 91.

Chapter V

1. Clarke, *History of McDonough County, Illinois*, 277.

2. To illustrate how late northern Illinois was settled compared to southern Illinois, a half dozen years after Illinois gained statehood, a person from Fort Dearborn (Chicago) doing county business had to travel to Lewiston in west central Illinois to conduct transactions.

3. The most noteworthy "keepers" associated with Canton were John Wright, Nathan Jones, the Reverend W. Jones, Lucius Parrish, Robert Stewart, Chauncey Driggs, and Theodore Sargent.

4. Active "agents" helping runaway slaves in and around Farmington included Dan Tanner, Riley Bristol, Joseph and Henry Cone, Phineas Chapman and A. B. Thomas. According to Chapman's Fulton County history, Thomas, on one occasion, harbored 14 fugitives. He helped large numbers of runaways escape during the time he was involved with the UGRR.

5. Ross, *The Early Pioneers and Pioneer Events of the State of Illinois*, 180–83.

6. Muelder, *Fighters for Freedom*, 121.

7. It was the first anniversary of the society's original convention at Alton in 1837.

8. It had been only 11 months since his martyred brother, E. P. Lovejoy, had been murdered.

9. *The Genius of Universal Emancipation*.

10. *Fulton County Life*. Reprinted from Canton Daily Ledger, 1916.

11. *Fulton County Life*. Reprinted from Table Grove Herald, 1914.

Chapter VI

1. LaSalle established Fort Creve Coeur in the area in 1680.

2. *The History of Peoria County*, 461.

3. Samuel Davis was an early Illinois newspaper man who had been neutral about abolitionists until the 1843 Peoria riot, at which time he joined the cause. His loyalty to the antislavery movement cost him dearly in June 1846,

when he was assaulted by a proslavery attacker close to his home. He and his son, who came to his father's aid, were both badly beaten before finally making it to safety inside their house.

4. *Western Citizen.*

5. See Muelder, *Fighters for Freedom,* 188.

6. Emma Chapin, in a letter to Wilbur Siebert, January 11, 1896, wrote "The Underground Railroad did not run through Peoria, but through the Harkness settlement near Farmington, Fulton County. Eli Wilson was an active agent then and though some fugitives were captured, many were sent on to liberty."

7. Letter from C. C. Cutter to Wilbur Siebert, September 27, 1898.

8. Roy later became minister of the Plymouth Church in Chicago, where he continued to help runaways avoid capture. Before the Civil War, he was embroiled for a time in the antislavery/proslavery politics of "Bleeding Kansas."

9. *Brimfield News.*

10. Letter to Wilbur Siebert from J. D. Huey, March 7, 1896.

11. *Elmwood Gazette,* April 26, 1906.

12. Handsome, intelligent, confident, articulate, and uncompromising, Douglass was the proslavery element's worst nightmare. He was born a slave, learned to read before he was ten and, after he escaped slavery, lived in Europe for two years. Abolitionist friends purchased his freedom and he returned to the United States. His lectures opposing slavery, usually delivered with convincing eloquence, had a profound effect on many who heard them. He established and edited the *North Star* for 17 years and after the Civil War, Douglass was marshall of the District of Columbia from 1877 to 1881 and served as minister to Haiti from 1889 to 1891.

13. Robert Ingersoll was a prominent attorney in the city of Peoria. He held openly agnostic views that often made him a figure of controversy. Originally he was a Democrat but he joined the Republican Party during the Civil War and in 1867 he was appointed attorney general of Illinois. Ingersoll was defeated in the election for governor of Illinois in 1868.

14. Douglass, *Life and Times of Frederick Douglass,* 560–62.

15. *Elmwood Gazette,* July 30, 1936.

16. *Elmwood Gazette,* April 11, 18, 25, 1907.

17. "One of the most active workers in the anti-slavery cause was Deacon Nathaniel Smith, of Lawn Ridge, a God-fearing blacksmith and member of the church militant, who could stroke hard blows in debate and back them up if need be with sledge hammer accompaniments in defense of right. He assisted many slaves on the road to freedom, and was always ready to turn out by day or night with his team. The first human chattel that passed through his hands was a closely pressed negro, who was brought from Princeville hid beneath a feather bed. He safely delivered him at the next station. The next was a poor fugitive, who lay hid under a bridge at Farmington all day, while the pursuers raged all around him. A third was concealed some time beneath a brush heap. One was a Baptist minister of the gospel. Once there came a load of seven in a covered wagon. One of the party lay beneath a log when his master on horseback jumped over it without finding him. A lady nearly white came along, who had been a slave to the Rev. Mr. Ely, of Baltimore. She was a stewardess on a boat, and finding her saintly owner designed selling her planned an escape and got safely through, but her husband, who was a free man, was arrested for assisting her and served a long term in a Southern penitentiary. A young man came through from Farmington who was hidden beneath a wagon box upon which his master, who was searching for him, sat down with an assistant and talked over their plans. They asked the 'agent' if the fugitive was about, and were told they could search the premises. Mr. Smith's house became noted, and he was once honored with a column notice in the St. Louis *Republican,* to which he replied. Once he traveled in the stage with an irate slave-holder searching for fugitives, and after learning all the latter's plans, disclosed himself. The man evinced a strong desire to make mince-meat of the Abolitionist, but the latter's brawny fists and resolute demeanor convinced him that discretion was the better part of valor" (Ellsworth, *Records of the Olden Time; Fifty Years on the Prairie,* 564–65).

Chapter VII

1. Siebert, *The Underground Railroad from Slavery to Freedom*, 97.

2. Flavel Bascom, who was a Knox College trustee and, starting in 1849, the minister of the old colony church in Galesburg, wrote, "The members and the ministry of this Church have always been in favor of carrying radical anti-slavery principles into politics as well as into religion. They have insisted on voting as well as praying for liberty. And she has done what she could to save the country, and give liberty to her oppressed millions" (Bascom, "A Historical Discourse Commemorative of the Settlement of Galesburg," 21).

3. George Davis apparently used whatever seemed the safest place available to hide runaways. He concealed fugitives in his house, barn, and haystack and when transporting "cargo," he would hide them in between "stations" if he thought he was being followed.

4. Cooley, "Illinois and the Underground Railroad to Canada," 82.

5. Humphrey, *Centennial History of Illinois*, 171.

6. Letter to Wilbur Siebert from George Churchill January 29, 1896.

7. *Galesburg Evening Mail*, February 1, 1900.

8. Chapman, *History of Knox County, Illinois*, 214–15.

9. A year earlier, on July 4, 1837, the Galesburg colony celebrated the day by forming a antislavery society. In the spring of 1906, E. S. Willcox, a Knox College professor before the Civil War and later Peoria public librarian, delivered a speech to the Knox County Historical Society at Beecher Chapel on the Knox College campus. He recalled that as a boy growing up in Galesburg, the Fourth of July was always an antislavery meeting day. "But our pronounced abolitionism made us a by-word and anathema to all the country round. Since we had then no large hall or opera house for our big gatherings, our Fourth of July celebrations which were invariably anti-slavery meetings, were often in summer held in large arbors built of boughs and branches hauled by wagon loads from Henderson Grove and erected on or near the site of your present Union Hotel. Here I

first felt the inspiring influence of a really great orator — Ichabod Codding — one of the greatest I ever listened to" (Willcox, "Reminiscences of Galesburg," 10–11).

10. *Peoria Register and Northwestern Gazetteer*.

11. Muelder, *Fighters for Freedom*, 117.

12. Fletcher, *Our Secret Constitution*, 102.

13. *Peoria Register and Northwestern Gazetteer*.

14. "For most free blacks involvement in the underground railroad was a natural outcome of their personal relationships. Since nine of every ten African Americans were slaves, almost every free black person either had been a slave or had family members or friends in slavery. As one historian explained, 'Practically every clump of Negro settlers in the free states was an underground depot by definition.' Fugitive slaves were some of those most directly involved in underground railroad activities, thereby risking their own recapture" (Horton and Horton, *Hard Road to Freedom*, 143). Susan (Aunt Sukey) Van Allen Richardson is an illustration of a former slave who was willing to take such risks.

15. Chapman, *History of Knox County, Illinois*, 210–11.

16. In the southeast corner of Iowa, in the Yankee town of Denmark, where Asa Turner lived and in the Quaker colony of Salem, two flourishing Underground Railroad centers existed. In Salem the main depot was the house of Henderson Lewelling. A short distance to the west of these two communities, the town of Keosauqua also provided hideouts for fugitives, but it was in Denmark that the remarkable Turner lead the region's resistance to slavery. He was for a brief time a minister in Quincy before moving to Iowa where he became one of the most important Underground Railroad conductors anywhere in the Prairie or Hawkeye states. George F. Magoun, the first president of Iowa College (now Grinnell College) wrote in 1899 that "it will surprise no one to know that fugitives for freedom were always welcome at the Denmark parsonage and in neighboring Christian homes. The village, it must be confessed, had the name of being one of the stations on the Underground Railroad. Masters from Missouri often crossed the Lower Des Moines and the south-eastern corner of Iowa in pursuit of run-

aways, or came up the Missouri by boat.... All in those days could tell of 'hair-breath escapes.' Once two 'Danes' crossed to Pontoosuc, Ill., on [a] ferryboat with a Missouri 'claimant,' the object of his search lying flat on the bottom of the Denmark wagon, snugly covered with some sort of lading for market" (Magoun, *Asa Turner: A Home Missionary Patriarch and His Times*, 290). Turner was familiar with the landscape on both sides of the Mississippi River, connected to nearly every "agent" in western Illinois and eastern Iowa and was mostly likely known to Missouri slaves. Turner was one of the first individuals to visit abolitionists Thompson, Work, and Burr in jail after their arrest in Missouri for aiding runaways. But like Quincy and Galesburg in Illinois, Denmark's Underground Railroad activities were not appreciated by numerous others who came to live in that part of Iowa. Charles Blockson (*The Underground Railroad*, 189) quotes a story in the *Fort Madison Plain Dealer*, May 27, 1857, as saying "To the disgrace of the County and State, Denmark has the name of being a rendezvous of men, who occasionally engage in negro-stealing, at the same time professing the religion of the gospel. Men of less shrewdness have been hanged — have received their just desserts — for engaging in practices of which respectable citizens of Denmark have been accused." Blockson also recounts the rescue adventure of Denmark's ardent abolitionist Theron Trowbridge, a deacon in the town's Congregational Church. Trowbridge once encountered an escaped slave girl who told him of having to abandon her child on a farm close to Kahoka, Missouri. He armed himself, rode into the "show me" state and two days later brought the child to the mother. Many fugitives moved out of these southeastern Iowa communities toward Burlington on the Mississippi River, which lay just across the water from Illinois. It was only 35–40 miles from the Burlington area to Galesburg. In Burlington lived abolitionist and Congregationalist minister William Salter, who was that community's most important UGRR operator. Salter was familiar with Knox College's abolitionist reputation, having been acquainted with the school's second president, Jonathan Blanchard, in the mid–1840s.

17. Chapman, *History of Knox County, Illinois*, 210–11.

18. Ibid., 211.

19. Ibid., 211–12.

20. See Muelder, "A Hero Home from the War." (Monograph on Blacks in the Galesburg Community.)

21. Thomas Richardson married Susan Van Allen in 1856.

22. Perry, *History of Knox County, Illinois*, 762–66.

23. The Quakers who Davis refers to were most likely arriving from the Iowa community of Salem where UGRR friends operated.

24. A Presbyterian school existed in Cedar Township, Knox County (then called Cherry Grove) from 1840 to 1868; only a cemetery remains.

25. *Semi-Centennial Celebration*, 19–20.

26. One of William's brothers, Hugh, attended Dr. David Nelson's antislavery Mission Institute in Quincy and another brother, George, went on to worldwide fame as the inventor of the Ferris wheel.

27. Gettemy, *A Memoir of Silvanus Ferris*, 201, 203–206.

28. Bonham, *Fifty Years' Recollections with Observations and Reflections on Historical Events*, 523–24.

29. *Galesburg Republican Register*, June 20, 1904.

30. *Galesburg Republican Register*, October 3, 1891.

31. Calkins, *They Broke the Prairie*, 229.

Chapter VIII

1. Leeson, *Stark County, Illinois*, 122–24.

2. Delano, untitled article, *West Jersey Harvest Home*, 80–82.

3. Muelder, *Fighters for Freedom*, 76.

4. S. G. Wright moved to Toulon, Illinois, in 1848 from western Stark County. He moved there after having been made minister of the town's Congregational Church two years earlier.

5. McKinzie, "Congregational Church, Toulon, Illinois, 1846–1921," 521.

6. This is most likely one of the times Fulton County's Luther Birge was charged and taken before the court for helping fugitive slaves escape.

7. This reference is to the legal matters associated with the capture of Susan Richardson and four other runaway slaves in Knox County.

8. Letter to Dr. H. M. Hall from S. G. Wright, August 25, 1885.

9. The controversial and uncompromising John Cross eventually moved to Lee County and continued with vehemence his antislavery and Underground Railroad activity at Temperance Hill. "Rev. John Cross, a Presbyterian minister, lived at Temperance Hill and named the place Theoka, but for some reason it has outlived that name. Mr. Cross was a warm advocate for human freedom, a friend and fellow worker with Owen Lovejoy, and was imprisoned at Ottawa for his services as conductor on 'the under-ground railroad.' He made no secret of his work. He posted bills in Mr. Bliss's bar room side by side with Frink and Walker's stage route advertisement:— 'free ride on the Underground Railroad,' and signed his name 'John Cross, Proprietor.' He had a pair of horses, one cream colored and the other bay, with which he took his passengers, who were flying from slavery to freedom, often gotten through from here to Chicago in a day, sometimes having as many as four passengers. Palestine Grove being but about forty miles from the Mississippi River, it was easily reached by those who were sheltered and directed by other friends of the slave, who often helped them on their way to this point. These under-ground depots were stationed all along the way from 'Dixie's Land' and the station-agents were in communication with each other" (Kennedy, "Reflections of the Pioneers of Lee County," 108–109).

10. Mr. Jones is probably the Deacon W. Jones who resided in Canton at that time.

11. This is undoubtedly Ichabod Codding who was a noted Illinois abolitionist and orator.

12. On occasion slaves were given Christmas papers allowing them to travel during the holidays in order to visit family or friends nearby.

13. *Western Citizen*, February 23, 1847.

14. This entry in Wright's journal is another example confirming the fact that western Illinois abolitionists and Underground Railroad operators were well connected with each other for years before the Civil War. The James Burr that Wright mentions is the same man who was in prison in Missouri in the early 1840s, with his friends George Thompson and Alanson Work, for trying to help slaves escape.

15. Fremont County, Iowa, rests at the extreme southwestern corner of the state. Wilbur Siebert lists over 30 individuals alone in that county as Underground Railroad activists. The next county to the east is Page, where in the late 1850s an incredibly daring raid was carried out by five UGRR operators, aimed at crossing over into Missouri in order to carry out fugitives. The conspirators hailed from Amity (now College Springs), a community conceived and organized in the notoriously abolitionist Illinois town of Galesburg. These ultra antislavery crusaders on one occasion audaciously drove 60 miles into the slave state below them and brought out 15 runaways upon their return to southern Iowa. These people were undoubtedly in cahoots with their western Illinois UGRR brethren.

16. Todd, *Early Settlement and Growth of Western Iowa and Reminiscences*, 134–37.

17. Muelder, *Fighters for Freedom*, 314.

18. In 1858, during the campaign for the United States Senate, seven debates were held throughout Illinois between Stephen Douglas and Abraham Lincoln. S. G. Wright's reference is to debate number five held on the Knox College campus in Galesburg on October 7th. The speeches were made from a stage at the east end of the main building of Knox College and the crowd was estimated to be well over 10,000. Lincoln was most likely aware of the town and school's abolitionist reputation and it was probably not an accident that it was at this debate, before a significant number of supporters, that he delivered his first strong denunciation of the immorality of Douglas' position on slavery.

19. Wright, "Wright's Journal."

20. To "frank" means to give easy passage or pass freely.

21. Bateman et al., *Historical Encyclopedia of Illinois and Knox County*, 536–37.

22. Augustus Dunn settled in West Jersey Township in early 1836 and was selected as Stark County's first sheriff in 1839. Slave trackers received no sympathy or help from Sheriff

Dunn. He was a Union soldier during the Civil War and he was badly wounded twice.

23. Liberty Stone moved to Illinois in 1833. "He was a pronounced abolitionist and connected with the famous Underground Railroad in Illinois. One child [of his] was named Celia Lovejoy for the wife of the martyred Elijah Lovejoy" (*Stark County News*, July 6, 1893). Following the death of his wife Julia in 1853, Stone married Thankful Lesan.

24. From the Greek; a hymn of thanking, a song of joy or triumph.

25. The vault of heaven, the sky or upper air. The whole phrase "to make the Welkin ring" is to make a loud noise.

26. Letter from Harriet Hall Blair to Wilbur Siebert, January 28, 1896.

27. Letter to Wilbur Siebert from James Buswell, n.d.

Chapter IX

1. Wolf, *On Freedom's Altar*, 49.

2. Owen Lovejoy thought of settling in Knox County but was persuaded by Edward Beecher to make his home instead in Princeton. His ties to the Galesburg and other Knox County abolitionists were strong for he came to serve on the board of examiners at Knox College and in 1846 he lectured to the school's Adelphi Literary Society.

3. The crawl space over the front hallway of his house was used to hide fugitive slaves.

4. Matson, *Reminiscences of Bureau County*, 336–37.

5. John Howard Bryant, an early and highly respected citizen of Bureau County, was twice elected to the state legislature before the Civil War.

6. Author of the famous poem "Thanatopsis."

7. Bradsby, *History of Bureau County, Illinois*, 163.

8. Matson, *Reminiscences of Bureau County*, 360, 362–63.

9. Siebert, *The Underground Railroad from Slavery to Freedom*, 404.

10. Ibid., 404.

11. Matson, *Reminiscences of Bureau County*, 364–65.

12. Ibid., 360–62.

13. Letter to Sarah Lovejoy from Justice Olds, May 17, 1874.

14. Magdol, *Owen Lovejoy: Abolitionist in Congress*, 39.

15. Owen Lovejoy was a member of the Illinois State Legislature from 1855 to 1857.

16. Horton and Horton, *Hard Road to Freedom*, 137.

17. A lustrum was a ceremony in ancient Rome to purify people and was held five years after the census.

18. Speech by Owen Lovejoy on the floor of the U. S. House of Representatives, February 21, 1859, published in Washington, D.C., by Buell Blanchard Printers, 1860.

19. Bradsby, *The History of Bureau County, Illinois*, 335–36.

20. Jones, *Lincoln and the Preachers*, 65.

21. Henry Ward Beecher was a famous minister, orator and lecturer. He was one of the nation's leading antislavery advocates and an enthusiastic supporter of women's suffrage. He was the brother of Edward Beecher and Harriet Beecher Stowe.

22. Letter (copy) to Mrs. Owen Lovejoy from Francis R. Carpenter, May 18, 1865.

Chapter X

1. Robinson and Moore, *History of Illinois*, 134.

2. The national story most often recalled about a fugitive traveling by rail to freedom was that of Henry "Box" Brown. He had himself placed in a box two feet eight inches deep, two feet wide and three feet long. He was sent from Richmond to Philadelphia, where friends were waiting to carefully cut him out of the container. Henry Brown moved to Boston and became actively involved there with the UGRR.

3. Randall, *The Civil War and Reconstruction*, 83.

4. Ryan, "A Chapter from the History of the Underground Railroad," 23.

5. Clarke, *History of McDonough County, Illinois*, 279.

6. Four years later, the Illinois Senatorial election of 1858 between Stephen Douglas and Abraham Lincoln served as a prelude to the

presidential election of 1860. The 1858 Senate campaign in Illinois, which centered around the "slavery question," also had the effect of catapulting Lincoln's name and reputation across the nation. The seven debates throughout the Prairie State that year (Ottawa, Freeport, Jonesboro, Charleston, Galesburg, Quincy, and Alton) helped the fledgling Republican Party better establish itself for its first major national victory two years later.

7. Democrat James Buchanan gained the White House by defeating Fremont in the 1856 presidential election.

8. Clark E. Carr was a prominent Republican, who rose from Galesburg postmaster to the minister to Denmark (1889–1893). He was a very successful lawyer and once served as president of the Illinois Historical Society.

9. Carr, *My Day and Generation*, 333.

10. Overton, *Burlington West*, 41.

11. Robinson and Moore, *History of Illinois*, 160.

12. The correspondence of Emma Chapin to Wilbur Siebert is one of the most important communications he received about the Illinois UGRR because she was the daughter of William T. Allan, one of Weld's "Seventy." Chapin would have been privy during much of her early life to the doings of the abolitionist movement in the Prairie State. Her father and family were well-known crusaders associated with the Illinois antislavery cause. William T. Allan was the central figure during a mob riot in Peoria at an antislavery society meeting in 1843, previously described in chapter 6. In her letter to Siebert, Chapin describes the night of the mob violence: "The Peoria Pres. Church was called an anti-slavery church & during the time Father Allan had charge of it he was in the employ of the Ill. Anti-Slavery Society & lectured a good deal through the state. At an anti-slavery meeting in his own church one evening, a mob assembled, headed by a saloonkeeper. They carried off one wheel from the carriage of Mr. Pettingel, a friend of my father and prominent anti-slavery [man].... The meeting was broken up and threats were made to take my father down to the river, cut a hole in the ice & 'chuck him in.' His friends besought him to leave the city, but he stood his

ground and was not hurt." Allan lectured against slavery in Bureau, Stark, Knox, and Peoria counties. He moved to Geneseo in 1844, a community close to the Rock River, where his first wife died and he then married Emma Chapin's mother. Here he joined the activities of the Underground Railroad with his brother, James.

13. Letter from W. C. Collins to Wilber Siebert, n.d.

14. Chapman, *History of Knox County, Illinois*, 211.

15. Calkins, *They Broke the Prairie*, 228.

16. League of Women Voters, *Know Your Town*, 6.

17. Conger, *History of the Illinois River Valley*, 411.

18. *Galesburg Republican Register*, January 25, 1900.

19. This is the same John Bryant mentioned in chapter IX who, with his brothers Arthur and John, were well-known UGRR agents in Bureau County. All three men were closely associated with Owen Lovejoy.

20. Bradsby, *History of Bureau County, Illinois*, 163.

21. Finkelman, "Slavery, the 'More Perfect Union,' and the Prairie State," 267.

22. "A Rambling Sketch of Some of Our Earlier Colored Residents," *Galesburg Post*, 9.

23. Turner, *The Underground Railroad in Illinois*, 6.

24. Merkel, "The Underground Railroad and the Missouri Borders, 1840–1860," 284.

25. Drake et al., *Black Metropolis: A Study of Negro Life in a Northern City*, 36.

26. Ibid., 37–38.

27. Naively considered by some at the time as a final solution to the issue of slavery in the territories, the Compromise of 1850 was a last gasp effort by Congress and President Fillmore to hold the United States together. The most unacceptable feature of this agreement to abolitionists was the inclusion of a much more stringent Fugitive Slave Law. It was African Americans, of course, who were the most infuriated by the passage of the new Fugitive Slave Law for it clearly sent the signal that the federal government was now under the thumb of the proslavery element. The other significant

parts of the Compromise of 1850 were: (1) California admitted to the Union as a free state, (2) the ending of the slave trade in the District of Columbia, and (3) allowing the people of the Utah and New Mexico territories to decide the issue of slavery for themselves.

28. On February 12, 1851, the *Oquawka Spectator*, in Henderson County, reported a mass meeting against the Fugitive Slave Law and the following week noted "we understand that there was quite an animated discussion on the subject of the Fugitive Slave Law at Hutchinson's Grove." John Conger also relates that "one element in the intensification of feeling between the North and South sprang out of the return of runaway negroes escaping north on their way to Canada. The fourth and fifth decades of the nineteenth century, especially after the Compromise of 1850 with its strengthened fugitive slave act, produced increased hostility between North and South. And the escaping negroes received a new sympathy in Illinois whose anti-slavery citizens helped create a tool for their aid and comfort known as the Underground Railway" (*History of the Illinois River Valley*, 407).

29. Cooley, "Illinois and the Underground Railroad to Canada," 77–79.

30. Berlin and Rowland, *Families and Freedom*, 95.

31. Berlin et al., *Free at Last*, 104–105.

32. In the fall of 1863, just months after the Battle of Gettysburg, Barnabas Root entered the Knox College Preparatory Department and eventually enrolled in the college. He graduated from Knox in 1870 and is one of the first black to earn a college degree in Illinois.

33. A photocopy of the original handwritten letter can be seen in Litvin, *Voices of the Prairie Land*, 180.

34. *Quincy Whig Republican.*

35. See Boydstun, Boydstun family papers, for an interview by John Boydstun, Knox College class of 1944, with James Oliver Washington.

36. Calkins, *They Broke the Prairie*, 227.

37. Slavery had existed continuously in North America at least as far back as the 1520s, when Spanish settlers brought black indentured servants with them to Georgia.

38. McCullough, *John Adams*, 104.

39. The Missouri Compromise allowed Missouri to join the Union as a slave state and Maine as a free-state and excluded slavery north of parallel 36°30'.

40. Antislavery men and women saw the Mexican War as an obvious excuse to justify slavery's westward extension. From the moment U.S. president James Polk ordered General Zachary Taylor to advance his troops from Corpus Christi, Texas, to the Rio Grande River in early 1846, the foremost issue that faced the nation for the next 20 years centered around the abolition of slavery.

41. The Dred Scott decision (1857) delivered a jolting body blow to antislavery forces when the United States Supreme Court ruled 6–3 that Congress had no constitutional power to exclude slavery from the territories.

42. Vidal, *The Last Empire: Essays 1992–2000*, 167.

Bibliography

Books

Abzug, Robert H. *Passionate Liberator: Theodore Dwight Weld and the Dilemma of Reform*. New York and Oxford: Oxford University Press, 1980.

Angle, Paul, and Richard L. Beyer. *Handbook of Illinois History*. Springfield: Illinois State Historical Society, 1943.

Asbury, Henry. *Reminiscences of Quincy, Illinois*. Quincy, Ill.: D. Wilcox & Sons, 1882.

Bancroft, Frederic. *Slave Trading in the Old South*. Baltimore: J.H. Furst, 1993.

Barnes, Gilbert Hobbs. *The Anti-Slavery Impulse 1830–1844*. New York and London: D. Appleton-Century, 1933.

Berkin, Carol, and Leonard Wood. *Land of Promise*. Glenview, Ill.: Scott Foresman, 1983.

Berlin, Ira. *Generations of Captivity: A History of African-American Slaves*. Cambridge, Mass. and London, England: Belknap Press, 2003.

Berlin, Ira, Barbara J. Fields, Steven F. Miller, Joseph P. Reidy, and Leslie S. Rowland. *Free at Last*. New York: The New Press, 1992.

Berlin, Ira, and Leslie S. Rowland. *Families and Freedom*. New York: The New Press, 1997.

Berry, Mary Frances, and John W. Blassingame. *Long Memory: The Black Experience in America*. New York and Oxford: Oxford University Press, 1982.

Bial, Raymond. *The Underground Railroad*. Boston: Houghton Mifflin, 1995.

Blassingame, John W. *The Slave Community*. New York and Oxford: Oxford University Press, 1979.

_____. *Slave Testimony*. Baton Rouge: Louisiana State University Press, 1978.

Blight, David W. *Freedom: The Underground Railroad in History and Memory*. Washington: Smithsonian Books, 2004.

_____. *Race and Reunion: The Civil War in American Memory*. Cambridge, Mass. and London England: Belknap Press, 2001.

Blockson, Charles L. *Hippocrene Guide to the Underground Railroad*. New York: Hippocrene Books, 1994.

_____. *The Underground Railroad*. New York: Simon and Schuster, 1987.

Bobrick, Benson. *Testament: A Soldier's Story of the Civil War*. New York: Simon and Schuster, 2003.

Boles, John B. *Black Southerners 1619–1869*. Lexington: University Press of Kentucky, 1984.

Bonham, Jeriah. *Fifty Years' Recollections with Observations and Reflections on Historical Events*. Peoria, Ill.: J.W. Franks & Sons, 1883.

Bordewich, Fergus M. *Bound for Canaan: The Underground Railroad and the War for the Soul of America*. New York: HarperCollins, 2005.

Boyer, Richard O. *The Legend of John Brown: A Biography and a History*. New York: Alfred A. Knopf, 1973.

Boyes, W. F., and E. R. Jelliff. *Annals of Knox County*. Galesburg, Ill.: Republican Print, 1918.

Bridges, Roger D., and Rodney O. Davis. *Illinois: Its History and Legacy*. St. Louis: River City Publishers, 1984.

Brown, William Wells. *The Slave Narrative of William Wells Brown*. New York: Penguin Books, 1993.

Buckmaster, Henrietta. *Flight to Freedom, the Story of the Underground Railroad*. New York: Dell, 1958.

Calkins, Ernest Elmo. *They Broke the Prairie*. Urbana and Chicago: University of Illinois Press, 1937.

Campbell, Stanley W. *The Slave Catchers*. Chapel Hill: University of North Carolina Press, 1968.

Carmody, John M. *Missouri: A Guide to the "Show Me" State*. New York: Duell Sloan and Pearce, 1941.

Carpenter, Allen. *Illinois: Land of Lincoln*. Chicago: Children's Press, 1968.

Carr, Clark E. *The Illini*. Chicago: A.C. McClurg, 1905.

_____. *My Day and Generation*. Chicago: A.C. McClurg, 1908.

Carr, Kay J. *Belleville, Ottawa, and Galesburg*. Carbondale and Edwardsville: Southern Illinois University Press, 1996.

Carter, William. *Middle West Country*. Boston: Houghton Mifflin, 1975.

Coffin, Levi. *Reminiscences*. Cincinnati: Robert Clarke, 1876.

Coleman, J. Winston, Jr. *Slavery Times in Kentucky*. Chapel Hill: University of North Carolina Press, 1940.

Conger, John L. *History of the Illinois River Valley*. vol. 1. Chicago: S.J. Clarke, 1932.

Davidson, Alexander, and Bernard Stuve. *A Complete History of Illinois from 1673 to 1873*. Springfield: Illinois Journal Co., 1874.

Dillion, Merton L. *Benjamin Lundy and the Struggle for Negro Freedom*. Urbana and London: University of Illinois Press, 1966.

Douglass, Frederick. *Life and Times of Frederick Douglass, Written by Himself. His Early Life as a Slave, His Escape from Bondage, His Complete History to the Present Time*. Hartford, Conn.: Park Publishing, 1882.

Drake, St. Clair, and Horace R. Cayton. *Black Metropolis: A Study of Negro Life in a Northern City*. New York: Harcourt, Brace, 1945.

Drew, Benjamin. *The Refugee: The North-Side View of Slavery or The Narratives of Fugitive Slaves in Canada*. Reading: Addison-Wesley, 1969.

Dumond, Dwight Lowell. *Antislavery: The Crusade for Freedom in America*. Ann Arbor: University of Michigan Press, 1961.

Ellsworth, Spencer. *Records of the Olden Time: Fifty Years on the Prairie*. Lacon, Ill.: Home Journal Steam Printing Establishment, 1880.

Fletcher, George P. *Our Secret Constitution: How Lincoln Redefined American Democracy*. New York and Oxford: Oxford University Press, 2001.

Fogel, Robert William. *Without Consent or Contract: The Rise and Fall of American Slavery*. New York: W.W. Norton, 1989.

Ford, Thomas. *A History of Illinois*. Chicago: S.C. Griggs, 1854.

Franklin, John Hope. *From Slavery to Freedom*. New York: Alfred A. Knopf, 1967.

Franklin, John Hope, and Loren Schweninger. *Runaway Slaves*. New York and Oxford: Oxford University Press, 1999.

Frazier, Harriet C. *Runaway and Freed Missouri Slaves and Those Who Helped Them, 1763–1865*. Jefferson, N.C. and London: McFarland, 2001.

Gara, Larry. *The Liberty Line: The Legend of the Underground Railroad*. Lexington: University of Kentucky Press, 1967.

Gettemy, Charles Ferris. *A Memoir of Silvanus Ferris 1773–1861 and a Genealogy of His Descendants*. Boston, Mass., 1935.

Goodwin, Hal. *The Real Book about Stars*. Garden City, N.Y.: Garden City Books, 1951.

Hagedorn, Ann. *Beyond the River: The Untold Story of the Heroes of the Underground Railroad*. New York, London, Toronto, Sydney, and Singapore: Simon and Schuster, 2002.

Hallwas, John E. *McDonough County Heritage*. Macomb: Illinois Heritage Press, 1984.

Harris, N. Dwight. *The History of Negro Servitude in Illinois*. Chicago: A.C. McClurg, 1904.

Harrold, Stanley. *The Abolitionists and the South*. Lexington: University Press of Kentucky, 1995.

Hart, John Frazer. *The Rural Landscape*. Baltimore and London: Johns Hopkins University Press, 1998.

Bibliography

Havighurst, Walter. *Land of Promise: The Story of the Old Northwest Territory*. New York: Macmillan, 1946.

Hicks, John D. *The Federal Union*. Berkeley, Calif.: Houghton Mifflin, 1952.

Hicks, Peter P. *To Awaken My Afflicted Brethren: David Walker and the Problem of Antebellum Slave Resistance*. University Park: Pennsylvania University Press, 1997.

Horton, James O., and Lois E. Horton. *In Hope of Liberty: Culture, Community and Protest among Northern Free Blacks, 1700–1860*. New York: Oxford University Press, 1997.

_____. *Hard Road to Freedom: The Story of African America*. New Brunswick, N.J. and London: Rutgers University Press, 2001.

Hudson, J. Blaine. *Fugitive Slaves and the Underground Railroad in the Kentucky Borderlands*. Jefferson, N.C.: McFarland, 2002.

Hughes, Langston. *The Collected Works of Langston Hughes, Volume 1, The Poems: 1921–1940*. Columbia and London: University of Missouri Press, 2001.

Hume, John F. *Abolitionists*. New York and London: G.P. Putnum's Sons, 1905.

Humphrey, Grace. *Illinois: The Story of the Prairie State*. Indianapolis: Bobbs-Merrill, 1917.

Hurt, R. Douglas. *Agriculture and Slavery in Missouri's Little Dixie*. Columbia and London: University of Missouri Press, 1992.

Jensen, Richard J. *Illinois: A Bicentennial History*. New York: W.W. Norton, 1978.

Jones, Edgar DeWitt. *Lincoln and the Preachers*. New York: Harper and Brothers Publishers, 1948.

Jordan, Philip D. *William Salter -Western Torchbearer*. Oxford, Ohio: Mississippi Valley Press, 1939.

Litvin, Martin. *Voices of the Prairie Land,* vol. 1. Galesburg, Ill.: Mother Bickerdyke Press, Historical Collection, 1972.

Macy, Jesse. *The Anti-Slavery Crusade*. New Haven: Yale University Press, 1920.

Magdol, Edward. *Owen Lovejoy: Abolitionist in Congress*. New Brunswick, N.J.: Rutgers University Press, 1967.

Magoun, George F. *Asa Turner: A Home Missionary Patriarch and His Times*. Boston and Chicago: Congregational Sunday School and Publishing Society, 1889.

Matson, N. *Reminiscences of Bureau County*. Princeton, Ill.: Republican Book and Job Office, 1872.

McCullough, David. *John Adams*. New York, London, Toronto, Sydney, and Singapore: Simon and Schuster, 2001.

McDougall, Marion Gleason. *Fugitive Slaves, 1619–1865*. New York: Bergman Publishers, 1967.

McFeely, William S. *Frederick Douglas*. New York and London: W.W. Norton, 1955.

McPherson, James M. *Battle Cry of Freedom*. New York: Oxford University Press, 1988.

Meltzer, Milton. *The Black Americans: A History in Their Own Words, 1619–1983*. New York: Harper and Row, 1987.

Morison, Samuel Eliot. *The Oxford History of the American People*. New York: Oxford University Press, 1965.

Muelder, Hermann R. *Fighters for Freedom: The History of Anti-Slavery Activities of Men and Women Associated with Knox College*. New York: Columbia University Press, 1959.

Nelson, Ronald E. *Illinois: Land and Life in the Prairie State*. Dubuque, Iowa: Kendall/Hunt, 1978.

Overton, Richard C. *Burlington West*. Cambridge, Mass.: Harvard University Press, 1941.

Patten, Jennie M., and Andrew Graham. *History of the Somonauk United Presbyterian Church*. Chicago: Patten and Patten, 1928.

Pease, Theodore C. *The Story of Illinois*. Chicago: A.C. McClurg, 1925.

Perry, Lewis, and Michael Fellman. *Anti-Slavery Reconsidered: New Perspectives on the Abolitionists*. Baton Rouge and London: Louisiana State University Press, 1979.

Peters, Pamela R. *The Underground Railroad in Floyd County, Indiana*. Jefferson, N.C.: McFarland, 2001.

Pirtle, Carol. *Escape Betwixt Two Suns*. Carbondale and Edwardsville: Southern Illinois University Press, 2000.

Potter, David Morris. *The Impending Crisis, 1848–1861*. New York: Harper and Row, 1976.

Randall, J. G. *The Civil War and Reconstruction*. Boston: D.C. Heath, 1953.

Ripley, C. Peter. *Witness for Freedom*. Chapel

Hill and London: University of North Carolina Press, 1993.

Robertson, Stacey M. *Parker Pillsbury: Radical Abolitionist, Male Feminist.* Ithaca, N.Y.: Cornell University Press, 2000.

Robinson, L. E., and Irving Moore. *History of Illinois.* New York, Cincinnati, and Chicago: American Book, 1909.

Ross, Harvey Lee. *The Early Pioneers and Pioneer Events of the State of Illinois.* Astoria, Ill.: Stevens. Reprinted by Ruth M. Davis, 1970.

Sage, Leland L. *A History of Iowa.* Ames: Iowa State University Press, 1974.

Saunders, Delores T. *Illinois Liberty Lines.* Farmington, Ill.: Farmington Shopper, 1982.

Schwieder, Dorothy. *Iowa: The Middle Land.* Ames: Iowa State University Press, 1996.

Sellen, C. J. *Review of the Commerce, Manufactures, and the Public and the Private Improvements of Galesburg: Containing a Brief History of Knox College, and Sketches of the First Settlement of the Town.* Galesburg, Ill., 1857.

Sernett, Milton C. *North Star Country: Upstate New York and the Crusade for African-American Freedom.* New York: Syracuse University Press, 2001.

Siebert, Wilbur H. *The Mysteries of Ohio's Underground Railroad.* Columbus, Ohio: Long's College Book Company, 1951.

_____. *The Underground Railroad from Slavery to Freedom.* London: Macmillan, 1898.

Simon, Paul. *Lovejoy: Martyr to Freedom.* St. Louis, Mo.: Concordial Press, 1964.

Sorin, Gerald. *Abolitionism.* New York, Washington, and London: Praeger, 1972.

Stampp, Kenneth M. *The Peculiar Institution.* New York: Alfred A. Knopf, 1956.

Stewart, James B. *Wendell Phillips: Liberty's Hero.* Baton Rouge and London: Louisiana State Press, 1986.

Still, William. *The Underground Railroad.* Philadelphia: Porter and Coates, 1872.

Stowe, Harriet Beecher. *Uncle Tom's Cabin.* New York: Signet, 1998 (reprint).

Sutton, Robert M. *The Heartland: Pages from Illinois History.* Lake Forest, Ill.: Deerpath, 1982.

Thompson, George. *Prison Life and Reflections.* Dayton, Ohio: United Brethren Printing, 1857.

Todd, John. *Early Settlement and Growth of Western Iowa and Reminiscences.* Des Moines: Historical Department of Iowa, 1906.

Todd, Lewis P., and Merle Curti. *Rise of the American Nation.* New York: Harcourt, Brace, 1964.

Turner, Glennette. *The Underground Railroad in Illinois.* Glen Ellyn, Ill.: Newman Educational Publishing, 2001.

Vidal, Gore. *The Last Empire: Essays 1992–2000.* New York, London, Toronto, Sydney, and Auckland: Doubleday, 2001.

Walker, Juliet E. K. *Free Frank.* Lexington: University Press of Kentucky, 1983.

Walters, Ronald G. *The Anti-Slavery Appeal: American Abolitionism after 1830.* Baltimore and London: Johns Hopkins University Press, 1976.

Weld, Theodore. *American Slavery as It Is: Testimony of a Thousand Witnesses.* New York: American Anti-Slavery Society, 1839.

Wilson, Carol. *Freedom at Risk: The Kidnapping of Free Blacks in America 1780–1865.* Lexington: Kentucky University Press, 1994.

Wilson, Douglas L., and Rodney O. Davis. *Herndon's Informants.* Urbana: Ill.: University of Illinois Press, 1998.

Winks, Robin W. *The Blacks in Canada: A History.* New Haven: Yale University Press, 1971.

Wolf, Hazel Catherine. *On Freedom's Altar: The Martyr Complex in the Abolition Movement.* Madison: University of Wisconsin Press, 1952.

Young, E. H. *A History of Round Prairie and Plymouth: 1831–1875.* Chicago: Geo J. Titus Book and Joe Printer, 1876.

County Histories

Bradsby, H. C. *History of Bureau County, Illinois.* Chicago: World Publishing, 1885.

Chapman, Charles C. *History of Fulton County, Illinois.* Peoria, Ill.: Chas C. Chapman, 1879.

_____. *History of Knox County, Illinois.* Chicago: Chas C. Chapman, 1878.

Clarke, S. J. *History of McDonough County, Illinois.* Springfield, Ill.: D.W. Lusk Printer and Binder, 1898.

Gregg, T. H. *History of Hancock County, Illinois.* Chicago: Chas C. Chapman, 1888.

Hamilton, Oscar B. *History of Jersey County, Illinois.* Chicago: Munsell, 1919.

The History of Peoria County. Chicago: Johnson, 1880.

Kett, H. F. *Past and Present of Rock Island County, Illinois*. Chicago: Ottaway and Colbert Printers, 1877.

_____. *Past and Present of Warren County, Illinois*. Chicago: Ottaway and Colbert Printers, 1877.

Kiner, Henry L. *History of Henry County*. Chicago: Pioneer Publishing, 1910.

Lesson, M. A. *Stark County, Illinois*. Chicago: M.A. Lesson, 1887.

Perry, Albert J. *History of Knox County, Illinois*, vol. 1. Chicago: S.J. Clarke, 1912.

Shallenberger, E. H. *Stark County and its Pioneers*. Cambridge, Ill.: B.W. Seaton, Prairie Chief Office, Book and Job Printer, 1876.

Tillson, John. *History of the City Quincy, Illinois*. Revised and corrected by Hon. William H. Collins by direction of the Quincy Historical Society. Chicago: S.J. Clarke, 1886.

Newspapers

Alton Observer Extra. Alton, Illinois, September 28, 1837.

Brimfield News. Brimfield, Illinois, August 20, 1936.

Bureau County Republican. Princeton, Illinois, n.d. but probably republished after 1922. Owen Lovejoy's papers, the Reverend William Moore, DeKalb, Illinois.

Canton Weekly Register. Canton, Illinois, December 15, 1910.

Chicago Daily Tribune. Chicago, Illinois, June 25, 1874.

_____. November 7, 1926.

Elmwood Gazette. Elmwood, Illinois, April 26, 1906.

_____. April 11, 1907.

_____. April 18, 1907.

_____. April 25, 1907.

_____. July 30, 1936.

Fulton County Life. Published as supplement of the *News and Cuba Journal*. January 8 and 22, February 5, and March 12, 1969.

Galesburg Evening Mail. Galesburg, Illinois, February 1, 1890.

_____. February 1, 1900.

_____. June 19, 1909.

Galesburg Register. Galesburg, Illinois, March 18, 1882.

Galesburg Republican Register. Galesburg, Illinois, July 29, 1876.

_____. August 5, 1876.

_____. October 3, 1891.

_____. January 25, 1900.

_____. June 20, 1904.

The Genius of Universal Emancipation. Hennepin, Illinois, February 26, 1839.

LaHarper. LaHarpe, Illinois, November 17, 1893.

Marshall County Republican. Reprinted from the *Princeton Republican*. March 26, 1869.

The Peoria Daily Transcript. Peoria, Illinois, February 25, 1859.

_____. March 10, 1896.

Peoria Register and Northwestern Gazetteer. Peoria, Illinois, July 14, 1838.

Quincy Whig Republican. Quincy, Illinois, March 21, 1863.

Stark County News. Toulon, Illinois, May 30, 1862.

_____. July 6, 1893.

Western Citizen. Chicago, Illinois, 1842–59.

Other Sources

Aldrich, D. W. *Portrait and Biographical Album of Knox County, Illinois,* Chicago: Biographical Publishing, 1886.

Annewalt & Lawrence's 1867 Galesburg Directory, Burlington, Iowa: Merchant Printing, 1867.

Bartlett, G. K. from field copy of Kathleen Williams. "How Did Uncle Joe Get Home?" (interview with 92-year-old former slave, Joseph Higgerson, Summer 1937, Sadalia, Missouri). In *Missouri Slave Narratives Volume 10* of *Slave Narratives: A Folk History of Slavery in the United States from Interviews with Former Slaves*. Federal Writers' Project of the Works Progress Administration for the State of Missouri, 1936–1938. Online collection of the Library of Congress. www.loc.gov.

Bascom, Flavel. *A Historical Discourse Commemorative of the Settlement of Galesburg*, Galesburg, Ill., Free Press Book and Job House, 1866.

Bateman, Newton, Paul Selby, W. Seldon Gale,

and George Candee Gale, eds. *Historical Encyclopedia of Illinois and Knox County.* Chicago and New York: Munsell, 1899.

Berfield, Karen. "Julian Bryant: Fair Treatment of Blacks in the Ranks," *Civil War Times Illustrated* 22, no. 2 (April 1983): 36–41.

Blanchard, J. *Sermon on Slave Holding.* Cincinnati, Ohio, October 20, 1841.

Blazer, D. N. "The History of the Underground Railroad of McDonough County, Illinois." *Journal of the Illinois State Historical Society* 15 (1922).

Boydstun, Charles. Boydstun family papers. Knox College Archives.

Bridges, Roger D. "Dark Faces on the Antebellum West Central Illinois Landscape." *Western Illinois Regional Studies* 6, no. 2 (Fall 1983): 67–80.

Bulletin of Knox College Fifty Year Club 12 (1959).

Chambers, E. P. *Reminiscences of Early Days.* Knox College Archives.

Cooley, Verna. "Illinois and the Underground Railroad to Canada." *Transactions of the Illinois State Historical Society* (1917): 76–98.

Delano, James. *West Jersey Harvest Home,* 1925. In *Illinois Liberty Lines* by Delores T. Saunders. Farmington, Ill.: Farmington Shopper, 1982.

Dempsey, Terrell. "Heroes, Previously Unnamed, Played an Important Role in Our History." *Hannibal Courier Post,* February 24, 2001.

Dewey, J. L. *County Directory.* Galesburg, Ill.: Liberal Book and Job Office, 1868.

Finkelman, Paul. "Slavery, the 'More Perfect Union,' and the Prairie State." *Illinois Historical Journal* 80 (Winter 1987): 248–69.

Gale, George Washington. *A Brief History of Knox College, Situated in Galesburgh, Knox County, Illinois.* Cincinnati, 1845.

Gara, Larry. "The Underground Railroad in Illinois." *Journal of the Illinois State Historical Society* 56 (Autumn 1963): 508–28.

Garretson, O. A. "Traveling on the Underground Railroad in Iowa." *Iowa Journal of History and Politics* 22 (1924): 418–53.

Illinois Atlas and Gazetteer. Freeport, Maine: Delorme Printing, 1991.

Illinois: Official Highway Map. Springfield, Ill.: Department of Transportation, 1999.

Kennedy, Inez A. *Reflections of the Pioneers of Lee County.* Dixon, Ill.: Inez A. Kennedy, Publisher, 1893.

League of Women Voters, *Know Your Town.* Galesburg, Ill.: League of Women Voters, 1968.

Lee, George R. "Slavery and Emancipation in Lewis County, Missouri" *Missouri Historical Review* 65, no. 3 (April 1971): 294–317.

Letter to Dr. H. M. Hall from S. G. Wright, August 25, 1885. Stark County Historical Society, Toulon, Illinois.

Letter (copy) to Mrs. Owen Lovejoy from Francis R. Carpenter, May 18, 1865. Bureau County Historical Society, Princeton, Illinois.

Letter to Sarah Lovejoy from J. H. Olds, concerning capture of slave "John," May 17, 1874. Bureau County Historical Society, Princeton, Illinois.

"The Lincoln-Douglas Debate, Galesburg, Illinois, October 7, 1858." Willcox family papers. Knox College Archives.

McKinzie, Clarke. "Congregational Church, Toulon, Illinois, 1846–1921." *Journal of the Illinois State Historical Society* 13 (1921): 504–37.

Merkel, Benjamin G. "The Underground Railroad and the Missouri Borders, 1840–1860." *Missouri Historical Review* 37 (October 1942–July 1943): 271–85.

Moore, W. K. "An Abortive Slave Uprising." *Missouri Historical Review* 52, no. 2 (January 1958): 123–26.

Muelder, H. R. *A Hero Home from the War.* Galesburg, Ill.: Knox College Library, 1988.

Page, Gordon Paul. *Elmira through the Ages.* Kewanee, Ill.: B & B Printing, 1990.

"A Rambling Sketch of Some of Our Earlier Colored Residents." *Galesburg Post.* Quarterly supplement of the *Home Towner.* Winter 1934.

Rand McNally Atlas of American History. Skokie, Ill.: Rand McNally, 1999.

Rasson, Terry. *Remembering the Flight to Freedom: The Underground Railroad in Illinois.* Springfield, Ill.: Historic Illinois, 1999.

Richardson, William A., Jr. "Dr. David Nelson and His Times." *Journal of the Illinois State Historical Society* 13, (January 1921): 433–63.

Bibliography

Ryan, John H. "A Chapter from the History of the Underground Railroad." *Journal of the Illinois State Historical Society* 8 (April 1915): 23–30.

Schmidt, O. L. "Somonauk United Presbyterian Church." *Journal of the Illinois State Historical Society* 18 (October 1925): 694–720.

Semi-Centennial Celebration, First Church of Christ, 1837–1887. Galesburg, Ill.: Galesburg Printing Company, 1887.

Sevenson, Brenda E., and C. Peter Ripley. *Underground Railroad.* Washington, D.C.: National Park Service, 1998.

Siebert, Wilbur H. Materials collected by Professor Wilbur H. Siebert and research students, Columbus, Ohio, Ohio Historical Society, 1962, microfilm 2 Reels: mm., Illinois Underground Railroad, Illinois Historical Society, Springfield, Illinois.

Taylor, Ella Hume. "History of the Congregational Church of Geneseo." *Journal of the Illinois State Historical Society* 20 (April 1927): 112–27.

White, Grace E. "Bred Slaves Like Stock" (interview with former slave Hannah Jones). In *Missouri Slave Narratives Volume 10* of *Slave Narratives: A Folk History of Slavery in the United States from Interviews with Former Slaves.* Federal Writers' Project of the Works Progress Administration for the State of Missouri, 1936–1938. Online collection of the Library of Congress. www.loc.gov.

Willcox, E. S. "Reminiscences of Galesburg." Willcox family papers. Knox College Archives.

Wright, Samuel G. "Wright's Journal." 1839–65, Knox College Archives.

Index

Numbers in *bold italics* indicate pages with illustrations.

191